CITIZENS' WEALTH

'This book sets out a compelling case for why governments investing public wealth on behalf of citizens have a duty to generate returns responsibly. Cummine's thought-provoking analysis convincingly makes both the moral and practical case for responsible investment among sovereign wealth funds.'
—James Gifford, founder of the United Nations Principles for Responsible Investment and Senior Fellow, Initiative for Responsible Investment, Harvard Kennedy School

'While over the last decade many rich nations ran up tremendous debts, others – and several emerging countries – accumulated huge stocks of assets. Having a sovereign wealth fund is a big help for macroeconomics; running it well is a big challenge for local politics. This book offers a useful account of how these funds have come into being and how they should evolve in the future. Recommended reading for policymakers all over the world.'
—Andrés Velasco, former Minister of Finance, Chile (2006–10), and Professor of International Development, Columbia University

'How can the substantial assets of sovereign wealth funds be managed transparently, invested ethically, and used to fight inequality? With bold, accessible arguments Angela Cummine shows that the key is more democratic governance to ensure that sovereign citizens directly control the wealth in their fund and receive the benefits of it. Highly recommended.'
—Leif Wenar, Chair of Philosophy and Law, King's College London

'This book raises important questions about how the growth of sovereign wealth funds potentially affects the relationship between the state and its citizens. While some will have reservations about certain proposals in the book, this topic deserves the attention of researchers, citizens and policymakers alike.'
—Martin Skancke, Chair of the United Nations Principles for Responsible Investment (UNPRI) and former Director General of Norway's sovereign wealth fund

'Angela Cummine's searching treatment of the topic and the inevitable politics that surround these funds provides an invaluable *aide memoire* for governments and their communities establishing or rethinking their sovereign funds.'
—David Murray, Inaugural Chair, International Forum of Sovereign Wealth Funds and former CEO, Australian Future Fund

'It is rare to come across a book on SWFs that attempts to redefine the debate at the most fundamental level. Angela Cummine's well-researched and ambitious work tries to do just that, raising a number of highly relevant and contentious points. Whether you agree or disagree with her analysis and conclusions, if you are interested in SWFs – read it! It will force you to think through some of the most fundamental tenets of SWF design and management.'
—Andrew Rozanov, Associate Fellow, Chatham House and originator of the term 'sovereign wealth funds'

'*Citizens' Wealth* makes a powerful case for reform in the sovereign wealth fund community. These giant sovereign funds play an outsized role in the global economy today but Angela Cummine questions if they truly benefit the peoples of their respective countries, and she demands they do more to resolve critical economic and social issues facing current

generations. *Citizens' Wealth* is a call to arms and a must-read for policymakers, professionals and citizens interested in the next chapter on how sovereign wealth should be managed.'
—Scott E. Kalb, Executive Director, Sovereign Investor Institute, Institutional Investor and former CIO and Deputy CEO, Korea Investment Corporation (KIC)

'The topic of sovereign wealth funds is as dauntingly difficult as it is important in modern political economy. Angela Cummine's treatment offers all that one could want in a normative analysis of this topic – in particular, a detailed and compelling account of the institutional possibilities for democratic control of these funds. This is a fine and immeasurably helpful piece of work.'
—Jeremy Waldron, Professor of Law, New York University

'Angela Cummine's important new book show us what sovereign wealth funds are, where they have come from, what they have done, what they can do and what they should do. It is a brilliant and timely contribution to a debate about managing states' finances that we all need to have.'
—Christopher Pierson, Professor of Politics, University of Nottingham

'Angela Cummine's fresh and compelling analysis of sovereign wealth funds shows how wise Norway was to create a sovereign fund and what might have happened if the UK had had the foresight to do the same when oil was plentiful and fetched a high price.'
—Iain McLean, Professor of Politics, University of Oxford and Vice President of Public Policy, The British Academy

'*Citizens' Wealth* is an excellent, timely and engaging examination of sovereign funds. It deals with the important issues of institutional design and governance of sovereign wealth to ensure effective management of public wealth in the people's interest.'
—Dr Khalid Alsweilem, Former Head of Investment, Saudi Arabian Monetary Agency and Fellow, Harvard Kennedy School Belfer Center

'This is a very well-written and well-researched book with a unique take on the role of sovereign funds in our economies, societies and indeed communities. Dr Cummine brings a fresh perspective on sovereign funds, adopting as her key lens of analysis and understanding an often underappreciated constituency and stakeholder: a country's own citizens. She adeptly argues for the rights of citizens within – and their key role in the management of – sovereign funds. In so doing, she asks (and convincingly answers) questions that are very useful in clarifying the roles and responsibilities of these ever-popular government-managed (and citizen-owned) entities. Well worth reading!'
—Dr Ashby Monk, Executive Director, Global Projects Centre, Stanford University and author of *Sovereign Wealth Funds: Governance, Legitimacy and Global Power*

'Angela Cummine in *Citizens' Wealth* makes an informative, thorough, and aspirational case for the democratization of sovereign wealth. Students of sovereign wealth will benefit from her thoughtful presentation even if they do not agree with all of her well-articulated arguments.'
—Ted Truman, author of *Sovereign Wealth Funds: Threat or Salvation*, Senior Fellow, Peterson Institute for International Economics and Former Assistant Secretary of the US Treasury

CITIZENS' WEALTH

WHY (AND HOW) SOVEREIGN
FUNDS SHOULD BE MANAGED BY
THE PEOPLE FOR THE PEOPLE

ANGELA CUMMINE

YALE UNIVERSITY PRESS
NEW HAVEN AND LONDON

For information about this and other Yale University Press publications, please contact:
U.S. Office: sales.press@yale.edu   yalebooks.com
Europe Office: sales@yaleup.co.uk   yalebooks.co.uk

Typeset in Adobe Caslon Pro by IDSUK (DataConnection) Ltd
Printed in Great Britain by Gomer Press Ltd, Llandysul, Ceredigion, Wales

Library of Congress Control Number: 2016023601

ISBN 978-0-300-21894-7

A catalogue record for this book is available from the British Library.

10 9 8 7 6 5 4 3 2 1

To my parents
for leading me to the starting gates

My sister
for encouragement from the sidelines

and

Christian
for seeing me across the finish line

CONTENTS

List of figures and tables   ix
Acknowledgements   x
Abbreviations   xiii

1   Introduction: The Santiago dilemma   1

Part I The blessings and burdens of sovereign wealth

2   Do sovereign funds make nations richer?   19
3   Whose wealth is it: state's or citizens'?   36
4   The Tsipras point: control of and benefit from community   58
    wealth

Part II Democratizing sovereign funds

5   No accumulation without representation!   71
6   Dirty money: generating sovereign wealth ethically   93
7   Role models of community control: Norway and New Zealand   113

Part III Distributing sovereign wealth

8   Show me the money! Citizen benefit from sovereign wealth   135
9   Owner-state or owner-people: lessons from Alaska   160
10 Fighting inequality with sovereign wealth   182

Part IV What next?

11   Past the peak? The future of sovereign wealth accumulation   195
12   Transforming sovereign funds into community funds   207

Appendix 1: The world's sovereign wealth funds   218
   (as at April 2016)
Appendix 2: Select sovereign wealth fund definitions   224
Appendix 3: Truman scoreboard of sovereign wealth   226
   funds (2009–12)
Endnotes   229
Bibliography   253
Index   272

FIGURES AND TABLES

Figures

1.1	Rise in SWF establishment over time	6
2.1	Sovereign wealth in the universe of public capital	26
2.2	Global public assets under management by category, 2015	27
5.1	The architecture of popular control: condominium and SWF	80
8.1	Alaska Permanent Fund historical returns, 1985–2013	142
8.2	Public support for different uses of mineral wealth in Mongolia, 2008–14	146

Tables

2.1	Sources of public finance	22
5.1	Popular control devices for SWFs based on the condominium model	78
8.1	Models of benefit distribution for SWF returns	154
9.1	Summary of 2011 original survey results on public conceptions of the Alaska Permanent Fund Dividend	170–1

ACKNOWLEDGEMENTS

This book benefited from the help and guidance of multiple people and organizations. My greatest debt is to Stuart White at the University of Oxford. I am grateful for his mentorship and intellectual influence throughout the shaping and execution of this research. Also from the Department of Politics and International Relations (DPIR) within the university, I am appreciative of the advice and support at various stages of Iain McLean, Liz Frazer, Alan Ryan, David Miller, Marc Philp, Louis McNay, Marc Stears, Elizabeth Greenhalgh and Rasangi Prematilaka. Tommy Peto and Joshua Cova's excellent research assistance informed Chapters 2 and 11 respectively. I am grateful for their detailed, timely help, as well as the DPIR's financial support which made their research assistance possible.

Beyond Oxford, the academic mentorship of Karl Widerquist has been influential, as was an early conversation with Leif Wenar on the structure of this project. Jeremy Waldron's and Christopher Pierson's feedback on an earlier version of this material helped advance this project. The material on Alaska in Part III benefited from the local expert assistance and feedback of Cliff Groh, Gregg Erickson and Scott Goldsmith, in particular the collation and interpretation of original data in Juneau and Anchorage. Thanks are also owed to the Wetherby family in Anchorage for their generous help with field research in 2011.

Outside academia, I am indebted to David Murray, the inaugural Chairman of both the International Forum of Sovereign Wealth Funds and the Australian Future Fund, who was particularly generous with his thoughts on the proper role and regulation of sovereign wealth funds and in facilitating access to the world of sovereign investment professionals. Thanks to sovereign wealth fund officials from Norway, Alaska, Australia, New Zealand, the United Arab Emirates, Hong Kong, Singapore, Botswana, Chile, Kuwait and Qatar, who cannot be named here, but who offered their time and frank thoughts.

In the SWF world, acknowledgement must also go to experts at I nvestec Asset Management as well as Khalid Alsweilem, former Chief Information Officer of the Saudi Arabian Monetary Agency, for helpful exchanges on the governance and design of sovereign investors, shared while undertaking joint research with the Harvard Kennedy School, which are drawn on in this work. I am also grateful for the insights gained into public investors during my time at the OECD's International Investment team in Paris, and at the Official Monetary and Financial Institutions Forum (OMFIF) and Institutional Investor's Sovereign Wealth Centre, both in London. The research of all three organizations informs this book.

Generous scholarships and financial grants have also supported this research. Chief thanks go to the Rhodes Trust and the British Academy. Additional thanks to the Jenkins Memorial Fund, the Scatcherd European Scholarship, the Society of Applied Philosophy, the Rothermere American Institute, and the DPIR and New College at the University of Oxford.

For helping this book come to life, huge thanks to my editor at Yale University Press, Taiba Batool – for commissioning, championing and refining this manuscript. Thanks also to the anonymous reviewers of this work, whose feedback at proposal and draft manuscript phase was very helpful. The production of the book has been greatly assisted by Rachael Lonsdale, Ann Bone and the thorough editorial assistance of Rachel Hulett at Stellenbosch University.

On a more personal note, I am grateful to many friends and family across the globe whose encouragement and assistance was vital. In partic-ular, the steady support of UK friends Caz, Anna and Lily, as well as the excellent editorial assistance and support of Nicholas Zweck in London. In Sydney, the long friendship and sage publishing advice of Alison Hurbert-Burns. In Zimbabwe, the Harare family – Paul, Trina, Heinrich, Amanda,

Christoph, Ilaria, Richard, Emma, Tobs, Lucy, Tim, Victoria and Avi – for making Zim a home in which such a project could germinate. And my Swedish family, spread across the globe, thanks for their ongoing support across large distances. Above all, there is my Australian family: Andrew and Gerard, who have encouraged pursuit of the creative; Juliette, for empathetic philosophizing; and Lee, who always makes us smile. The book is dedicated to my parents, John and Lyndall, my sister, Sally, and my husband, Christian, whose love, wisdom and encouragement make such work possible.

March 2016

ABBREVIATIONS

APF	Alaska Permanent Fund
APFC	Alaska Permanent Fund Corporation
AUM	assets under management
BC	Basic Capital
BoP	balance of payments
CCA	citizen's capital account
CDC	Caisse des Dépôts et Consignations (France)
CI	Citizen's Income (Basic Income)
CIC	China Investment Corporation
EI	ethical investment
ESG	environmental, social and governance (factors)
ESSF	Economic and Social Stabilization Fund (Chile)
EU	European Union
GAPP	Generally Accepted Principles and Practices ('Santiago Principles')
GDP	gross domestic product
GIC	GIC Private Ltd (Singapore) (until 2013, Government Investment Corporation of Singapore)
GPF	Government Petroleum Fund (Norway)
GPFG	Government Pension Fund Global (Norway)
HDF	Human Development Fund (Mongolia)
HRADF	Hellenic Republic Asset Development Fund (Greece)

IFSWF	International Forum of Sovereign Wealth Funds
IMF	International Monetary Fund
ISIF	Ireland Strategic Investment Fund
IWG	International Working Group of Sovereign Wealth Funds
LIA	Libyan Investment Authority
NBIM	Norges Bank Investment Management (Norway)
NGO	non-governmental organization
NII	Net Investment Income (Singapore)
NIR	Net Investment Return (Singapore)
NIRC	Net Investment Returns Contribution (Singapore)
NPRF	National Pensions Reserve Fund (Ireland)
NSIA	Nigeria Sovereign Investment Authority
NWF	national wealth fund
NZSF	New Zealand Superannuation Fund
OECD	Organisation for Economic Co-operation and Development
PCC	Police and Crime Commissioner (England and Wales)
PFD	Permanent Fund Dividend (Alaska)
PNG	Papua New Guinea
PRF	Pension Reserve Fund (Chile)
RI	responsible investment
SAFE	State Administration of Foreign Exchange (China)
SNA	System of National Accounts (United Nations)
SOE	state-owned enterprise
SWF	sovereign wealth fund
UAE	United Arab Emirates
UN	United Nations
UNPRI	United Nations Principles for Responsible Investment

Introduction: The Santiago dilemma

The revenue . . . of government . . . may be drawn either, first, from some fund which peculiarly belongs to the Sovereign or commonwealth, and which is independent of the revenue of the people; or secondly, from the revenue of the people.

Adam Smith, *The Wealth of Nations*, 1776

In mid-2006, the streets of Santiago were flooded with protestors. Effigies of the new finance minister, Andrés Velasco, were ablaze as citizens demanded a bigger share of Chile's historic copper boom.[1] The metal's soaring price had quadrupled in just four years, generating unprecedented budget surpluses for the world's largest copper producer. But much of the windfall was going into two newly established sovereign wealth funds (SWFs), tasked with saving the country's boom proceeds for a rainy day.[2]

The move to quarantine a chunk of Chile's burgeoning wealth in these sovereign funds was not popular. The country's developing status and persistent income inequality meant many ordinary Chileans favoured expenditure of the copper revenues on welfare-enhancing projects.[3] A May 2006 poll revealed that two-thirds of Chileans wanted the government to spend, not save, the copper windfall. Demonstrators chanted 'The copper money is for the poor people',[4] as President Michelle Bachelet's approval ratings dipped to a historic low.[5]

But the finance minister had a different concern. With copper receipts constituting 60 per cent of the national budget, the South American nation was worryingly exposed to metal price volatility. Wishing to avoid the boom and bust fate of commodity dependent neighbours Mexico and Argentina, Velasco set out to ensure Chile would have something to show for the good times. In 2006, he initiated a series of fiscal reforms, including the creation of the Pension Reserve Fund (PRF) and Economic and Social Stabilization Fund (ESSF) to save and store commodity proceeds. The PRF and ESSF were tasked with financing pension and social welfare obligations, and buffering Chile's economy in an economic downturn, respectively.

Both sovereign funds were capitalized by 2007 as the government reported a budget surplus quadruple that of just four years earlier. But Chile's economic growth was slowing. Public anger intensified. When the government refused to draw down despite the financial crisis, students and workers escalated demands for improvements in living standards.

But one year later, the protests ceased and Velasco's vindication came. In mid-2009, the price of copper tanked, falling 50 per cent within a few months. Chile's growth hit negative figures. Unemployment soared to 10 per cent. Thanks to boom-time discipline, the government was able to stimulate recovery by drawing down the ESSF and PRF revenues to fund urgent social spending. At 2.8 per cent of GDP, close to US$4 billion, Chile's stimulus package of tax breaks for business, job-creating public works and investment in mining was one of the largest in the world. Two to three times higher than other Latin American governments, it even outstripped America's 2 per cent stimulus effort.

Chile escaped catastrophe, experiencing only a minor recession despite massively declining government income. By converting some of its finite copper flow into permanent financial stock, the government had ammunition to contain the economic jolt. The ESSF and PRF proved an indispensable component of the state's fiscal apparatus. When they left office in 2010, Bachelet and Velasco boasted the highest approval ratings of any president and cabinet minister since Chile's return to democracy. The government's popularity was greater during the global recession than it ever was during the copper boom years. Velasco went from villain to hero.

In the same protest-plagued capital of Santiago during 2008, leaders of the world's major sovereign wealth funds finished drafting a set of principles on the governance, accountability and investment practices of SWFs. Remarkably, those principles, finalized amid Chile's internal furore over the use of its sovereign wealth, largely ignore the domestic implications of sovereign funds. Today, the Santiago Principles are the leading international framework for guiding, evaluating and influencing the behaviour and design of sovereign funds.[6] Yet, they continue to overlook the fundamental question of how these funds help or harm local sponsor communities.

This is the 'Santiago dilemma'. Chile's experience demonstrates that sovereign funds can be as much a cause of conflict within, as a source of help to, a community that chooses to create (sponsor) such a fund. Yet the leading best-practice principles on these funds, named after the Chilean capital in which they were finalized, largely overlook the significance of SWFs for the domestic citizen–state relationship.

This neglect of sovereign funds' impact at home is also rife in scholarly and regulatory discussion of SWFs.[7] Despite substantial analytical attention paid to sovereign funds, most of it focuses on their international significance. Given their geography, this is not surprising. Many are located in East Asia, the Middle East and Africa,[8] leading to a characterization of the SWF phenomenon as a 'redistribution of wealth and economic and financial power from the United States, Europe, and other mature industrial economies to countries perceived to be less firmly grounded in similar economic, financial, and political mores'.[9] As a result, recipients of SWF investment in the West have often viewed sovereign funds cautiously, anxious about their use as tools for realizing the strategic or political goals of their state sponsors.[10] For this reason, much extant research on SWFs focuses on their investment behaviour[11] and geopolitical implications[12] for the global economy. Policy deliberations at the international[13] and domestic[14] level also focus on regulating sovereign funds as transnational investors. This asymmetric focus on SWFs as global market actors is largely to blame for the predominantly international orientation of the Santiago Principles.

It is surprising, however, that this almost exclusive international focus on the ramifications of SWFs continues amid the ongoing fall-out from the worst financial and economic crisis since the Great Depression. In many states, government debt is at record levels, the global economy is sluggish and economic inequality worsens. Welfare spending continues to contract at a time when more citizens find themselves unemployed, living longer and in need of protection from the vicissitudes of global economic dislocation. Lack of interest in the domestic dynamic of the substantial growth of government wealth in such an era is striking. How can more governments be growing wealthier, while seemingly fewer citizens enjoy the benefits of such wealth?

This becomes even more baffling given that one of today's most pressing and talked-about policy challenges – economic inequality – is ultimately an *intrastate* challenge. As influential French economist Thomas Piketty observed in his seminal treatise on the distribution of twenty-first-century wealth, 'the inequality with respect to capital is a far greater domestic issue than it is an international one. Inequality in the ownership of capital brings the rich and poor within each country into conflict with one another far more than it pits one country against another.'[15] Taking this idea a step further, since the proliferation of sovereign funds places more capital in government hands, SWFs may pit citizen and state against one another unless that capital is used and managed in a way that reduces rather than entrenches inequality in capital ownership.

Unfortunately, such conflict over SWFs *is* occurring. Indeed, Chile is not alone in experiencing domestic disputes over its sovereign wealth. As shown throughout this book, similar episodes of conflict between state and citizen over SWFs have plagued societies at the national, state and local level on every continent. From disagreements over how to invest public wealth ethically in Norway, Australia and New Zealand, to tussles for control over sovereign wealth in Korea, China and Nigeria, to controversy over the raiding of sovereign funds and use of SWF returns in Alaska, Mongolia, Ireland and Russia, the proper treatment of sovereign wealth is a thorny issue confronting numerous communities. And such issues are likely to become more important. The global collapse in commodity prices since 2014 and China's dramatic economic slowdown mark the beginning of a new era of reduced potential for sovereign wealth accumulation, reigniting debates around when and how to draw down national savings in SWFs. Yet a proper understanding of and guidance on the role of sovereign funds within their local sponsor communities is still lacking.

This book seeks to correct that oversight. It offers the first domestically oriented account of the impact of sovereign wealth funds on the citizen–state relationship, highlighting how sovereign funds can both help and hinder citizens' interests, and proposing reforms to ensure they do more of the former and less of the latter. By drawing on examples from across the SWF world, I demonstrate how the three core activities of a sovereign fund with the greatest domestic impact – the investment, management and distribution of a community's sovereign wealth – at times overlook or even undermine the best interests of citizens in the sponsor community. Even in developed, stable democracies, on which this book focuses, the design and behaviour of SWFs can lead to undemocratic, unethical and unjust outcomes for citizens. This is despite the vast, often untapped potential of sovereign funds to promote the social welfare and prosperity of sponsor communities significantly in all manner of political and economic contexts. Accordingly, this book proposes a set of principles for ensuring that the design, management and use of sovereign funds enhances any positive (or contains any detrimental) impact on the establishing community, whether a nation, state or city. If embraced, such principles could help transform sovereign funds managing sovereign wealth into community funds managing citizens' wealth.

Sovereign funds, community funds and citizens' wealth

Aspiring to transform sovereign funds into community funds holding citizens' wealth requires an understanding of each concept – sovereign funds, community funds and citizens' wealth – and how they differ.

Sovereign wealth funds are the best known of the three. Although the term is barely a decade old, first coined in 2005 by SWF commentator Andrew Rozanov,[16] the rapid and prolific rise of these funds has commanded global attention. At the start of 2016, more than sixty governments globally possessed almost eighty funds,[17] the majority of which were established after the year 2000 (see Figure 1.1).[18] Their rapid increase in number has been matched by an explosive growth in the total value of SWF assets,[19] leading to their characterization as a new 'power broker' in the global economy.[20]

Yet, though the term is new, the reality of sovereign funds long predates their twenty-first-century rise to prominence. France's Caisse des Dépôts et Consignations (CDC), established in 1816 following Napoleon's depletion of the public coffers,[21] competes with the Texas Permanent School Fund

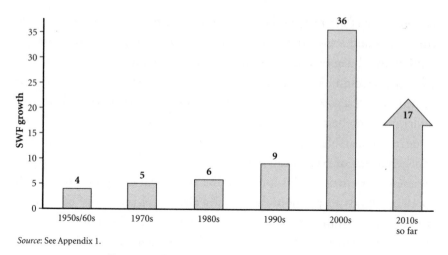

Source: See Appendix 1.

Figure 1.1 Rise in SWF establishment over time

founded in 1854 for the oldest SWF, depending on the definition of SWF used.[22] The Kuwait Investment Authority set up in 1953 marks the first wave of twentieth-century establishment phases,[23] which by 2000 had produced over twenty sovereign funds. All this occurred prior to the 2005 birth and subsequent official embrace of the SWF moniker by the International Forum of Sovereign Wealth Funds (IFSWF) in the Santiago Principles.

The 'community fund' concept is much less established, despite also recently emerging after a similarly lengthy, unnoticed gestation. In 1997, Welsh economist Gerald Holtham first used the term to describe an earlier proposal by economics Nobel Laureate James Meade for a state-owned fund created in the name of the community.[24] Meade's idea was for government to hypothecate a portion of the state's revenues into a commercially managed investment fund, which could offer an additional financing tool for worthy public policy. Such a fund would 'cascade' public wealth across generations and ensure that government revenues enjoyed some relationship to increases in the value of capital.[25] Neither writer appeared aware of the resemblance between their community fund idea and the real world institution of the sovereign fund.

Meade and Holtham were not alone in articulating a community-fund vision. The original version of this concept had a long incubation period in one of the world's most famous texts. Adam Smith, the grandfather of modern economics, quoted in the epigraph, first sketched the idea of a fund comprised of return-generating assets forming part of a state's financial artillery in his 1776 tome *The Wealth of Nations*. The revenue for the sovereign's fund would come from profit or interest derived from stock or land owned by the state,[26] and, if managed properly, would offer greatly improved returns on state property, augmenting the public coffers. While the lion's share of government revenue would still come from taxation – 'the revenue of the people' – together, these two revenue streams could help defray the 'necessary expenses of the commonwealth'.

When, 200 years later, Meade laid out his 'community-fund' vision, presumably unaware of Smith's writings on the topic, he too suggested that governments build up a public fund of financial assets, but seeded by running large budget surpluses. He argued for governments to use this additional revenue to cover gaps in education and healthcare spending and to fund a universal basic income for all citizens.[27] This stakeholder vision sought to ensure that all community members held a stake in their public wealth, both directly through a basic income payment and indirectly through properly financed vital public services.

A decade on, Holtham adapted the idea further. By this time, the fiscal profile of most nations with advanced economies had changed. Against the late 1990s backdrop of recurrent deficits, Meade's idea of a surplus-financed investment fund seemed improbable, yet the need for a more secure funding source for critical overheads like health, education and pensions was becoming more pressing.[28] In response, Holtham developed a more modest vision: a fund seeded with privatization receipts and capital taxes instead of surpluses, with its use of returns limited to funding basic critical services rather than a more ambitious basic income scheme.

Around the same time, several American and British thinkers proposed similar ideas, although none adopted the 'community-fund' label. Across the Atlantic, American journalist and political scientist Robert Kuttner argued that the US government should invest a proportion of its budget surplus in the equities market and place the returns into a fund to make grants to all newborn babies.[29] In 2000, public policy experts Gavin Kelly and Rachel Lissauer proposed a similar idea for a baby bond in Britain,[30] and in 2003, on the brink of the biggest wave of sovereign wealth fund establishment globally, political theorist Stuart White invited readers to '[i]magine that the state owns some proportion of the shares that are traded on the stock market' and that '[e]ach year the state receives a return on its various shareholdings. The combined returns on these holdings are then merged and used to help finance a range of public projects.'[31]

By this time, as many as twenty sovereign wealth funds existed around the world, investing government capital in equities and bonds. However, none of the community-fund proponents made the connection.[32]

Finally, in 2014, Holtham loosely connected the two ideas advocating the creation of a community fund for Britain on an SWF model.[33] Where previously his writings depended on having to '[i]magine the consequences of [the state] having a national patrimony of say, £50 billion invested in equities',[34] he now acknowledged the SWF phenomenon, recognizing the resemblance of select sovereign funds in Norway and Singapore to his community fund ideal. Most recently, British financial journalist and inequality expert Stewart Lansley advocated the conversion of SWFs into *social* wealth funds that could help combat inequality domestically.[35] So too did political philosopher Martin O'Neill, who emphasized the role that sovereign wealth funds can play in realizing Meade's proposal of tackling wealth inequality through collectivizing returns to capital.[36]

Today, with the large-scale emergence of SWFs, there is no longer any need to imagine the state's potential as a capital owner. Sovereign funds make real this aspiration, at least in form. Yet still too few philosophers and economists make the connection, let alone consider the possibility of SWFs as community funds. Similarly, as I show, too few extant sovereign funds are explicitly designed to be, or actually operate as, funds for citizens. This is despite all the potential benefits they offer to members of a sponsor community, whether a city, state or nation, explored throughout this book. As Part I shows, sovereign funds can make their sponsor communities richer and fairer if designed properly and if their domestic ownership status is made clear. Parts II and III go on to show how greater citizen control over, and direct benefit from, sovereign wealth helps promote more just, equal and democratic societies. In the absence of such citizen-centric design, sovereign funds are likely to remain as Adam Smith described: funds that 'belong to the Sovereign or commonwealth', managing assets that are 'independent of the revenue of the people'.

The SWF ownership quandary

Is it even possible then for sovereign wealth to be the *citizens'* wealth? The idea that sovereign wealth in SWFs could or should be citizens' rather than government wealth is only valid insofar as these two concepts are distinct.[37] As Chile's experience highlights, and as this book goes on to show, vagary dogs the question of whether SWF assets are primarily the property of states or citizens, causing confusion, competition and conflict within numerous SWF-sponsor communities. Moreover, these squabbles occur irrespective of how democratic the government is that is managing those sovereign funds, suggesting a fundamental uncertainty about the owner-ship status of sovereign wealth itself. Since this uncertainty plagues the real-world operation of SWFs, a preliminary goal of this book is to resolve any deeper, destructive ambiguity surrounding SWF ownership.

Chapter 3 seeks to help by asking 'Whose wealth is it: state's or citi-zens'?' Looking to formal definitions and descriptions of sovereign funds is not much help. There is no single universally accepted definition of an SWF in regulatory or scholarly discourse. Sovereign funds themselves even contest the label's meaning. Some dispute their status as such, while others embrace the term and identity. The Santiago Principles attempted to resolve the confusion, offering a widely agreed definition of SWFs as 'special purpose investment funds or arrangements, owned by the general government . . . for macroeconomic purposes'. Yet, as Chapter 3 elaborates, even this attempt to impose a consensus understanding of sovereign funds as 'government owned' has plainly not succeeded in practice. Real-world rivalry between states and their citizens over sovereign wealth persists. Recent episodes of conflict have occurred in states as diverse as China, Australia, Ireland, Mongolia, Alaska, Nigeria and Libya, among others. This suggests that neither stage of economic development nor type of political regime immunizes communities from struggles over their sover-eign wealth.

For some, this may seem like a straw-man debate. On a contemporary view of representative government, Adam Smith's distinction between the sovereign and the people's revenue might seem mistaken or, at best, outdated. In modern democracies, citizens elect their lawmakers to under-take the activities of government on their behalf, including managing the public coffers. By definition, therefore, a public asset like sovereign wealth *is* the citizens' wealth. There can be no cause for conflict, then, if a government manages these assets in an accountable, transparent manner that ultimately promotes the interests of citizen constituents regarding this wealth. Promisingly, examples of such accountable, democratic governance in the practical world of sovereign wealth management exist and are drawn upon as exemplary throughout this book.

Yet, cases of conflict over sovereign wealth in both more and less democratic polities still occur, despite the adoption of respectable levels of transparent, accountable SWF management. As long as confusion lingers over the proper ownership of these assets and the balance of rights between state and citizen that this implies, the risk of domestic conflict over SWFs persists.

Towards a solution: a principal–agent framework of SWF ownership

To help reduce conflict over SWFs, I propose applying a principal–agent framework to the citizen–state relationship that can guide the governance of SWF assets. Under this classic theory of the state, inherited from seventeenth-century philosopher John Locke, government is an agent for, and under the control of, its principal, the people. The principal–agent conception of the citizen–state relationship implies a set of fiduciary principles that require the people to maintain control over their government agent. One such principle is that all property obtained by the agent in the course of acting on the principal's behalf belongs to the principal and must be managed exclusively and solely for their benefit. On this view, then, citizens are the rightful owners of sovereign wealth. It is their interests and rights that must be promoted in relation to SWFs, not those of state agencies and governments who enjoy physical and legal possession of SWFs.

Elaborating on the precise rights and interests of citizens over SWFs which flow from this fiduciary understanding of the state is the next step. The framework only does part of the job: it acts as a blocking claim, preventing the idea of government as ultimate owner of state property; but it fails to articulate what citizen ownership of such property, including sovereign wealth, would look like. Chapter 4 takes up that task, drawing on the insights of property theory. If owners must typically enjoy control and benefit rights to their property, then this should extend to citizen-owners of sovereign wealth. But how can citizens, as a collective, *control* a piece of shared property like a sovereign fund? And how should they *benefit* from it? As individuals, or a group? Directly or indirectly? What aspects of SWFs should this apply to in practice?

Citizenship ownership in practice

These questions assume a grasp of how local citizens currently control and benefit from sovereign wealth, if at all. I identify three main areas of SWF behaviour that impact upon citizens' potential to own their funds: the management, investment and distribution of sovereign wealth. This list is not exhaustive. Consider that the question of whether to establish an SWF in the first place and how it is funded will also have implications for a community. For instance, should a government be spending on present-day needs rather than saving for future generations? In a climate-conscious age, is it even appropriate to encourage the establishment of sovereign funds with commodity receipts if those windfalls are generated through the exploitation of fossil fuels? Will placing large portions of public wealth in quarantined government funds help democratize a government, or corrupt it? While such issues are touched on throughout the book, they do not form a central focus because they leave unaddressed the very real and pressing issues facing existing funds.

Consider how SWF management impacts upon sponsor communities. Sovereign funds are playing an increasingly important role in the management of government windfalls and income surpluses. The injection of sizeable chunks of national savings into capital markets through SWFs is both a blessing and a burden for sponsor communities.[38] On the one hand, sovereign funds offer improved potential for public-wealth maximization. On the other, they do so by exposing large chunks of public wealth to the vicissitudes of global financial markets. Indeed, sovereign funds are part of a growing trend in which the long-term prosperity of many nations is increasingly entwined with the financial economy.[39] In an era of heightened volatility in financial markets, the need for accountability and transparency in national wealth management intensifies.

Problematically, sovereign funds can be designed and managed in a way that hinders such accountability. SWFs are frequently established as separate, independent authorities, outside the traditional organs of state. Even when SWFs are located within finance ministries or central banks, they are often exempt from the same degree of answerability or transparency as other parts of the bureaucracy. Transparency is particularly lacking in those funds established as segregated investment tranches within central banks.[40]

Add to this the accountability challenges posed by the actual task of SWF investment management. A basic rationale for sovereign funds is to enable a portion of national capital to be invested in higher risk assets with the aim of yielding higher returns than is typically possible through central banks and Treasuries. This demands a more specialized, complex set of asset-management skills than traditional investment activities in central banks and Treasury departments. As a result, the key task of investing SWF assets is often outsourced to the financial industry or managed in-house within sovereign funds by specially recruited financial managers with a more sophisticated investment capability.[41] While this promises potentially higher returns on national savings than possible through conventional state agencies, it raises accountability concerns given the redistribution of state capital from public coffers to private markets and often to the direct control of 'arm's-length' asset managers. All of these features of SWF management beg the question: who should control the *management* of sovereign wealth (and how)?[42]

The second way in which SWFs impact upon the members of their establishing communities is through their investment activity. The 'special status' of government investors as public actors[43] has sparked debate about whether SWFs – more so than private investors – should marry their investment strategies with laudable social goals. This could involve constraining the investment universe of SWFs to assets considered ethical according to the values of the community whose public capital is invested, or requiring the fund to invest so as to promote certain policy goals of the state actively.[44]

Implicit in these debates is a view that unique ethical obligations attach to government investors since, unlike other institutional investors, SWFs make investment decisions on behalf of an entire political community of citizens.[45] Sovereign funds therefore implicate citizens in their investment choices when they allocate stocks of national wealth to particular assets. They do so in a coercive manner since citizens rarely enjoy the kind of exit option from sovereign funds that they do with a pension or other form of private investment fund. Instead, governments, and their arm's-length fund managers, choose on behalf of citizens. A community may be opposed to child labour but discover that its national fund has channelled millions of dollars to fashion brands that manufacture their wares in sweatshops.

For some, the unique public nature of SWFs is a basis for demanding that more stringent ethical standards should apply to sovereign funds relative to peer institutional investors.[46] Others, including some SWFs, have rejected demands that they be subject to higher moral standards on the grounds that this constrains their ability to generate optimal returns.[47] There is a possible justice cost, they argue, to this constrained investment universe in that it deprives domestic communities of potential wealth, 'adversely impacting the living standards of both current and future generations'.[48]

On either view, though, there is an implicit sense that special obligations attach to SWF investment practices by virtue of the *public* status of their invested capital,[49] irrespective of whether the investment is undertaken by public or private sector managers. As more states establish these funds, governments assume new responsibilities as well as enhanced capability to influence market behaviour through their SWFs. Questions naturally follow as to how SWF *investment* decision-making should be governed to ensure that the values and collective conscience of a sponsor citizenry are protected and promoted through deployment of its sovereign wealth. A second key question for this book, then, is how should a community *invest* its sovereign wealth?

The third area of domestic impact by SWFs concerns the *distribution* of their revenue streams. Knotty questions persist regarding the potential use of SWF income (i.e. the annual returns generated on fund investments). How should a government use the fund's investment returns? Should it reinvest returns into the fund principal or allocate the income to immediate expenditure? For, even though the investment of sovereign wealth is often outsourced to private managers, SWF returns remain at the behest of their state sponsor. As Chile's experience showed, when managed successfully,

SWFs offer a new financing tool in the government policy kit, boosting the state's redistributive potential.

America and Europe have also witnessed this transformative power of SWFs for the public purse. In 1977, the Alaska Permanent Fund (APF) started with initial seed capital of $2.7 million.[50] Today, it is valued at over $53 billion,[51] making it one of the largest public asset managers in the US.[52] Even more dazzling is the growth of Europe's largest sovereign fund, the Norwegian Government Pension Fund Global (GPFG). The GPFG only received its first net transfer of $310 million (NOK 2 billion) twenty years ago.[53] Today, it is valued at approximately $825 billion, making it the largest SWF in the world.[54]

Naturally, these impressive new levels of public wealth trigger competing demands over its use. As the assets, number and power of SWFs grow, so too do proposals for their expenditure. Current suggestions include employing SWFs as development funds,[55] anti-poverty tools,[56] mechanisms for addressing human rights injustices,[57] and financing sources for egalitarian distributive schemes like Citizen's Income (an unconditional income payment at regular intervals to all adult citizens) and Basic Capital (a one-off lump-sum grant of assets to all adult citizens upon maturity).[58] Remarkably, the current debate lacks a basis for adjudicating between these possible applications and recommending the most appropriate use for SWF income streams. A third key issue, then, for community sponsors of SWFs is how should they *distribute* their sovereign fund earnings?

These dilemmas show that SWFs turn governments into managers, investors and distributors of wealth in a manner that causes both anxiety and optimism for the domestic citizen–state relationship. Sovereign funds have the potential to realize *or* subvert the goals and values of their sponsor communities. Yet meaningful ownership of SWFs requires that citizens be able to control and benefit from their funds. They must be able to ensure that the local impact of a sovereign fund is welfare enhancing, not diminishing; that it facilitates rather than obstructs the shared goals of a community. Accordingly, the model of citizen ownership defended in this book recommends principles to help transform SWFs into community funds that citizens directly control and benefit from. That is, to convert sovereign wealth into citizens' wealth.

Parts II and III of this book consider the case for citizen control and benefit rights to sovereign wealth respectively. I propose substantially increased democratic control over SWF management and investment through a range of measures, including an enhanced ability for citizens to influence and constrain the boards and management of SWFs directly; an ethically constrained investment mandate for all funds to ensure citizen values are better protected and promoted in the investment of sovereign wealth; and greater transparency and direct accountability to citizens in SWFs' everyday operations. I also recommend more direct benefit rights for citizen-owners to fund income through individualized distribution of investment returns or direct investment in community-enhancing projects. The book's main argument is that all these measures will help ensure that the government manager of an SWF is truly the agent of its principal, the people, and that sovereign wealth is the citizens' wealth.

Transforming sovereign funds into community funds

Realizing the proposed model of citizen ownership over sovereign wealth has far-reaching practical implications for the design and operation of sovereign funds. The final crucial task of this book, then, is to assess the feasibility and desirability of my suggested reforms. To this end, Parts II and III compare current practice among SWFs to the proposed theoretical ideal, demonstrating that the idea of citizens' wealth in sovereign funds is far, although not impossibly distant, from current institutional practice. The real-world comparison focuses on the strengths and weaknesses of role-model funds, highlighting what they do well and isolating what could be improved to ensure that SWFs operate first and foremost as the property of citizens, not their representative governments. The most detailed analysis focuses on funds in developed democracies, in particular those of Norway, New Zealand and Alaska. The SWFs in these communities are already exemplary in the SWF world for their democratic management (Norway), responsible investment (New Zealand and Norway) and fair distribution of sovereign wealth returns (Alaska). Their experience offers invaluable insight into how communities – whether national, provincial or local – with sovereign funds should design and run them to reflect and promote citizens' best interests. Yet, each has still faced challenges in reaching political consensus between state and citizen on the most desirable management and use of their sovereign wealth. Considering how to refine the governance of role-model funds located in prosperous, accountable conditions better isolates whether the proposed reforms are feasible in any real-world setting or are entirely utopian. The analysis suggests cautious optimism about the possibility of such improvements in analogous democratic settings, but patience with regards to a larger-scale roll-out of reforms across the SWF community.

Finally, Part IV considers what should happen next. After reaching an optimistic conclusion in Chapter 11 about the future of sovereign wealth accumulation despite declining commodity revenues and other challenges to global economic growth, Chapter 12 recommends plausible amendments to the Santiago Principles to achieve citizen-ownership of sovereign wealth. If adopted, they would encourage sovereign funds to be more accountable, just institutions in their local communities. Only then can the 'Santiago dilemma' of how to leverage the potential blessings while minimizing the possible burdens of sovereign funds be resolved. If embraced, these reforms will transform *sovereign* funds into *community* funds, funds run by the people, for the people.

PART I

THE BLESSINGS AND BURDENS OF SOVEREIGN WEALTH

2

Do sovereign funds make nations richer?

Britain has spent its pot of black gold. Norway saved a large chunk and
now is sitting on a big pile of money.

Stewart Lansley, economist and financial journalist, 2015[1]

In 1969, the Ekofisk oilfield, one of the most important oilfields in the
North Sea, was discovered in the sea's Norwegian sector. The Forties oilfield,
the largest in the North Sea, was discovered on the United Kingdom side in
1970. By the mid-1970s, production had begun, providing a huge boost to
government revenues for both the UK and Norway. Forty-five years later, in
2014, total tax revenues from North Sea oil to the UK government had
amounted to almost £200 billion,[2] while the Norwegian government has
raised approximately £522 billion in equivalent taxes (6.17 trillion krone).[3]

Both countries discovered the same resource, in the same place, at the
same time, with similar revenue streams. And yet in 2016, Norway had a
sovereign wealth fund worth $825 billion, and has used it to buy over 1 per
cent of global equities and real assets, such as a £348 million, 50 per cent
stake in a major shopping centre in Sheffield, England. The UK, on the
other hand, appears to have nothing so tangible to show for its oil riches,
though at a conservative estimate it could have had an SWF worth £350
billion by 2012.[4]

This observation has caused consternation in the British press over the
past few years, with accusations that politicians squandered this vast

wealth.[5] The UK, it was feared, had missed a unique chance to capture and augment a new source of national wealth, with the extent of its failure reflected in the mirror of Norway's enormous sovereign fund. Why is Norwegian oil money being deployed to buy prize assets in the UK, while the UK has no oil money to spend in Norway? Does the UK have a lower level of public wealth as a result of failing to set up a sovereign wealth fund?

The answers to these questions depend partly on what the UK did with its North Sea revenue stream.[6] They also rely on a proper understanding of exactly what sovereign wealth is and how it affects a nation's bottom line. Placing different types of government revenue – whether resource windfalls, surplus foreign reserves, privatization proceeds or public pensions – into a quarantined sovereign wealth fund *can* dramatically boost national savings. But the creation of an SWF alone does not automatically affect net public wealth. In many cases, a new sovereign fund will simply reflect a reorganization of the national balance sheet. Whether it ultimately helps generate additional wealth for a community will depend on three factors: the type of underlying capital used to seed a fund; successful investment of fund assets; and disciplined, sustainable saving and spending of fund earnings over time. A decently seeded, rule-governed fund, the assets of which are invested prudently and managed in a disciplined way, *can* enrich a nation, but an SWF alone is no guaranteed jackpot of permanent prosperity.

What is sovereign wealth?

The definition of a sovereign wealth fund in the Santiago Principles identifies the main underlying assets for sovereign funds, which could be considered a description of sovereign wealth: 'SWFs are commonly established out of *balance of payments surpluses, official foreign currency operations, the proceeds of privatizations, fiscal surpluses, and/or receipts resulting from commodity exports.*'[7] This definition of an SWF has been adopted by the International Monetary Fund (IMF) in its *Balance of Payments Manual* and by the United Nations accounting definitions,[8] although the term 'sovereign wealth' itself is not defined in either of these documents.

In the absence of a precise definition, assume that sovereign wealth is that wealth held *within sovereign funds.*[9] Sovereign wealth, then, appears to have multiple sources or forms: balance of payments (BoP) and fiscal surpluses, foreign exchange and privatization proceeds, and commodity receipts.[10]

Such an interpretation immediately raises a host of questions for governments and their citizens. Does that mean that only governments with SWFs possess sovereign wealth? The UK clearly possesses its North Sea revenues; it hasn't used them to seed a sovereign fund, so is there no such thing as British sovereign wealth? Does that in turn make Britain poorer than Norway, which converted its equivalent resource revenues into sovereign wealth by creating a sovereign fund?

Similarly, Americans might wonder if they have any national sovereign wealth given the lack of a federal-level SWF for the US. Yet America has the highest number of sovereign funds of any country in the world, boasting nine state-level funds. Does that mean that Alaskans, Texans and the residents of Wyoming, West Virginia, Alabama, New Mexico, Louisiana, Utah and North Dakota are all richer than Americans in other states, at least in terms of sovereign wealth?

Citizens of states which are not resource rich may also be perplexed. Think of China or South Korea, whose central banks boasted enormous foreign reserves for years before they set up their sovereign funds with a portion of their 'surplus' foreign exchange reserves as seed capital. Does that mean China and Korea only possessed sovereign wealth from 2007 and 2005 respectively, after they each created their sovereign funds? If so, did China or Korea's total national wealth change when it established these respective funds?

Understanding sovereign wealth as that capital sitting in SWFs also implies that many nations have only just acquired new levels of wealth given the establishment spree of sovereign funds this century. This latest global spike in SWF creation has fed a view of sovereign wealth as 'fresh' financial capital.[11] Yet, such an impression is for the most part misguided. While the growing use of SWFs in the finance architecture of modern states is new, the capital used to seed them typically comes from established sources of public revenue. Compare the funding sources for SWFs set out in the Santiago Principles (BoP surpluses, foreign exchange gains, privatization proceeds, fiscal surpluses, commodity receipts) with traditional sources of public finance, as set out in Table 2.1. All sources of sovereign wealth (bold in the table) appear in the traditional list of revenue sources for government.

Table 2.1 Sources of public finance

Appropriated resources	Market transactions	Other sources
Commodity receipts from physical resources	Borrowing/bonds	**Privatization/lease of assets**
Taxation/fiscal surpluses	**BoP surpluses**	**Privatization of inventory**
Social security payments	Dividends on equity loans	**Foreign exchange gains**
Printing money	Interest income on loans	Dividends from public agencies
Fines and most fees	Fees for some services	

Source: Adapted from Abelson (2003), table 18.1, p. 322.

This cautions against viewing sovereign wealth as a 'fresh', distinct source of public capital. SWFs are not a 'get rich quick' scheme and sovereign wealth is not necessarily 'new' public capital. Most often, sovereign wealth comes into being through a transfer of some existing public asset from one part of the state's national accounting apparatus to another (an SWF). Since transfers are not wealth-creating as such, states do not automatically become richer just by creating and seeding a sovereign fund.

There are two occasions, however, when sovereign wealth *does* constitute 'new' public wealth. The first is when a community makes a new natural resource discovery and chooses to place that revenue into a sovereign fund. Several such discoveries have dramatically enhanced the balance sheets of governments around the world, whether or not those fresh revenues are placed in a sovereign fund. The accidental discovery in 1948 of the Ghawar oilfield in Saudi Arabia catapulted the newly formed Gulf nation from a sparsely populated desert state to a global energy superpower. Alaska's 1967 discovery of Prudhoe Bay oilfield was another game-changer, providing a singular new source of public revenue nine times the size of its then state budget. More recently, the futures of Mozambique and Mongolia looked more promising following massive gas and mineral discoveries. Standard Bank has estimated that reserves of liquefied natural gas off the northern Mozambique coast could add $39 billion to its economy in the next twenty years, boosting GDP per capita from approximately $650 in 2013 to $4,500 by 2035.[12] Mongolia boasted the world's highest GDP growth in 2011 at 17 per cent on the back of vast mining operations exploiting its impressive gold, coal and copper reserves. For the relatively poor, landlocked nation of 3 million people, the promised wealth flows are transformative, with GDP growth anticipated to average 12 per cent in the coming decade.[13]

Most nations cannot hang their hopes of a richer future on the remote chance that they are sitting atop undiscovered resource wealth. Thankfully, there is a second way in which SWFs promise 'new' wealth for all nations, whether rich in commodities or not. Irrespective of a fund's underlying assets, a sovereign fund generates investment income for its sponsor community if successfully invested in financial markets. The returns earned on the investment activities of a sovereign fund constitute a new revenue stream for governments. This revenue stream can be quite substantial if a community chooses to reinvest annual returns back into the principal of its sovereign fund.

Recent research by the Harvard Kennedy School demonstrated just how significant the potential for creating and augmenting sovereign wealth is through a simply invested SWF portfolio.[14] The analysis compared the difference a rule-based sovereign fund investing resource windfalls in bond and equity markets could have made to the accumulation of national wealth in three oil-producing nations: Saudi Arabia, Nigeria and Azerbaijan. A number of counterfactual scenarios were constructed by applying simple savings rules that would have seen these countries make regular deposits into a savings fund and then invest that capital for a return in a balanced 60/40 global equity/bond portfolio.

The research showed that all three countries failed to properly capitalize on the upward trend in revenues they experienced between 2000 and 2013, either from the rise in oil prices or increase in oil production. As their government coffers swelled, there was scope for even greater accumulation of assets through higher savings *if* transfers to a sovereign fund had occurred on a rule-governed basis, and returns earned by that fund had been reinvested into the SWF principal and allowed to compound.

On a best-case scenario, Saudi Arabia could have accumulated assets of around $1 trillion by 2013, outperforming its actual asset accumulation in the same period by roughly $300 billion. Nigeria and Azerbaijan also accumulated fewer assets than would have been possible under a simple savings rule with reinvestment of returns into a sovereign fund. Strikingly, Nigeria has little to show by way of saved assets from this boom period, with actual savings amounting to around $7 billion by 2013, compared with possible total savings of between $98.5 billion and $113.2 billion. For Azerbaijan, the difference is less dramatic but still significant. In mid-2014, its sovereign wealth fund held around $38 billion in assets, but with a basic savings rule and reinvested income from an SWF, Azerbaijan could have amassed anywhere from $40 billion to $55 billion.

Sovereign wealth and a nation's net worth

If a government wished to exploit the wealth-enhancing potential of a sovereign fund, when and how will creating an SWF have this effect? Both the UK and Norway were beneficiaries of a genuinely new source of national wealth at precisely the same time. Yet only Norway converted that fresh income into sovereign wealth through an SWF, seemingly making itself richer in the process.

That conclusion is a little too hasty. Whether Norway's national bottom line actually improved more than Britain's depends on what the UK did with its North Sea spoils and how that affected its total national wealth compared with the counterfactual of it having set up an SWF. Since not all nations establish sovereign funds with a new resource windfall, or indeed commodity revenues, we need a better, broader grasp of exactly how sovereign wealth, no matter what its origin, can enhance a nation's total wealth.

Several recent works have advanced our conceptual understanding and measurement of national wealth. Much credit goes to Thomas Piketty, who, along with several other economists, has amassed a comprehensive historical dataset, drawing on leading data sources and standards,[15] on the relationship between private and public wealth. Piketty sets out a clear definition of national wealth as 'the total market value of everything owned by the residents and government of a given country at a given point in time, provided that it can be traded on some market'.[16] National wealth, on this account, 'consists of the sum total of *nonfinancial* assets (land, dwellings, commercial inventory, other buildings, machinery, infrastructure, patents, and other directly owned professional assets) and *financial* assets (bank accounts, mutual funds, bonds, stocks, financial investments of all kinds, insurance policies, pension funds, etc.), less the total amount of financial liabilities (debt)' owned by individuals and the government.[17]

This corresponds to what the UN terms the 'net worth of the nation'. In the UN System of National Accounts (SNA),[18] the main official data source on what constitutes wealth, this is defined as 'the difference between the total value of non-financial and financial assets and the total value of liabilities of an economy'.[19] On both the SNA's and Piketty's approaches, national wealth is a stock measure.[20] It corresponds to the total wealth owned at a particular point in time; this stock comes from the wealth appropriated or accumulated in all prior years combined.

There are two main owners of national wealth: governments and individuals. Private wealth is owned by individuals, corporations and other non-state entries, while public wealth is owned by government. The government as owner includes central, subnational and local levels of government and covers 'all public agencies',[21] including government bodies, towns and social insurance agencies.[22] Adding together the public and private capital of a nation gives you the total national wealth of that nation, the same wealth of nations of which Adam Smith spoke.

As sovereign wealth is government owned, it falls within the *public* component of national wealth. More specifically, it is a component of *financial* public wealth. As Piketty explains, public assets also tend to come in two main forms:[23]

1 Non-financial: 'meaning essentially public buildings, used for government offices or for the provision of public services, primarily in health and education: schools, universities, hospitals, etc.'
2 Financial: 'governments can own shares in firms, in which they can have a majority or minority stake. These firms may be located within the nation's borders or abroad. In recent years ... sovereign wealth funds have arisen to manage the substantial portfolios of foreign financial assets that some states have acquired.'[24]

What's so special about SWFs as wealth generators?

Piketty's description rightly stresses the increasingly important role played by SWFs in helping governments own and invest financial assets. Yet sovereign funds are only one means through which governments manage their financial wealth. Indeed, governments hold stock and investments through a variety of entities, including state-owned enterprises (SOEs), public pension funds, central bank reserves[25] and Treasury-held deposits, loans and securities.

Figure 2.1 places SWFs alongside the other major entities available to states for holding and managing financial wealth. It also helps situate sovereign wealth within the broader universe of public capital, both in its financial and non-financial forms. The right-hand side of the diagram consists of non-financial assets, or what Swedish economists Dag Detter and Stefan Fölster term 'public commercial assets'. They include SOEs in this definition.[26] Here, I follow the IMF classification of SOEs as a financial asset, but much work remains to be done on how exactly states define, classify and account for their financial and non-financial assets.[27]

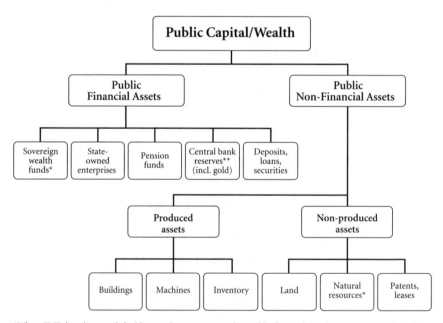

*Where SWFs have been seeded with natural resource proceeds, a public financial asset has originated on the right-hand side of the graph in the non-financial public assets.
**Where SWFs have been seeded with financial assets from the central bank, one type of public financial asset has been created with a different public financial asset.

Source: Adapted from IMF (2013).

Figure 2.1 Sovereign wealth in the universe of public capital

As SWFs are just one of several instruments through which sovereigns manage financial wealth, why focus only on the wealth-enhancing potential of sovereign funds? This query becomes more pressing when SWFs' smaller wealth holdings relative to peer public entities are acknowledged. As captured in Figure 2.2, SWFs in 2015 were estimated to hold 22.5 per cent of global public financial assets, with the remainder sitting in central banks and public pension funds.

However, the focus on SWFs is still justified on two counts. First, although the bulk of public financial wealth sits in other entities at present, the wealth-creating potential of sovereign funds is greater than that of central banks and public pension funds. The mandate of central banks is restricted to managing reserve assets for safety and liquidity, not return. That is precisely why several nations with excess reserves, including China, Korea and Singapore, removed a portion of their surplus foreign exchange assets from their central banks and allocated them to a separate sovereign fund, tasked with a higher risk–return strategy.[28]

In contrast, the money in public pension funds ultimately belongs to public sector employees on whose behalf the state makes contributions, *not* the government investing those pension assets on their behalf. It is this liability and ownership profile that distinguishes public pension funds

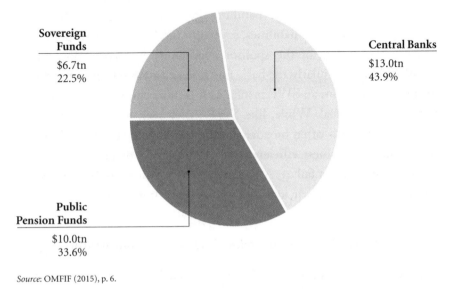

Sovereign Funds
$6.7tn
22.5%

Central Banks
$13.0tn
43.9%

Public Pension Funds
$10.0tn
33.6%

Source: OMFIF (2015), p. 6.

Figure 2.2 Global public assets under management by category, 2015

from SWFs. Fixed liabilities mean pension funds must be invested more conservatively than SWFs, limiting their relative wealth-creating potential. Even if they perform exceptionally well, the legal entitlement of individual claimants to those assets means they ultimately will disappear from the state's coffers into the private savings of pensioners. There are, however, a number of SWFs that fall into the category of 'reserve' or 'contingent' public pension funds, which some governments have created to cover potential shortfalls in their pension liabilities. Governments are not legally obliged to use such funds for this particular purpose, nor are those fund assets owned by individuals, even though one day they may be used to help offset government liabilities through distribution to individual pensioners. But as the government sponsor is free to use these assets for a different purpose, they are distinct beasts from public pension funds. Such funds include the Chilean Pension Reserve Fund, Australian Future Fund and the New Zealand Superannuation Fund, all of which are officially SWFs and whose assets count as sovereign wealth.

The second reason for looking closely at SWFs within the universe of public finance managers is that sovereign funds' raison d'être is to assist governments with the preservation and augmentation of a nation's financial wealth. Unlike central banks, treasuries and public pension funds, which seek to manage financial assets to serve other policy goals such as controlling currency supply, handling government financial flows or funding superannuation liabilities, sovereign funds' essential purpose is to enhance the welfare of the sponsor community by maximizing public wealth holdings. Similarly, the basic function of a state-owned enterprise is distinguishable from an SWF insofar as it is more commercial and operational than financial. While, like SWFs, they seek to increase national capital, their task is often broader, aiming to promote economic development, improve business efficiency in certain sectors or provide a service where there is market failure. A comprehensive treatment of SWFs ensures focus on the most explicit, ambitious public wealth investor.

When and how do sovereign funds boost public wealth?

We have seen that if an SWF has been seeded from revenues of items already on the public balance sheet then, by definition, it cannot affect net public wealth. If a government uses official currency reserves to create an SWF, then it has merely reorganized its balance sheet. The same applies for the monetization of non-financial assets used to create an SWF: natural resources, government land and buildings, SOEs, etc., are all already part of public wealth. When a government uses those assets to create an SWF, all that has happened (in the first instance) is that the government has reorganized its public wealth by realizing the monetary value of those assets through their sale or exploitation.

Similarly, when a government issues new debt to raise funds to seed an SWF, there is *no* effect on public wealth. Although government assets have indeed increased in that scenario, government liabilities have been raised by exactly the same amount. Thus, there has been no change to net public wealth. In short, SWFs that come from balance sheet reorganization do not affect net public wealth simply by virtue of being created; so SWFs seeded from natural resource revenues,[29] privatizations[30] or from debt issuances[31] do not themselves affect net public wealth.

Of course, in the long run they will affect net public wealth if a sovereign wealth fund generates higher rates of return than the initial value of those assets. So, a sovereign fund generating positive returns and re-investing those returns into the fund will generally outperform the value of unexploited natural resources in the ground and the unrealized market value of a state-owned asset.[32] An SWF is also a net gain even when seeded by debt if the rate of return of the fund is higher than the interest rate on the debt product used to finance the fund. All these scenarios result in an SWF *increasing* net public wealth in the long run. The converse is that if there is a financial crash, or for some reason the SWF underperforms, then the SWF might decrease net public wealth in the long run.

An SWF could only affect net public wealth if the funds *do not* originate from sources already on the public balance sheet as stock, such as BoP or fiscal surpluses. These sources of public finance reflect a temporary increase in government revenues in any given year. A government may choose to carve out a portion of these and store them in an SWF. Or it may choose to keep it in the Treasury coffers. Either way, better annual performance in either of these areas results in a new, positive contribution to public wealth.

In theory, then, when the UK did not establish a sovereign fund with its North Sea proceeds, it did *not* necessarily squander these assets. If the value of its natural resources was already reflected in the national accounts when those assets were under the sea, it simply monetized that value when it exploited the assets for sale, converting one aspect of its public wealth from a non-financial to a financial asset.

Perhaps the UK still missed a chance to boost its overall wealth when it chose not to create a sovereign fund with its newly monetized public asset. However, even in the case of SWFs that are created with new revenue sources, it is not guaranteed that all such SWFs increase net public wealth. Assume for a moment that the UK's discovery of its North Sea resources in 1970 reflects as a brand new line item on the national balance sheet. The influx of revenue streams from this asset from 1970 onwards produces BoP surpluses, which the government can then use in one of four general ways besides establishing an SWF. These options can be pursued singly or in combination. Each has a distinct effect on net public wealth:

(i) Increased government consumption   If the government chooses to use its new revenues to increase spending on consumption goods such as nurses' and teachers' salaries, this would *not* affect the public balance sheet in any way. The new money comes in and immediately goes out in spending on overheads. One could view this as 'squandering' this revenue source, but that depends partly on how high the demand of the present generation is for better public services. For this reason, several developing nations such as Mozambique and India have decided against establishing sovereign funds with new resource windfalls, preferring to increase spending on heavily in-demand public services.

Moreover, when governments do choose to spend rather than save new revenue, some of the government expenditure will be received as income and saved by the private sector, contributing to private wealth, and hence boosting national wealth. If, instead, a government's newly received revenue is used to create an SWF, it will only increase national wealth by the amount it exceeds the contribution made by private sector savings, not by the full value of the SWF.

(ii) Increased government investment The government investment scenario involves a government allocating new revenues to investments

(capital expenditure) in roads, schools, hospitals, transport and communications infrastructure, or *financial* investments, for example in pension funds or social security funds. All of these options involve increasing the *stock* of government assets, whether financial or non-financial.

Alternatively, if that same revenue is instead used to create an SWF, then the SWF does *not* automatically increase net public wealth more than would occur if the government invested in infrastructure or a social security fund. Greater government investment in infrastructure or financial assets could be just as wealth-boosting as an SWF, or more so. That will ultimately depend on the return earned by each of those investments.

(iii) Tax cuts Using new revenue to fund tax cuts maintains government spending at its previous levels, but reduces the revenue taken in from taxes. The government's lost income from taxes is simply replaced by its new revenue source. This option sees *no* increase in total government assets.

However, since some proportion of tax cuts will be saved by the private sector, there will be an increase in private wealth from this policy. National wealth will therefore increase under this option. If, however, the new revenue is instead used to create an SWF, then, although this SWF does increase net public wealth compared to the alternative, it does not increase national wealth by the full value of the SWF. Indeed, if the entirety of the tax cut would have been saved, then there is no difference in national wealth between tax cuts and creating an SWF.

(iv) Deficit/debt reduction The final option available to governments in possession of a new revenue stream is to reduce the deficit or pay off outstanding government debt. This option allows the government to maintain its current spending level, but reduce its liabilities. As a result, net public wealth increases because the government has reduced or removed its borrowing costs.

Compared with this option, an SWF would not therefore increase net public wealth: an SWF increases government assets by the value of the new revenue; deficit/debt reduction decreases government liabilities by the value of the new revenue. Both these options increase net public wealth by the same amount. The only way in which an SWF would outperform debt or deficit reduction is if the returns earned on investing sovereign wealth are greater than the (now removed) cost of borrowing. If it costs a government 5 per cent to borrow capital, but it could earn 10 per cent through its SWF investments, it would be wise to use the new revenues for an SWF which could both help service the debt/deficit (5 per cent) and bring in future revenues (5 per cent).

Considering all four scenarios together, the creation of an SWF only affects public balance sheets positively if a given country's wealth has emerged from sources not already on public balance sheets *and* if it has not made decisions to invest that wealth elsewhere or to pay down public debt (both of which have the same *initial* effect as creating an SWF of increasing national wealth).

Yet, of those policy options that increase overall national wealth, the creation of an SWF is the only policy that bestows on a nation a tangible and easily identifiable financial legacy – in the form of a quarantined pot of financial assets. It may also be the option that most effectively raises and preserves national wealth *over time* by offering a more efficient and effective vehicle for value creation and growth through financial markets.

Is the UK worse off without an SWF?

If the UK had spent its North Sea oil revenues on government investments – in schools, hospitals or state-owned industries – then, initially, UK public wealth would have increased by just as much as if it had established an SWF. The wealth would simply have appeared differently on the balance sheet: instead of appearing in an SWF as a financial asset, it would have appeared as a 'building' or 'SOE' or 'inventory' item as a non-financial asset. In either case, public assets would have increased by the same amount. However, UK public sector net investment plunged from 2.5 per cent of GDP at the start of the Thatcher era to just 0.4 per cent by 2000.[33] It seems revenues, for the most part, were not invested.

If the UK government had used this wealth to reduce its fiscal deficit, or to reduce the stock of debt, Britain's public wealth would still have increased. Instead of putting the money into an SWF and increasing its assets, it could have been ploughed into debt reduction and decreasing liabilities. This would have also increased public net wealth *initially* by the same amount as establishing a sovereign fund. However, although net government debt did fall in the second half of the 1980s, it went straight back up again in the early 1990s, suggesting this was merely a cyclical effect.[34] It seems that the British government, unlike its Norwegian counterparts, failed to tangibly and lastingly increase public wealth with those same resource revenues.

In fact, it seems that in the UK 'the oil money enabled non-oil taxes to be kept lower'.[35] When the North Sea was providing maximum income, Nigel Lawson, Thatcher's Chancellor of the Exchequer, slashed income and other direct taxes: most notably, the top rate of tax came down from 60 pence in the pound to just 40 pence by 1988. Thus, the UK used the revenue to fund a public giveaway, primarily to higher rate taxpayers.

Does this mean that the UK's national wealth is lower than it could have been as a result? Not necessarily. Certainly, *public* wealth is lower as a result. But if UK taxpayers saved and invested the entirety of their tax breaks, then *private* wealth would have risen by an equivalent amount. Thus, if UK consumers behaved in this way, then the policies of both the UK and Norway would have identical effects on national wealth (which is made up of both public and private wealth). Indeed, many core macroeconomic models would predict that the establishment of an SWF and tax cuts would have exactly the same effect on national wealth; those models suppose that those receiving the tax cuts would invest the proceeds so that when the oil runs out, they (or their children) would be able to carry on as if nothing had happened.[36]

Some of this theoretical prediction was borne out in practice: much of that higher disposable income was used to invest in property and bid up house prices.[37] As a result, much of Britain's oil wealth has ended up in bricks and mortar, and so still contributed to the country's national wealth.[38] Nonetheless, the UK taxpayer did not save the entirety of the windfall. In general, tax cuts are almost never entirely saved,[39] and in this particular case the data do not look promising as far as saving most of those tax cuts is concerned.[40]

Consequently, although national wealth increased somewhat through greater private investment, it did not increase by as much or for as long as it would have done had the UK followed Norway in establishing an SWF. Nor did it necessarily increase as fairly as would have been the case if those wealth gains had been captured in a sovereign fund. Tax breaks for the top tax bracket effectively distribute the bulk of windfall revenues to a single higher-earning cohort of the population. The subsequent pouring of those savings into property investment, further fuelling the UK's affordable housing crisis, only amplified the unequal distribution of benefit from these windfalls. One might argue, then, that even though the difference in net impact on national wealth between creating a sovereign fund versus other spending and investment decisions with new revenues is negligible, there is a meaningful difference when it comes to the *fair* distribution of those new revenues and the subsequent national wealth they help create. Capturing temporary increases in national wealth in a sovereign fund offers government the potential to pursue a more equitable distribution of those wealth gains than other spending and investment options. Few of the alternatives for using new public revenues offer such a permanent, lasting and equally shareable increase to national wealth as a sovereign fund.

To create or not to create an SWF: that is the question

The contrasting experiences of Britain and Norway are instructive for communities pondering the creation of an SWF. The economic case for a sovereign fund will depend on the individual circumstances and objectives of a potential SWF-creator community. That decision should consider the macroeconomic context, the underlying asset used to generate sovereign wealth and the intended role of the sovereign fund within the overall policy framework of the sponsor government. Substantial research on these aspects of whether and when to set up a sovereign fund from an economic point of view has been conducted elsewhere.[41]

Politically speaking, the question of SWF creation is somewhat different in focus. It is ultimately a question about whether this is a desirable policy move for the domestic citizen–state relationship. When the divergent experiences of Norwegian and British sovereign wealth are juxtaposed, Norway's decision to establish a sovereign fund boasts several advantages over the UK's course of action. Norwegian governments and citizens can point to their GPFG and unequivocally state 'here is our oil money'. Their sovereign wealth is identifiable and easily quantifiable, enhancing the sense in which this public asset is accountable to both state and citizen. In contrast, British public debates tend to lament their 'squandered' North Sea windfalls, suggesting that Britons lack an observable legacy, financial or otherwise, from these revenues. Even though much of Britain's resource windfalls were captured as private wealth in housing and property, wealth *in this form* has failed to convey the same sense of a lasting community endowment as that bestowed by Norway's sovereign fund.

Norway's sovereign wealth is also now, in theory, permanent. By placing its resource windfalls in a sovereign fund, Norway converted its finite resource wealth into a lasting and transferable asset. This has ensured that the exploitation of this significant public asset did not just benefit those generations who were lucky enough to exploit and sell their North Sea riches, but that future generations will also experience and benefit from this capital as it can be preserved in the form of financial assets.

In Britain, the conversion of the UK's resource wealth into housing market gains has meant that only a certain segment of the home-owning population has enjoyed the inherited trappings of North Sea riches. Compared with Norway, Britain's failure to establish a sovereign fund perpetuated two inequalities: one intergenerational, the other national. Not all past citizens gained equally from those riches at the time of their creation (national inequality), nor have all current citizens enjoyed this bequest relative to their ancestors (intergenerational equality).

So, while an SWF is just one way of using government revenue to contribute to national wealth, it more than other policy options promises that the entirety of a public windfall remains a national and, most importantly, *public* asset, with the potential for more egalitarian distribution among citizens today and across time.

3

Whose wealth is it: state's or citizens'?

Accepting ... that the people of Alaska have ultimate sovereignty, we reject [the] conclusion that the people own the state's natural resources ... [T]he people of the State of Alaska have very clearly constituted the state as owner of the natural resources which give rise to the fund in question.

US Court of Appeals, Ninth Circuit, 1987[1]

In the 1980s, the citizens of Alaska took their government to court. Over a series of cases that went all the way from Alaska's district benches to the United States Supreme Court, Alaskans asserted their rightful ownership of the state's sovereign wealth. On that basis, they challenged their state government's right to tax annual dividends paid to each citizen from the returns earned by their sovereign fund, the Alaska Permanent Fund (APF). The people argued that they shouldn't be taxed on something that already belonged to them. The State of Alaska disagreed, asserting ultimate ownership of the sovereign fund and its underlying assets – proceeds from the exploitation and sale of Alaska's natural resources.

A decade earlier, in 1976, the Alaska government had established the APF to save and invest windfalls from the state's vast mineral resources. After a few years of successful management, the government began direct distributions of a portion of the APF's returns to Alaska's citizens. Known as the Permanent Fund Dividend (PFD), every year since 1982 all eligible citizens of Alaska who apply have received a personal cheque for their per-capita share of a proportion of the fund's annual earnings. A resident of Alaska who has received all thirty-four annual PFD payments from 1982 to 2015 has received a total of $39,100.[2] That amounts to $56,100 in 2016 dollar terms. This distribution of Permanent Fund returns ensures that each Alaskan receives their individual share of the state's collective wealth.

For that very reason, the taxation of the PFD caused some ire back in its early days. Some Alaskans wondered what right the government had to tax resources that already belonged to the people. Two such citizens initiated legal action, arguing that the dividend should be declared tax-exempt on two grounds. The first held that the dividend was a distribution of earnings from property – mineral deposits – belonging to the individual residents of Alaska, not the state. As shown in the epigraph, the appellate court rejected that argument, following the lower court in relying on language in the Alaska Constitution referring to *the state* as owner of Alaska's natural resources. The appellate court also ruled that, regardless, the dividend counts as income on a number of constitutionally accepted definitions and was therefore taxable.

The petitioners advanced a second argument, arguing 'that because the state paid the dividends without expecting anything in return, it constituted a gift and gifts are not taxable'.[3] The appellate court found it difficult to dismiss this argument since it had concluded in the other suit that 'the people' did not own Alaska's resource wealth and therefore 'the state' did not owe them anything. Nevertheless, the gift argument was ultimately rejected on different grounds. The PFD was declared taxable. The state won.

The Alaska legal dispute is fascinating, not so much for the legal conclusion reached by the courts, but for the reasoning employed by the bench. The courts at the appellate level both treated the State of Alaska and its citizenry as independent and ultimately competing candidates for ownership of Alaska's sovereign wealth. This characterization reflected a deeper confusion within Alaska's community over the rightful owner of its sovereign wealth. Is it state property, managed primarily for the benefit of the sponsoring government and its agencies, or the people's property simply managed by governments on the citizenry's behalf?

These thorny issues persist today in Alaska. In early 2016, the Alaska State Legislature was considering a series of reforms proposed by Governor Bill Walker and Alaska state legislators to cap the dividend and redirect part of the Permanent Fund's earnings to help fund government in a more sustainable way. The reform proposals came about in response to a fiscal crisis in Alaska. With the dramatic drop in oil prices and falling production, Alaska's oil revenues have fallen 88 per cent from 2012 to 2016.[4] The state has been in deficit since 2013, with a massive projected shortfall of $3.6 billion out of a budget of $5.2 billion for the 2016 financial year. This is despite radical spending cuts that saw the budget slashed from $8 billion in 2012 to $4.8 billion in 2015. Oil revenues fell faster than spending, and although Alaska has a Constitutional Budget Reserve for precisely such occasions, at its current value of just over $6 billion, it will be empty within two years if tapped to cover deficits of this scale.

These fiscal challenges and proposed amendments to the Permanent Fund and popular dividend programme again raise fundamental questions about the balance of rights between government and citizen to Alaska's sovereign wealth. Lurking beneath these Alaska debates are unresolved issues about the status of state-owned assets which are of relevance to all communities. Can a state own something in its own right, for its independent benefit, and therefore appropriate a public asset for government use irrespective of the preferences of community members? If not, how should state institutions managing public assets be designed to ensure that a community's collective interest in and desire to benefit from such assets is respected? Where does this leave sovereign wealth sitting in government-controlled SWFs: whose wealth is it – the state's or the citizens'?

The Alaska case is not isolated. Tension abounds between states and their citizens over claims to sovereign wealth. Since the Alaska legal battle thirty years ago, conflict involving SWF assets has occurred across the developed and developing world, in democratic and non-democratic contexts. This chapter reviews some of those cases. If citizens and their state agencies are capable of asserting rival claims to sovereign wealth, whose claim should triumph and on what basis?

There are several steps to answering this question. First, we need to consider the intended owners. This task is tricky since policy and legal documents on SWF ownership identify an array of possible owners in the public sphere, spurring a definitional debate in both popular and academic discourse over the precise nature of a sovereign wealth fund. But we only need worry about this confusion if it causes problems in the practical world of sovereign wealth management. In fact, plentiful evidence of conflict over sovereign wealth exists. It displays in states as varied as China, Australia, Ireland, Nigeria and Libya, among others. Just this small sample of SWF conflicts suggests that the level of economic development and type of political regime fail to inoculate communities against struggles over their sovereign wealth. Accordingly, a universal strategy for resolving this harmful ownership ambiguity is needed. The chapter proposes such a strategy in closing.

SWF ownership in theory

Ever since its formal emergence in 2005, the term 'sovereign wealth fund' has been beset with definitional difficulties. There was never and still is no 'single, accepted, fully operational definition of sovereign wealth funds',[5] with a lack of agreement about the most fundamental terms in the debate.[6] That has created complications for identifying the funds' intended and actual owners.

Some have blamed this definitional elusiveness on the opaque nature of SWFs, with public availability of information about fund operation, size and management varying between funds and over time.[7] Others point to the heterogeneous nature of SWFs and the absence of an archetypal fund.[8] Still others point to the hybrid public–private nature of SWFs,[9] making them simultaneously public actors responsible to citizens in their sponsoring state and investment destinations, and market actors, accountable to their financial managers operating with profit motives.[10]

However, there is a different diagnosis. While these factors are undoubtedly important, the definitional confusion around SWFs is in large part driven by ambiguity surrounding their precise ownership. A review of early definitions in scholarly, policy and organizational literature is presented in Appendix 2. The sample reveals not only the proliferation of definitions of 'sovereign wealth fund', but also the extent of inconsistency between them when it comes to their ownership. The source of the ambiguity appears to be the malleable term 'sovereign'.[11] Within the sample, the list of explicit or implied owners is extensive. While each is some actor associated with the public sphere, the list varies substantially in degree of abstraction, with intangible entities such as 'the state', 'government', 'nation', 'citizens' and 'the country' identified as owners alongside more specific candidates like 'the bureaucracy' or particular organizations like the 'central bank' or 'Treasury'.

One explanation for this inconsistency is that the terms used are *not* necessarily intended to refer to different public entities. Rather, they may be used synonymously to express the same broad idea of public ownership. Indeed, casual commingling of terms is a persistent feature of ordinary language and academic discourse where the 'public sphere' is concerned. Consider the regular conflation of words like 'state' and 'nation';[12] 'nation' and 'country';[13] 'government' and 'state';[14] and 'state' and 'citizenry'.[15] A Deutsche Bank definition of SWFs (included in Appendix 2) is illustrative of this interchangeable use of public sphere concepts. It explicitly identifies 'the state' as SWF owner, while simultaneously using the terms 'public', 'government' and 'central bank' to describe the source and character of its assets.

The semantic slipperiness plaguing formal SWF definitions may be overstated. To some extent, this disparity reflects the variety of actual ownership arrangements in place between SWFs and their state sponsors. As Professor of Economics at Peking University HSBC Business School and author of *Sovereign Wealth Funds: The New Intersection of Money and Politics* Christopher Balding observed, 'Countries have taken various approaches to the relationship between sovereign wealth funds and governments. Some SWFs are managed by the finance ministry, some by the central bank, and others by nominally independent entities.'[16] The variety of possible SWF owners may simply reflect the funds' varied institutional arrangements. All the different terms may simply be proxies for the wider concept of a public ownership.

But how does the idea that SWFs must be managed *separately* from entities like the central bank and outside traditional organs of state like the Treasury sit alongside the idea of 'the state' as owner? When we look to the real-world experience of sovereign wealth ownership and management, a demand for definitional precision becomes more urgent. On the ground, there is deep disagreement and confusion over these funds' legitimate owner(s). Any theoretical consensus on the meaning of 'sovereign' in the SWF moniker must also translate into a practical consensus within communities that possess sovereign funds.

Conflict and confusion over sovereign wealth

Looking around the world of SWFs today, rivalry between governments and their people over sovereign wealth is commonplace. Citizens may conflict with a particular government, political party or state agency over the proper status of SWF assets. Alternatively, different arms of the state may compete with each other, vying for control over sovereign wealth. Such conflict is often destructive, hindering effective and accountable management of public wealth and corroding trust in the domestic citizen–state relationship. It is vital, then, to understand exactly when and how such conflict over SWF assets manifests.

To this end, contemporary episodes of discord over sovereign wealth are considered in five distinct nations: Australia, Nigeria, Ireland, China and Libya. All differ vastly in terms of political regime and socioeconomic development.[17] Yet all share a common experience of disagreement over the ownership status of their SWF assets. Sometimes this results from simple *confusion* over the status of sovereign wealth that frustrates accountable and effective management of a nation's capital (Australia, Nigeria). Other times, rights to sovereign wealth are deeply contested, with outright *conflict* occurring, either among state actors (China) or between state and citizen (Ireland, Alaska, Libya). The necessary course of action, then, is to minimize potential for confusion and outright conflict over sovereign wealth. As long as the ownership of SWFs remains ambiguous, such discord may occur in any community that has, or wishes to establish, a sovereign fund.

These episodes of discord contain three clear themes. One is that public sphere actors compete over sovereign assets irrespective of the social, political and economic character of the sponsor. The variety of cases here includes poor and prosperous states in more and less democratic polities, cautioning against the inference that government and citizen rivalry over SWFs is purely a function of less accountable power structures in non-democratic regimes.

The second theme is that government is not always a unified force *against* the citizenry. It is both susceptible to its own internal rivalries, as demonstrated by China's experience, discussed shortly; as well as capable of better promoting the welfare of citizens in certain circumstances. Think of Chile's internal discord in 2008 over the proposed use of its sovereign wealth discussed in Chapter 1. During the copper price boom, the government's decision to quarantine its resource windfalls in new sovereign funds deeply angered Chileans. But when the copper price fell, the government's unpopular decision was vindicated as the country was able to ride out the difficult financial times without inflicting too much financial pain on the ordinary Chileans. Disagreement between state and citizen here was the result of government taking an unpopular but wise and long-term view over the best use of a community's sovereign wealth.

This links to the third theme, that the presence of conflict does not always result in a bad policy outcome, but can signal a governance or accountability failure on the government's behalf. Ireland's experience over the radical reforms to its sovereign fund at the height of its financial crisis is a case in point. While those reforms breached best practice standards of SWF governance and counted for some as 'raiding' the nation's sovereign wealth,[18] given how well Ireland has recovered economically and financially, these measures may have, on balance, represented the most prudent decision for current and future citizens. That said, tension around these eventually sound reforms could have been minimized if there had been a clear conversation between state and citizens over the need for reform and the status of the country's sovereign wealth.

Compare the public conversation taking place in Alaska now and in recent years over its fiscal future and possible reforms to its sovereign fund. This debate displays deep differences of opinion within the community and among political leaders. But it has been conducted in an open, consultative manner with Governor Bill Walker attempting to explain the case for reform[19] through public consultation. Following Governor Walker's election in November 2014, the Governor's Office has conducted a budget survey, numerous conversations on a sustainable future, and meetings around the state to inform and seek public opinion on how to overcome Alaska's current fiscal challenges.[20] Organizations such as the Rasmuson Foundation[21] and Alaska Common Ground[22] are also facilitating state-wide meetings to inform citizens on the fiscal situation and various reform proposals. Whether Alaska can develop a budget plan that attracts widespread support remains to be seen. But so far, the differing views of state and citizens over Alaska's fiscal future have formed part of a wider public conversation around its sovereign wealth. Unfortunately, as the discussion below illustrates, the Alaska experience stands out as a novel effort to mediate and minimize conflict over sovereign wealth.

Confusion over sovereign wealth

Nigeria and Australia display recent instances of the type of confusion that Alaska suffered in the 1980s regarding the ultimate owner of its sovereign wealth. The resultant legal battle over the taxability of Alaska's SWF-financed dividends demonstrated in sharp, legal relief that contradictory understandings of who owns sovereign wealth can lead to outright rivalry between state and citizen.

Nigeria

In May 2011, Nigeria created the Nigeria Sovereign Investment Authority (NSIA) to improve the management of Nigeria's oil revenue and distribute resource profits more evenly between current and future generations.[23] The NSIA's key objective is to build 'a savings base for the Nigerian people'.[24] The establishing bill also vests ultimate ownership of the fund in the 'people of Nigeria',[25] but requires that this ownership interest be protected by all levels of the Nigerian government through shared management of the NSIA: 'All ownership interest in the Authority shall be held by the Federal, State, Federal Capital Territory and Local governments of the Federation on behalf of the people of Nigeria.'[26]

The bill's language is striking, not only for its explicit reference to 'the people' as owner of the state's resources, but also for the implicit notion of government-as-fiduciary contained in the description of the sovereign fund management. The NSIA is government owned and controlled, but only for the purpose of the government acting as an *agent* for the Nigerian people, the fund's ultimate owner and intended beneficiary.[27]

Despite this, the state-level government threatened the existence of the fund in its early days, asserting a claim to a portion of the NSIA's underlying assets.[28] In August 2011, Nigeria's thirty-six state-level governors challenged the fund's constitutionality.[29] The governors demanded 'their' share of federal revenue be removed from the NSIA and returned to the states. In the words of one governor: 'it is *our* money and *we* need it. We are faced with so many challenges beyond the scope of our financial capacity and we cannot have a situation where the federal government will compel us to save money by not giving us *our* full dues from the Federation Account.'[30]

The governor's language is revealing. The country's oil revenues are conceived of as belonging in part to state *governments* specifically. There is no acknowledgement that resource windfalls channelled to the NSIA are earmarked for *all* Nigerians, the same Nigerians in whose interests all levels of governments are meant to act. On the contrary, the state governors' protest showed disregard for the motivation behind the new SWF to better manage Nigeria's resource wealth in the interests of the people following years of mismanagement of oil revenues.[31] The protest significantly delayed the NSIA's establishment and operationalization, highlighting how such ambiguity around the ownership status of sovereign wealth can frustrate its proper management.[32] Local politics is undoubtedly part of the explanation, but so, it seems, is the exploitable ambiguity surrounding sovereign fund ownership. Even when an SWF is explicitly set up in the interests of 'the people', and the government's ownership interest is plainly set out as fiduciary in nature, the fund's ownership remains contestable by different public sphere actors.

Australia

At the same time, confusion plagued sovereign wealth in the mature democracy of Australia. Disagreement over what to do with the windfalls from Australia's then commodity boom exposed widespread misunderstanding over whether the country's existing sovereign wealth fund belonged to the government or the people. Between 2010 and 2013, Australia enjoyed record income from the super commodity boom and the insatiable resource appetite of Australia's biggest export partner, China. It sparked a debate on whether to establish a national SWF for the benefit of all Australians. A sizeable corpus of politicians, commentators and high profile figures called for an SWF to preserve unprecedented profits from

Australia's finite resource base to ensure Australians of both today and tomorrow could benefit from the nation's wealth.[33]

Interestingly, the country already possessed an SWF that aimed to serve the interests of present and future Australians. Yet few seemed aware of the entity, despite it holding close to AU$100 billion in assets.[34] Just like Chile, Australia's SWF was intended as a contingency fund to help the government cover shortfalls in its forecast public pension bill. Australia had created the Future Fund in 2006 with a one-off transfer of trade surpluses. The main difference between the Australian and Chilean funds was that rather than support a universal pension systems, the Future Fund was intended to finance pension liabilities of federal public servants from 2020 in the event that future governments *were unable to cover the bill.*

The former Treasurer responsible for establishing the Future Fund, Peter Costello, put the lack of public awareness of Australia's existing sovereign fund down to ambiguity around its ownership:

> The confusion in Australia arises from the difference between ownership and purpose [of the Future Fund]. By definition a sovereign wealth fund is owned by a sovereign power – in our case, *the government* . . . The specific purpose it is earmarked for is the growing liability of public sector pensions . . . But the money in the Future Fund is *not owned by public servants.* Public servants did not pay any money into it. It was built by budget surpluses. That money belongs to *all of us* and not just to us, but to future generations.[35]

Peter Costello's imploring of the Australian public to realize that this is 'their' money and not the government's highlights the potential for confusion over proper ownership. This is especially likely when governments' use of sovereign wealth fails to serve a citizenry's notion of the public interest. Australians' lack of general awareness of the Future Fund and the confusion around its ownership identified by the former Treasurer suggests that it is not viewed in the public imagination as a fund for 'the people'.[36] Rather, it is seen (if at all) as a fund for offsetting the government's liabilities as an employer.[37] Even in established democracies, then, a lack of clarity around the ultimate ownership of sovereign wealth can hinder awareness and in turn accountability of a nation's public wealth.

Competition and conflict

In some states, ambiguity around SWF ownership goes beyond confusion, causing conflict and competition between state and citizen or among state actors. Three cases of such conflict follow, presented in order of increasing severity. Ireland experienced contestation over its sovereign wealth, which could have been minimized or mediated through proper consultation with the public. Arguably the country made a defensible through controversial decision regarding its sovereign wealth, albeit one into which Irish citizens should have enjoyed much greater input.

China demonstrates the potential for intrastate conflict over sovereign wealth, with different arms of the state fighting for control SWF assets.

Finally, Libya underscores the extent to which governments can abuse their power over the management of sovereign wealth in the absence of clear, transparent ownership and government structure.

Ireland

The experience of Ireland during the financial crisis illustrates the potential for government–citizen tension over sovereign wealth in the absence of citizen input into sensitive decisions around SWF assets. In 2010, the Irish government controversially directed its SWF, the then National Pensions Reserve Fund (NPRF), to invest in Ireland's struggling banking industry. This move contravened the spirit and the law of the NPRF, a fund set up in 2001 to help offset Ireland's long-term projected pension shortfalls and social welfare costs in light of its ageing population. The Irish fund was protected from drawdowns until 2025, after which it was legally obligated to 'meet as much as possible of the costs of social welfare and public pension services' until 2055. Its investment policy required the fund to secure the 'optimal total financial return' when investing its assets towards this end.[38]

Despite these protections, a 2010 requirement by the Irish government that the NPRF direct some of its investments to struggling local credit institutions effectively amounted to short-term tapping of the savings fund by the government.[39] An amended investment mandate for the NPRF portfolio reflected the new priority accorded to state needs: investments should help remedy 'serious disturbance(s) in the economy of the

State' and 'prevent potential serious damage to the financial system in the State'.[40]

The measure to redirect funding to ailing credit institutions was particularly controversial given its potential to compromise the fund's ability to generate optimal returns by treating the NPRF as last-resort financing for low-grade domestic investment. Even more contentious was the creation of a 'directed investments' portfolio within the NPRF under the personal direction of the Minister for Finance. These measures compromised the sense of the fund being quarantined from present-day political raiding, prompting public anger. Ireland's SWF no longer seemed to be the property of the Irish people, safeguarded for future public spending on their needs. Instead, it was under the direct control of the Irish government for its own use,[41] with the practical result that the holdings of the fund were decimated: from nearly €25 billion in seed capital down to just €4.2 billion in 2010.[42]

Three years later, the government completed the drawdown, again prioritizing immediate government over long-term citizen needs. Laws were introduced requiring that the NPRF's remaining assets, at the time worth €6.4 billion, be sold and reallocated to a domestic investment fund. The NPRF was effectively abolished, forced to sell off its international assets, and transfer the proceeds into the newly created Ireland Strategic Investment Fund (ISIF), established at the end of 2014. The ISIF formed part of a wider effort to spur economic growth through investment, as the government abandoned austerity policies.

The citizens of Ireland may ultimately benefit from this move, but at a price. Sovereign wealth specifically set aside to meet certain social needs (welfare and public pension payments from 2025) was reallocated to help the government kick-start the ailing domestic economy and protect state institutions in times of financial crisis. The decision was arguably prudent. Ireland's economic recovery is proving to be among the most impressive in the European Union. For two consecutive years in 2014 and 2015, Ireland enjoyed the title of fastest growing economy in the EU, though much of that was due to an export boom thanks to the falling price of the euro. Whether the radical redeployment of the nation's sovereign wealth away from long-term policy objectives to short-term policy needs will prove wise and just remains to be seen.

China

Conflict over sovereign wealth can also occur internally within the state between different public sector actors. Often such conflict involves different government agencies vying for control over sovereign wealth, to the detriment of the community which should benefit from that wealth. China offers an example of such harmful bureaucratic rivalry.

China boasts two of the world's largest and most high profile sovereign investors. The China Investment Corporation (CIC) and the State Administration of Foreign Exchange (SAFE) are estimated to hold over $1 trillion between them and regularly appear in the top five rankings of SWFs based on assets under management.[43] While SAFE sits within China's central bank, the People's Bank of China, CIC is an independent authority. Both funds are mandated to manage a portion of China's vast foreign reserves, currently the largest reserve holdings in the world at $3.6 trillion.[44]

SAFE has existed since 1979 and assumed its current form as a higher risk-taking investor with a tranche of foreign reserves in 1997. Little is known about the total holdings and investment behaviour of SAFE's investment portfolio. It is estimated to manage approximately $300 billion in foreign exchange reserves (but the Chinese authorities have never confirmed this total), thought to be allocated to equity and alternative investments overseas. CIC was created in 2007 as a separate entity mandated to diversify another portion of China's foreign exchange reserves into higher return assets. The CIC was initially capitalized with $200 billion in foreign reserves, purchased by the Ministry of Finance with funds raised through a 1.55 trillion yuan bond issuance. Today, it manages $747 billion.

China is the only country in the world to boast two sovereign investment vehicles – one within its central bank and one outside the traditional state apparatus – dedicated to managing excess foreign reserves for a return, not just liquidity. This exceptional situation is best explained by intense bureaucratic rivalry to control the country's sovereign wealth.

As China's reserves of US dollars swelled throughout the 2000s, the government's desire to diversify these holdings into more aggressive, global investment strategies increased. The Ministry of Finance proposed the creation of a new independent sovereign fund on the basis that SAFE lacked the skills to make higher-risk investments.[45] The central bank resisted, desperate to maintain control over its ever-growing stockpile of reserves. SAFE lobbied for a mandate expansion or the creation of a similar entity under the remit of one of its international subsidiaries to implement an offshore investment strategy. To prove it was up to the task, in early 2007, SAFE allocated up to 15 per cent of its reserves to higher-return, non-debt assets.[46] Through its Hong Kong subsidiary, it took small equity positions in some of the world's largest public companies. By mid-2007, it had disclosed holdings of up to $22.1 billion in FTSE 100 companies, equalling 0.75 per cent of the index's total market capitalization. These investments mark the beginning of SAFE's investment portfolio, born out of intense bureaucratic rivalry yet lacking a sound investment mandate.

SAFE's efforts were unsuccessful. The Chinese Investment Corporation was officially established in September 2007. Although the Ministry of Finance was not made outright owner of CIC, it was given managerial control over the fund and its officials dominated CIC's senior leadership ranks, as they still do today. As a placatory measure, CIC's articles of association mandated that five major government agencies – including the People's Bank of China and SAFE – could nominate one non-executive director to CIC's board of directors. Yet the inaugural chairmen of CIC's board of directors and board of supervisors were both former Ministry of Finance top officials and remained in this position from 2007 to 2013.[47]

Despite the efforts of China's leadership to appease its central bank, SAFE has competed rather than collaborated with CIC.[48] The ongoing competition has impacted CIC's institutional design and investment. As China analysts Liew and He observe:

> The CIC as it stands today is largely a product of the ongoing competition between two of China's key policymaking bodies over which one of them should manage and control the country's sovereign wealth. The contest over the CIC, between China's central bank, the People's Bank of China ... and the Ministry of Finance ... is derivative of the larger battle between them for influence over broad economic policy and control of the country's financial assets.[49]

The problem with such bureaucratic rivalry is that investment decisions have been driven more by the funds' institutional agendas than by the official wealth preservation and augmentation objectives for which they were created.[50] Moreover, institutional design decisions have been made on the basis of appeasing organizational egos, rather than according to best principles. For instances, CIC has never been given a stable funding mechanism as this would involve regular transfers of foreign reserves from SAFE to the CIC. Instead, it has received sporadic injections at the government's initiative: $30 billion in 2011 and $19 billion in 2012.[51] This unreliable funding arrangement poses challenges for CIC in planning its investment strategy and portfolio allocation.

This phenomenon is not unique to China. Contestation between state agencies and governments over management of a national sovereign wealth has affected a number of countries with 'excess' foreign reserves. This typically involves the government reallocating a portion of reserves from the central bank to another state agency, such as the Ministry of Finance or Treasury, or to an entirely independent authority. Such a move can provoke backlash from the central bank resisting a loss of control over 'its' capital. The Bank of Korea fought the establishment of the Korea Investment Corporation with foreign reserves in 2005. Today, the central banks of both Hong Kong and Taiwan are fighting attempts to create independent sovereign wealth funds with a portion of their respective foreign reserves.[52] Such bureaucratic bickering over valuable financial resources is perhaps not surprising; but if the precise ownership status of this capital were clearer, there would be less scope for state agencies to frustrate government agendas for managing these assets.

Libya

Libya supplies the most extreme case of citizen–state conflict over sovereign wealth. In early 2011, a question regarding the precise ownership of Libya's SWF, the Libyan Investment Authority (LIA), arose in the context of democratic uprisings against the Gaddafi regime. The violent suppression of these uprisings by the regime resulted in the United Nations Security Council imposing, among other things, an asset freeze on 'all funds [and] other financial assets and economic resources ... which are owned or controlled, directly or indirectly, by the Libyan authorities'.[53] The LIA was identified as an entity subject to the asset freeze on the basis that it was '[u]nder control of Muammar Qadhafi and his family, and [a] potential source of funding for his regime'.[54]

From an SWF ownership perspective, the resolution was controversial as it declared the supposedly 'government-owned' LIA the personal property of the sovereign family.[55] Prior to the resolution, the LIA held itself to be an asset of the Libyan state. Its purported mandate was to protect assets for future generations of Libyans. Internationally recognized as a legitimate SWF through its membership of the IFSWF,[56] official IFSWF documentation emphasized the LIA's ownership by the *state* of Libya.[57] This same documentation also described the LIA as a 'savings fund for future generations', and referred separately to Libyan citizens *and* the Libyan state as distinct but equal beneficiaries of the fund.[58]

Subsequent freezing of assets in compliance with the UN resolution reflected a growing view that the LIA was in fact the personal preserve of the ruler, Muammar Gaddafi, and his family.[59] The final determination by companies such as UK publishing house Pearson, in which the LIA held a 3.27 per cent stake, to freeze their holding was on the basis that the LIA was under the personal control of the Gaddafi elite.[60] Billions of dollars of Libyan assets were frozen abroad in America, Austria, Canada, Italy and elsewhere.[61]

As per the UN resolution, all income from frozen assets was to accumulate on behalf of the Libyan *people* and be released as soon as possible 'to and for the benefit of the people of the Libyan Arab Jamahiriya'[62] when a government capable of representing them was in place.[63] This process has been frustrated over the past five years as rival groups have asserted their status as the 'government' of Libya. The power struggle has spilled over to the LIA, with the emergence of two rival institutions, and their respective heads, asserting the right to control the nation's $67 billion in sovereign wealth assets.[64] A Tripoli-based group currently housed in the original LIA offices is headed up by AbdulMagid Breish, former chairman of the LIA until his resignation in April 2014. Breish asserts his authority to the current chairmanship based on a ruling by Libya's Court of Appeal that recognized him as leader. The other, Malta-based institution is headed by Hassan Bouhadi, appointed as official LIA chairman in October 2014 by the LIA's Board of

Trustees, which in turn was appointed by the internationally recognized government of Libya based in Tobruk. In March 2016, Britain's High Court recognized the Malta-based investment authority as enjoying 'continued operations' regarding the assets of the LIA.[65]

Even in the absence of a functioning government and despite these power struggles, LIA assets still accumulate on behalf of Libyan citizens. They attach to the continuous political entity of Libya, despite deep contestation over Libya's rightful government and sovereign-fund chairman.[66] While that is some comfort, the uncertainty surrounding the management of the LIA still costs the Libyan people. Of the $66 billion portfolio, 25 per cent is held in bonds and equities and is still frozen under international sanctions, 40 per cent is held in five active subsidiaries and 35 per cent is in cash deposits in the Central Bank of Libya in Tripoli.[67] Bouhadi argues that the frozen assets should be released as the LIA is missing vital opportunities to invest this capital more effectively. Bonds simply convert to cash on maturation, an undesirable outcome in a low-yield environment, while equity investments remain vulnerable to global stock-market volatility. The legal disputes over the fund chairmanship also hamper further saving as fund earnings are channelled to legal fees and dispute, rather than much-needed nation-building. The continuing vagary over the LIA's management underscores how crucial it is to clarify and institutionally protect the proper ownership of sovereign wealth.

The abuse of government control over sovereign wealth by a ruling family for its own personal gain is an extreme illustration of how radically the interests of state and citizen can diverge. While it is unsurprising that this occurred in a non-democratic setting, the acceptance of the LIA into an international forum of peer sovereign funds whose principles demand a degree of transparent and accountable management of SWF assets suggests that too little was understood both internally and internationally about the precise status of and control over Libya's sovereign wealth.

Establishing the rightful owner of sovereign wealth

How do we resolve uncertainty around the ownership of sovereign funds plaguing all manner of polities from mature and emerging democracies to authoritarian and despotic regimes? Though the drafters of SWF arrangements did not likely intend such ambiguity, the conflict within many communities wielding sovereign wealth shows that confusion exists and is even fuelled by the vagary. Even when governments take sound decisions regarding the use and management of sovereign wealth, a lack of clarity around the precise ownership status of SWFs can still cause tension and confusion between state and citizen.

As has already been seen, an international group of sovereign funds attempted to resolve some of the confusion by imposing an official definition in the Santiago Principles, which declared SWFs to be 'special purpose investment funds or arrangements, owned by the general government'.[68] Endorsing this definition means declaring sovereign funds *government* property. Recent definitional accounts of SWFs have moved in this direction, displaying a loose consensus around the idea of sovereign funds as 'government owned'.[69] However, as is clear from the above, theoretical agreement has not prevented a spate of real-world conflict over these assets.

This is in part explained by the ambiguity inherent in the very idea of government ownership. Even if everyone agrees that SWFs are government owned, there might be no consensus on what that idea itself means. Historical accounts of government and public ownership reveal how 'different versions of public ownership' have consistently produced 'complexities about ownership and control' due to the range of potential owners of 'public property'.[70] Property theorist Stephen Munzer suggests the owners of public property include 'the state, city, community, or tribe',[71] while fellow theorist Andrew Reeve observes that public ownership has been associated with a variety of entities, including 'the public, God, the state, the community, corporations and business firms, churches, charities and families'.[72] Even if there is consensus around *government* ownership of SWFs, the question of what government ownership implies remains open.[73]

A fiduciary framework for the citizen–state relationship

Resolving this confusion involves determining who or what is the ultimate owner of sovereign wealth, and indeed all public assets. Political theory is instructive on this point. A number of influential thinkers from Locke to Hobbes offer a conception of public power that casts the citizen–state relationship in fiduciary terms. Following Lockean political thought,[74] both the state and its institutions, including government, are agents for their principal, 'the people', and ultimately subject to their control. Crucially, anything that an agent obtains by virtue of an agency relationship *belongs* to the principal. On a fiduciary view of the citizen–state relationship, then, all public assets are simply held on trust by governments for their ultimate beneficiary, the people. The principal cannot own anything in their own right for their own benefit.

Lawyers refer to this as 'fiduciary state' theory,[75] while political philosophers have called it the 'political trust' metaphor.[76] Whatever the appropriate name, this conception of the citizen–state relationship was a commonplace means of understanding state power up until the earlier years of the twentieth century.[77] It has at times been overshadowed by the conceptual and analytical device of contract in theories of the state.[78] But a revival of this theory has begun[79] and has clear benefits in the case of sovereign wealth funds. It offers a framework for understanding the different roles and rights of states and citizens to sovereign wealth as a contested piece of public property.

In legal terms, the concepts of a fiduciary and a fiduciary duty arise out of a special relationship in which one party, in a position of vulnerability (the 'principal'), entrusts another party (the 'fiduciary' or 'agent') to act loyally on the principal's behalf, solely in the principal's interests and for their benefit alone. The fiduciary is then deemed to be under a 'fiduciary duty' to do so. They must place their personal interests below those of the principal's and not profit from the relationship. As Peter Birks, one of England's foremost legal scholars on trust law, observed: 'A fiduciary is someone whom one can trust and rely on, as a beneficiary can trust and rely on a trustee.'[80]

In essence, then, the fiduciary relationship is one of trust where that trust arises automatically by virtue of the character of the relationship.[81] Legal scholars Fox-Decent and Criddle argue that such relations have been generally recognized as arising in 'circumstances in which one party (the fiduciary) holds discretionary power over the legal or practical interests of another party (the beneficiary) and the beneficiary is vulnerable to the fiduciary's power in that he is unable to, either as a matter of fact or law, exercise the entrusted power'.[82]

The conceptual synergy with the citizen–state relationship is immediately apparent. The coercive and monopolistic nature of state power renders citizens vulnerable to their governments in an asymmetric manner. The state may choose to exercise its power in the interests of the citizens, but citizens often lack the means, factually or legally, to shield themselves against an abuse of state power. Nor may they carry out many of the functions that the state undertakes on the citizens' behalf. This is an unnegotiated, unequal relationship with substantial asymmetries of power and information. Citizens are therefore 'peculiarly vulnerable' in the characteristic sense of a beneficiary.[83]

While these properties of the citizen–state relationship have led legal theorists to view governmental authority in fiduciary terms, the citizen–state relationship is not a *legally* recognized fiduciary relationship. In law, such relations include agent–principal, director–corporate officer, doctor–patient, lawyer–client, trustee–beneficiary, partner–partnership and parent–child. The case for extending this principle to the citizen–state relationship has been persuasively put by a number of public law theorists.[84] There are also precedents for the application of the fiduciary concept to sovereign finance *in particular*.[85] However, with one recent exception, the framework has not yet been applied to sovereign funds.[86]

A principal–agent framework and SWFs

What are the implications of casting citizen–state relations in fiduciary terms for the specific entity of sovereign funds? Of the existing types of fiduciary relationship, the one that best approximates the citizen–state dynamic where public assets are at stake is the principal–agent relationship. As with all fiduciary relations, an agent is subject to a fiduciary duty to act solely for the benefit of the principal. But there is an additional obligation upon the agent to act only subject to the principal's *control*. The added emphasis on the principal's ability to control their agent gives rise to a series of obligations of the agent towards the principal, including an asset-ownership restriction. The restriction holds that any assets obtained by the agent in the course of the agency relationship are ultimately the property of the principal.

The main consequence, then, of applying a principal–agent framework to SWFs is that governments, in their capacity as sponsors of a sovereign fund, would become subject to a fiduciary-like obligation to act in the interests of the domestic community in establishing, managing and using an SWF. Any attempt by government or state agencies to exert control over sovereign wealth in a manner that serves their own interests (or the interests of some narrowly defined group within a domestic community), rather than the interests of the community at large, would be inimical to this principle.

What counts as a government acting 'in its own' interest and not that of the citizenry is contentious. The case studies above contained clear and less clear examples. Libya was an explicit case of government abuse of an SWF for the personal gain and profit of members of the ruling family. The Nigerian experience also highlights how a particular government pursuing its own narrow financial interests could jeopardize that of the citizenry more broadly. Government infighting in Nigeria delayed the establishment and effective operation of its new sovereign fund intended to improve the transparent management of the country's resource windfalls. Moreover, a particular level of government asserted that a portion of the fund's seed capital was owed to them specifically, contradicting the explicit fiduciary conception of ownership in the fund's founding documents.

A similar point could be made in relation to the Chinese funds. Competing elements of the Chinese public service frustrated the smooth and effective establishment and operation of their sovereign funds. The institutional design and investment mandates of both SAFE and CIC were influenced primarily by the intense rivalry between the central bank and the Ministry of Finance. Rather than creating an effective, fit-for-purpose sovereign investment entity, the design of CIC was a product of a placatory compromise, while SAFE was born out of an effort to maintain control over its reserves. Moreover, the investment decisions of both funds were regularly influenced by their mutual desire to outperform the other. Such funds could hardly be characterized as operating in a fiduciary-like capacity for the sole benefit of their sponsor communities.

The Irish and Australian cases are the least clear-cut. The Irish government's political tapping of Ireland's SWF may have violated citizen interests since the government depleted wealth earmarked for long-term social spending; however, it arguably helped serve the beneficial end of warding off economic collapse and stabilizing the banking system. It did so, though, at the extremely high cost of all but destroying the country's SWF.[87] The precedent that governments can raid quarantined public funds hypothecated for particular community needs when they have a crisis to resolve surely violates the fiduciary ideal of citizen–state relations.

In the Australian case, the general lack of knowledge among the Australian public regarding their established Future Fund suggests that citizens may only be aware of and thus able to properly monitor their SWFs when those funds are clearly perceived as promoting citizen interests. Such interests include accumulating national savings, infrastructure financing, intergenerational wealth transfer, funding social services and so on. If, instead, sovereign fund assets are earmarked for overheads of the government, either as an employer with liabilities or as the manager of the economy in need of extra assistance during a crisis, such uses may encourage a perception of *government* serving its own political or immediate policy needs. Directing sovereign wealth to emergency budget relief when it was not set up for that purpose, or allocating it to government sector pensions, may not necessarily violate a citizen's claim to this wealth, but the Irish and Australian cases suggest it may not sufficiently respect it either.

Next steps

The principal–agent model of citizen–state relations holds that the citizenry is always the ultimate owner of sovereign funds – and indeed all public assets. Since, on the fiduciary view, government and the state only exist to serve the interests of citizens, the possibility that governments may hold discrete interests in, or ultimately own SWFs is prohibited. Such a framework acts as a blocking claim – cautioning against the view that governments or states can own and manage SWF assets for their own ends, where those ends diverge from that of the citizenry. Any legal or official description of the funds as 'government-owned' or 'state-controlled' vehicles therefore must be read in light of this claim: that governments are mere agents of their principal, the people, serving as stewards of public wealth which ultimately belongs to citizens. Citizens are the true owners of sovereign wealth. Such a move resolves the SWF ownership question and offers a foundation for deriving norms of good governance and management for SWFs. Developing and articulating those principles is the task to which the rest of this book now turns.

4

The Tsipras point: control of and benefit from community wealth

We want the state to control key sectors of the Greek economy so that
we can reap the benefits.

Alexis Tsipras, Prime Minister of Greece, 2015[1]

Greek national assets are up for sale – everything from vital infrastructure
such as Athens Water Supply, the country's main ports at Piraeus and
Thessaloniki and fourteen regional airports, to symbolic assets like the
2004 Olympic complex and the Hellenic Post. As part of Greece's third
bailout struck in July 2015, privatization proceeds from state assets must go
into an independent fund to help repay Greece's international creditors.

For many Greeks, this arrangement feels like selling off the family silver,
only to hand back the proceeds to those demanding its sale. It was report-
edly the sticking point that nearly scuttled the €86 billion three-year debt
relief programme and forced a Grexit from the eurozone.[2]

That the privatization idea was imposed on the Greek negotiators didn't
help. Greece had opposed privatization as a fundraising strategy from the
outset of its troubles. In 2010, when several German politicians controversially suggested Greece sell off its uninhabited islands and historic monu-
ments to pay down debt, Greek citizens responded by boycotting German
imports.

Despite the protests, the Hellenic Republic Asset Development Fund
(HRADF) was established in 2011 to oversee a privatization programme.

Known as Taiped, this initial fund was expected to generate €50 billion in sale proceeds within five years. But, by early 2015, only €3.2 billion sat in the fund. Most key infrastructure assets were unsold. When the Syriza party took office on an anti-austerity mandate at the start of 2015, it sacked Taiped's leaders and halted the sale of numerous assets. A near-completed purchase of ADMIE, Greece's electricity network operator, was cancelled.

ADMIE is now for sale again and the privatization programme rolls on as part of the current debt relief agreement. But this time Greek Prime Minister Alexis Tsipras secured two concessions: the privatization fund must be run from Athens, not Luxembourg as the creditors had wished; and part of its capital must be invested in Greece. The final deal allocated half of the new fund's anticipated €50 billion to recapitalizing local banks and a quarter to local investment in Greece, leaving the remaining €12.5 billion to pay off creditors. In short, Greeks wanted *control* over and *benefit* from the privatization fund holding the proceeds of their national assets.

It is no surprise that the two conditions insisted upon by the Greeks to render the privatization fund acceptable were greater control and benefit, for these are the two core components of property rights. Pleas for more local control and benefit are ultimately pleas of ownership. Greek citizens wished to exert control over and benefit from the HRADF assets so that the fund would truly feel like *their* property. In that respect, Tspiras's demands reinforce the appropriateness of a fiduciary conception of citizen rights over public financial assets elaborated in the previous chapter. That model holds that sovereign wealth ultimately belongs to the people in their capacity as principal over their government agent. As agents can only act subject to their principal's control and for their benefit, citizens must have power over, and benefit from, a government's management and use of SWFs.

Recognizing that citizens must enjoy control over and benefit from their sovereign wealth is just the first step towards ensuring sovereign funds feel like the people's property. But questions remain as to exactly what a fully fleshed-out model of citizen ownership of SWFs would look like in practice. In Greece's case, support for the new fund required a degree of local power over the fund's management and more direct benefit through domestic investment in Greece of its capital. Sending this public money offshore to be managed abroad, before being transferred to international creditors, removed any sense of the HRADF as a Greek community fund. This chapter investigates what the equivalent measures would be for citizen-owners in the case of SWFs. I examine the specific ways in which citizens can exert control over, and extract benefit from, sovereign wealth to ensure it is their wealth.

The 'Tspiras point' for sovereign funds

Alexis Tsipras's demands for local power over the Greek privatization fund involved more domestic control over its management and investment and more direct benefit from the use of its capital. Similar demands can be made regarding those same aspects of a sovereign fund's design and behaviour. The extent to which sovereign funds already permit local control over their management and investment or ensure that citizen-owners benefit from their capital varies from fund to fund. But an overall sense of what is expected of SWFs in this regard is decipherable from the Santiago Principles.

In this chapter, I take a closer look at those three aspects of an SWF's design and behaviour touched upon in Chapter 1 that most affect the domestic citizen–state relationship: fund management; investment of fund assets; and use of SWF returns. Examination of existing scholarly and regulatory treatments of SWFs, including the Santiago Principles, reveals that discussion of citizen control and benefit is either absent or thin in these areas. More work is needed to ensure sovereign funds reach the 'Tsipras point' of sufficient local control over and benefit from sovereign wealth to count as community funds.

Control of fund management

The issue of control over SWFs has arisen in geopolitical analyses of sovereign funds. The primary concern in those discussions is whether SWFs are instruments of their sponsoring states for political or non-financial purposes.[3] The early phase of the SWF debate was dominated by recipient country anxiety as to whether 'governments would use their SWFs to buy control of large "national champion" firms in key sectors'.[4] Consequently, the question of SWF control focused on *what* sovereign funds gain control over through their investments;[5] whether they exert influence over these acquired assets;[6] whether this is for particular strategic ends;[7] and what arm's-length governance procedures would quarantine sovereign funds from political interference.[8] In short, the SWF control agenda has been dominated by what sovereign funds control, not who should control SWFs and how.

By contrast, the priority here is to determine who should ultimately *control the management of SWFs*, whether citizen or state, private or public sector, and which governance model best gives effect to the preferred control arrangements. The Santiago Principles offer minimal guidance on this type of control issue. There is little discussion of what 'government control' should consist of and how this should be exercised. The occasional principle implicitly supports enhanced control of domestic communities over their sovereign funds (since the framework's stated intention is to improve the understanding of home countries about their SWFs),[9] but there is no direct reference to the role of citizens as owners/stakeholders, nor any reference to popular control rights.[10]

Even if the Santiago Principles' latent intention is to enhance citizen control, the mechanisms put in place to encourage this are inadequate. In terms of transparency, the principles are widely regarded as weak compared to global norms.[11] The founder of the term SWF, Andrew Rozanov, has observed that 'the term "transparency" does not appear once in the actual text of the principles',[12] although seventeen principles explicitly invoke a requirement for 'public disclosure'.[13] These principles typically relate to the fund's organization, objectives, legal arrangements and institutional structure. Principles concerning more substantive issues such as the fund's investment portfolio (including size, composition, allocation, risk indicators and returns) are not subject to public disclosure requirements. They are simply governed by internal accountability mechanisms such as timely, accurate and regular reporting to their sovereign owner (typically the relevant national government), leading SWF analyst Ted Truman to characterize the principles as 'essentially meaningless in terms of public disclosure and accountability'.[14] Other mechanisms that could support domestic accountability and control are not mentioned.

Investment management

The discussion of SWF investment does not fare much better when it comes to citizen control. Although SWF investment strategies dominate much of the discussion on SWFs, the focus is typically on how SWFs should manage their portfolios as long-term investors seeking to generate optimal risk-adjusted returns. The discussion is by nature technical, focusing on the characteristics of state-sponsored funds and how this affects their asset allocation (should funds hold more equity, debt, cash or alternative assets?) and risk management.

These financially oriented analyses of SWF investment performance are now complemented by a different set of questions about the possibility of responsible investment of sovereign wealth. Inspired by Norway's adoption of an ethical investment mandate for its SWF, an embryonic literature has emerged, pressing other sovereign funds to follow suit.[15] It is largely descriptive, recounting the design of the Norwegian model and how the ethical investment mandate works, and lauding Norway's commitment to global justice through investing.[16] However, these analyses have by and large failed to ask why this obligation is incumbent on *government* investors in particular, leaving it vulnerable to a major objection to ethical investment by SWFs: namely, that ethical investment places SWFs at a disadvantage relative to other market participants in generating maximum returns for their ultimate beneficiaries, the domestic population of the SWF's home state.[17] Whether there is a normatively significant difference between government and other investors is therefore fundamental to the resolution of the ethical investment debate.

Equally neglected within this debate is the impact of SWF investment decisions on the sponsor community. Understanding the ways in which a sovereign fund's investment may implicate or benefit a citizenry while generating a community's shared wealth is essential to determining what is necessary for a people to exercise sufficient control over their fund.

The Santiago Principles remain guarded about the possibility of an ethical investment mandate. Since the drafters were at pains to quell the anxieties of recipient countries regarding the presence of non-financial motives for SWF investment, the text of the document is careful to emphasize that SWF investments must be motivated by and managed solely on financial and economic grounds. Principle 19 states that: 'The SWF's investment decisions should aim to maximize risk-adjusted financial returns in a manner consistent with its investment policy, and based on economic and financial grounds.'[18] Subprinciple 19.1 does allow some flexibility on this point, stating that if 'decisions are subject to *other than* economic and financial considerations, these should be clearly set out in the investment policy and be publicly disclosed'.[19] The explanation and commentary on this subprinciple makes clear that this exception was specifically entertaining the possibility of an ethical investment mandate by sovereign funds.[20]

The Santiago Principles therefore countenance the possibility of an ethical investment mandate. They stop short, however, of stipulating whether government investors like SWFs *should* manage their investment strategies ethically, and, if so, how they should go about it. The scope allowed for ethical investment in Subprinciple 19.1 is also contradicted by past official policy statements by the IFSWF which insist that subjecting SWFs to extra-financial obligations when investing (for example, ethical considerations) compromises their ability to meet their overarching objective of generating returns for the long-term prosperity of their home state.[21] These neglected aspects of the SWF investment debate can be tackled by considering whether government investors have a unique status in the investor community that entails particular obligations when generating returns in private markets, and if so, what role the community should play in influencing the investment mandate of a sovereign fund in its quest to generate wealth on their collective behalf.[22]

Distribution

Once again, the question of how to use sovereign fund capital has received significant attention, but not from the perspective adopted here. The focus has largely been on the use of a fund's principal rather than its returns, and considered through a macroeconomic lens. A typical question is what policy purpose a sovereign fund should serve within the wider fiscal architecture of a state.[23] There is significant interest in the use of sovereign funds as mechanisms for managing commodity wealth in resource-rich nations.[24] Indeed, commodity management has been the dominant reason for establishing such funds, with many SWFs located in the Middle East and other resource-rich states.[25] Over the last several years, however, the ascendancy of commodity funds has been challenged by the rise of non-commodity sovereign wealth funds accounting for roughly 45 per cent of global SWF assets under management.[26] Moreover, recent research has explored how a state does not have to be 'resource rich' to establish a sovereign fund. The taxable asset base for a state extends far beyond natural resources, covering a whole array of public assets owned by or for the benefit of the domestic community that offer potential revenue for states to establish community funds.[27]

The growth of non-commodity funds should prompt a broader recasting of SWFs that complements this book's effort to transform sovereign funds into community funds. Beyond their narrow characterization as resource management mechanisms, they are increasingly considered essential tools in a state's economic apparatus.[28] This concerns not only how *the fund itself* can best assist in the management of a state's public finances (for example, through accumulating savings, currency stabilization or reserve management), but also how the *income* generated by any type of sovereign fund could be used within an SWF's home community to promote greater equality, democracy and justice.

Regrettably, on the returns distribution question, the Santiago Principles are so broad as to be largely meaningless. This is no doubt influenced by a desire to respect sovereignty. Indeed, to reach agreement on the Santiago Principles, the IFSWF had to ensure its wording did not violate members' preferences to be free to use their funds as they pleased.[29] The principles only require (at Principle 4) that that there 'should be clear and publicly disclosed policies, rules, procedures or arrangements in relation to the SWF's general approach to funding, withdrawal, and spending operations'. The explanation of the principles acknowledges that '[f]unding and withdrawal rules are specific to the type of SWF',[30] while the commentary goes on to observe that '[s]ome SWFs keep their capital and returns while others pay out targeted annual dividends'.[31] Subprinciple 4.2 elaborates slightly on withdrawals and expenditure of SWF capital, stipulating that spending should only occur on the fund's operating expenses.[32] However, no direction is given as to whether there should be distributions in the form of dividends to the present generation or to the national budget for other government expenditure that may benefit present and future citizens, nor on how to choose between these competing uses. More guidance is needed on desirable distribution options for SWF returns for sovereign funds that seek to be community funds for both present and future generations.

All in all, the Santiago Principles and wider scholarship around SWFs offer scant guidance on domestic control over, and benefit from, sovereign funds. The general absence of these themes in sovereign fund policy, especially from the best practice framework authored by SWFs themselves, shows there is little expectation for sovereign funds to possess the virtues Alexis Tsipras deemed necessary for Greece's national fund to feel like Greek property. There is a way to go, then, before achieving citizen ownership of sovereign funds in practice.

Global rights to sovereign wealth?

To fill this lacuna, the rest of this book considers *how* SWFs should be managed, invested and distributed to realize the ideal of citizen ownership of sovereign wealth. Consistent with the structure of property rights, the book is divided into a discussion of *control* and *benefit* privileges in Parts II and III respectively. Since the management and investment of sovereign wealth are fundamentally about control over SWFs assets, they are addressed in Part II. The issue of benefit is tackled in Part III where the distribution of SWF earnings is discussed.

Before proceeding, two reservations about the SWFs' domestic community fund ideal must be noted. First, this idea rests on an assumption that members of a given community (whether national, subnational or city-based) have a greater right to control, manage and use sovereign fund assets than groups outside their community borders. That is problematic for those who consider national boundaries irrelevant in determining our rights and responsibilities towards one another.[33] Proponents of this 'global justice' outlook might dispute the idea that citizens of certain communities have any prior or stronger claim to assets in national or state-level funds than citizens elsewhere in the world. But analysing SWFs' potential as domestic community funds automatically rules out the possibility of global rights to SWFs.

Such arguments often surface in discussions about the ownership of natural resources, where there is a view that territorial claims to resources are morally indefensible since the very existence of nation-states and territorial boundaries is arbitrary, a contingent fact of our political history. On that outlook, all resource windfalls might be best pooled into a global fund and redistributed throughout the world for the benefit of all humanity. Similar arguments could be made in regard to sovereign wealth that stems from budget surpluses or privatization proceeds.

This touches upon the second reservation, that a general discussion of sovereign wealth such as this book undertakes ignores relevant distinctions in the underlying assets of the funds. Should the principles for a fund's management and use differ depending on how an SWF was initially funded – whether through commodities, currency reserves or budget surpluses?

Dealing quickly with the second reservation first, the relevant asset of SWFs that demands scrutiny is the *public* wealth they hold, irrespective of the origin of that wealth. Since the primary concern here is to determine how governments can act responsibly on behalf of their constituents in the management and use of sovereign funds, it would be unhelpfully narrow to restrict the focus to only one type of fund – commodity, reserve excess or privatization surplus.[34] All sovereign wealth must be managed in citizens' best interests, regardless of how it is generated.

The other worry that a domestic ideal of a community fund is morally questionable from a global justice perspective is understandable, but exaggerated. Global justice advocates will be concerned with achieving similar objectives to those aimed at here – to ensure sovereign wealth is managed in a manner that is welfare-enhancing for its ultimate beneficiaries. But they will differ on the identity of those beneficiaries. So, global principles for the fair management and use of sovereign wealth are likely to be similar in content, but more expansive in reach, encompassing the global community of citizens.

Consider that domestic-level principles for enhancing local popular control over sovereign fund management could be similar in nature for endowing world citizens or states with sufficient control over a global SWF. They are likely to involve mechanisms for enhancing citizens' ability to monitor, influence, direct and interact with their SWF institution, whether those citizens are global or located in a particular domestic community. Equally, extending the distribution obligations of sovereign fund returns to global citizens could be done by maintaining national SWFs but pooling their returns into a global SWF for world redistribution or by establishing one global fund along the lines of Thomas Pogge's anti-poverty fund.[35] Finally, if SWF investment must be ethically constrained to protect citizens' values properly, then given the international nature of SWF investment, the adherence to such an obligation would automatically have a cross-border impact. Arguably, then, strengthening the ethical orientation of domestic-level investment mandates should have immediate ramifications for the justness of international capital flows, given the growing presence of SWFs in financial markets.[36]

There is thus good reason to believe that the extension of domestic principles to the global sphere might not prove difficult, so the analysis here could act as a blueprint upon which to build a global justice theory of SWFs. Even if a global justice outlook does produce substantively different principles, this should not prevent us from seeking to establish which principles apply to make SWFs, as they currently exist, more ethically satisfying institutions. This is logical for a first attempt to theorize the relationship between domestic communities and sovereign wealth, given that these funds are already influencing the lives and distributive landscape of the communities in which they reside. If, with time, the claims of global justice theorists prove persuasive, then the restriction of the community fund ideal to the domestic realm may be relaxed and their design revisited.

PART II

DEMOCRATIZING SOVEREIGN FUNDS

5

No accumulation without representation!

We are a community holding a banking licence.

Matthias Kröner, CEO of Fidor Bank, 2015[1]

A new bank has arrived on British soil. In September 2015, digital bank Fidor opened its UK doors. Or, more accurately, its webpages. Founded in Germany in 2009, Fidor is a purely online bank. It has no branches or call centres. Financial advisers have been replaced by community feedback. Customers and community followers use social media to offer ideas on its products and services, which at present include current accounts, savings bonds, transfer services and corporate accounts. The bank then takes this feedback to innovate, improve and develop products. Following consultation with its 300,000 'Smart Community' members, Fidor ran a campaign to reduce its lending rate by 0.1 per cent for every 2,000 'likes' it received on Facebook.

In the UK, Fidor is the first new retail bank to enter the market with a genuinely community-oriented philosophy. The bank's creators set it up as a place to exchange the 'know-how and experience' they believe ordinary people have when it comes to finance. A major motivation for the founders was to restore lost confidence in banking following the financial crisis by enabling customers to actively participate in the bank's decision-making and to shape the products and services they wanted. Any aspect of finance and money can be put on the discussion table. For Fidor, '[t]he community is a foundation and platform for "doing business"'.[2]

With a digital-only focus, Fidor does not yet offer the full suite of banking products that come with the branch and ATM network of traditional banks. This has posed some challenges for Fidor in gaining significant market share in Germany where scepticism about online businesses remains high. But its creators argue that it is precisely because of its digital business model that it can overcome the failings of conventional banks, which, despite their physical branches and helplines, regularly leave customers feeling disempowered and frustrated. This might help explain Fidor's rapid growth, securing 100,000 customers in Germany in five years and winning numerous awards for its transparent, innovative and interactive approach.[3] Fidor now hopes its community-oriented alternative will prove popular in the UK.

The Fidor model offers an intriguing precedent for democratic control over wealth and savings. If community influence over retail banking is not just desirable but feasible, then why not over sovereign wealth? The case for increased customer power over individual money in banks and greater citizen control over national wealth in sovereign funds share much in common. So, too, can the institutional responses. At Fidor, the 'personalised approach to banking gives every customer a voice in how [the] bank is run, as well as giving them unprecedented control – setting their own interest rates or naming the current account card that the bank will use'.[4] This chapter considers similar institutional possibilities for greater citizen control in the case of sovereign funds. It demonstrates why control over property is an essential part of ownership and how that right can be exercised over shared property like sovereign wealth. But sovereign funds are a peculiar beast in the architecture of modern states. They display a unique control dynamic relative to other public agencies given the need for their arm's-length management from government and their frequent outsourcing of investment activities to external asset managers. For this reason, existing mechanisms to allow for democratic control by a citizenry over its government and state agencies do not always map easily onto sovereign funds. In response, this chapter develops a specific model of enhanced popular control for SWFs. The model aims to strengthen citizens' direct and indirect control over SWFs by targeting both: their government agent who establishes and oversees an SWF; and SWF managers tasked with internal governance of the fund.

After considering the case for and against enhanced community power over sovereign wealth under this model, I recommend a set of reforms to

SWF management that offer a compromise between total quarantined professionalization of fund management and full direct democratic control by citizens. These reforms focus on three key initiatives to enhance citizen power over sovereign wealth: citizen election of board representatives; public input into the objective-setting documents of an SWF; and mechanisms to allow citizens to properly monitor SWF representatives' commitment to those fund objectives. They stop short, however, of supporting direct citizen control over the daily investment activities of sovereign wealth, which should remain the preserve of specialist investors.

Control over property

A core aspect of ownership is the ability to control one's property.[5] Control rights concern an owner's ability to be 'the final arbiter over what is to be done with a thing'.[6] They include the rights to possess, use, manage or transfer, give away and even destroy a piece of property.[7] To have control over property, then, an owner must maintain the primary say over the fate of the owned thing.

The question for this chapter is how a collective owner – the citizenry – can exercise such control rights over something like sovereign wealth. An initial glance suggests that some of the standard control rights may not be intelligible in the case of a sovereign fund. How might citizen-owners 'possess' an SWF in the way that an owner of a car or a house or clothing possesses their individual property? In those situations, physical control over the owned object seems intrinsic to the right to possess.

Even in the case of assets outside the immediate possession of legal owners, such as bank accounts or shares, owners still exert a reasonable degree of physical control over those assets through individualized rights to access and influence the property's fate. I can withdraw, transfer and use money from my bank account at the time and for the purpose of my choosing. My portfolio of shares may be sold, held or increased at my discretion. Citizen-owners of SWFs do not wield equivalent physical control over the sovereign wealth in their government coffers.

Other control rights are more conceptually compatible with the idea of sovereign wealth as citizens' property. It is possible to envisage the 'use' and 'management' of a fund and its assets by a collective, or its 'destruction' through legal unwinding or spending down for the benefit of the community. Even so, translating these ideas from individual to collective owners – from citizens to the citizenry – is not straightforward. How can any, let alone *all* citizens in a domestic community control the possession, use, management or destruction of an SWF when it is in the primary possession of a government, especially when it is the government that establishes and possesses an SWF, selects the use(s) for its capital, manages the fund by determining its investment strategy and appointing its managers, and regulates the duration of its existence. If control privileges are indispensable to property rights, we need to know how citizen-owners could exercise a degree of control over SWFs, whether as principals over their representative government agents or directly over a sovereign fund.

Democratic control over shared property

Democratic theory has much to offer on this point. Effective citizen control over government is a core ideal of democratic thought.[8] One of the most recent comprehensive accounts of democratic control, by leading political and social theorist Philip Pettit, emphasizes that a controlling agent must exercise both influence and direction over a process to enjoy control.[9] Applying this idea to the citizen–state relationship, Pettit argues that 'the people will achieve control over the state insofar as they attain influence, on the one side, and succeed on the other in using that influence to impose a suitable direction on government'.[10] Influence alone is insufficient. Any influence exercised must lead towards a suitable outcome, in the eyes of the people, to be constitutive of control.

To see how this could inform the establishment of democratic control over sovereign funds, consider whether Pettit's view of popular influence and direction is applicable to SWFs. Practically speaking, citizens are most likely to be able to influence sovereign funds through their representative government, which enjoys primary custody over an SWF. In democratic settings, influence over government is typically exercised through transparent elections and the appointment of officials mandated to implement the voters' will. On this procedural idea of democratic influence, the people choose between parties at election time, but 'do not otherwise control their political leaders'.[11] Even where there are free, fair and periodic elections, considerable freedom of discussion within the electorate and an accessible government responsive to public debate, there is still no guarantee that citizens' preferences will be represented. As Pettit observes, 'the people in a democracy do not control their government if they influence what it does, even influence it equally, but do not secure anything they might as a people value'.[12]

To enjoy *actual* control over government requires another ingredient: the ability to push government 'in a certain direction that is equally acceptable to all'.[13] Typically, this involves the citizenry articulating a purpose for government and cooperating in its promotion along with fellow citizens. The citizenry may either 'intentionally' or 'non-intentionally' impose a purpose they implicitly or explicitly endorse.[14] If there is *intentional* direction, the citizenry expresses a 'general will' or shared vision of the 'common good' through voting, which in turn tasks elected representatives with implementing this expressed agenda. A satisfactory notion of this public interest involves more than 'the intersection of private interests'. It demands that citizens form a view of the common good that recognizes every citizen's interest in living as an equal member of that community.[15] Citizens can then communicate this view to government by either forming a view on preferred policies and then selecting representatives likely to support those policies, or choosing preferred representatives and then relying on them to develop 'public-interest policies' on behalf of time-pressured, less informed citizens.[16]

The idea of intentional direction is problematic, however, since those representatives still have excessive discretion over what should count as the public interest. The *non-intentional* form of exerting popular influence over the direction of government is more promising. This idea holds that a process may be controlled even where the controlling entity does not exercise control intentionally. The classic example is that of the comatose patient whose general wishes, specified by the patient in health, dictate the treatment provided. The direction is non-intentional in that it follows *general wishes*, but still amounts to control.

In a political context, this can occur through utilitarian voting. Rather than the people actively forming a general common will for the purpose of imposing a collective *intentional* direction on government, instead all voters can simply vote on the basis of self-regarding preferences and thus produce an *unintended* direction for government.[17] Under this approach, the citizenry at large remains responsible for guarding against the misuse of unequal power.

How does all of this relate to SWFs? At present, no sovereign fund holds elections for its officials. All SWF personnel are government appointed, so citizens lack the first instance opportunity to directly exert 'influence without control' over sovereign funds. But this is only a problem if citizens are unable to push the government custodians of sovereign wealth 'in a certain direction that is equally acceptable to all' with regard to the management and use of their SWF. If citizens control the government custodian of an SWF, irrespective of whether or not they elect those custodians, then ipso facto they control their sovereign fund.

The presence of conflict and contestation between state and citizen discussed in previous chapters suggests that such directional influence over the treatment of sovereign wealth is often lacking. This is unsurprising. Very few governments, democratic or otherwise, have gone to election polls campaigning with manifesto promises to establish a sovereign fund or indicating how a proposed fund will be managed, invested and distributed in the long term. On the contrary, SWFs are often conceived and established as a result of internal government or Treasury policy, in between election cycles and subject to little popular input. In these circumstances, the likelihood of citizens being able to form a general will or develop private preferences on this policy issue for the purposes of applying intentional or non-intentional direction on government with regard to an SWF is extremely remote. These standard democratic procedures are therefore insufficient to promote direct popular control of sovereign funds.

Even if such policies were publicly debated and citizens formed systematic views on SWF policy following these debates and then expressed their views by electing a certain official to government or a particular party into power promising to implement those views, there is no guarantee that such an outcome would result in the desired ends since the sovereign fund itself is not subject to more direct mechanisms of democratic control. What about the ongoing behaviour of the funds which must be monitored, influenced and shaped between elections? A different approach is needed to ensure that citizens' preferred outcome regarding their community's sovereign wealth can be imposed upon government custodians of sovereign funds.

The institutional power model of control

Pettit suggests a model of control incorporating positive attributes of the 'intentional' and 'non-intentional' direction approaches, known as the 'institutional power' approach. If embraced, it would imply a balance between full direct democratization of sovereign funds, where citizen trustees would directly manage SWFs, and the status quo of total professionalization.

Pettit bases the institutional power model on a metaphor of condominium governance. Typically, residents in shared buildings elect a committee to manage the common affairs of their condominium. Ideally, the committee administers the collective business of the residents guided by universally endorsed terms of reference. These terms should be set out in a mission statement or constitution which identifies the overall purpose of the condominium's management in general terms.

This form of collective control incorporates both the influence and direction necessary for popular control. Influence is achieved through reliance on periodic elections to influence committee decisions through choosing representatives. It involves *directed* influence since the building managers must set out a universally endorsed mission developed by the residents. Everyone has the opportunity to equally participate in decision-making if they so choose. The set of demanding constraints limiting the powers of the committee ensure they are bound to act within the scope of this mission. Transparency requirements for decision-making empower the residents to ensure that the committee is responsive to their will and not to some external interest.

At the same time, this mode of control is less demanding than the 'intentional direction' approach since it does not require that the people entrust virtuous committee members with substantial discretion on what constitutes the public interest. Nor does it require the collective to have developed a general will on numerous policy questions other than the overarching question of the general purpose of its governing body. In the case of sovereign funds, a citizenry need not express a general will on more detailed and particular aspects of SWF governance, but they would need to develop and express a consensus view on the purpose and goals of the sovereign fund and the ways in which it should achieve these through its investment.

Realizing democratic control over SWFs

The institutional power model offers a basis for developing principles to institutionalize popular control rights over SWFs. Table 5.1 translates the core features of Pettit's condominium governance model into equivalent mechanisms for controlling SWF decision-making.[18] For the most part, many of Pettit's control elements are applicable to SWFs. Public debate could occur following a government announcement of an intention to

Table 5.1 Popular control devices for SWFs based on the condominium model

	Condominium popular control	SWF popular control
1	Residents elect committee members	Citizens could elect SWF board/governing body members
2	Residents set terms of reference for the committee	Citizens should set the content of an SWF's charter or constitutive documents
3	Residents exert influence over the committee in accordance with the terms of reference	Citizens should exert influence over SWF board/governing body members in accordance with the fund's founding documents
4	Committee decisions must be based on publicly available information	The government/board should publicly release information about the SWF decisions
5	Residents should be able to debate committee decisions and performance in light of their published reasons	Citizens should be able to debate SWF board decisions and performance in light of publicly released information
6	Committee members' powers must be regulated	Government/board members' powers must be regulated
7	Residents must have certain inalienable rights in relation to their property	Citizens must have a set of clearly stipulated inalienable rights in relation to their SWF

Source: Petit (2012) and author.

establish an SWF. Public hearings could be conducted to allow citizens to express their views on the merits of the idea following education and awareness sessions on the proposal. If there is support for an SWF, further public consultation could be conducted through participatory democratic forums (discussed in more detail below) on the fund's purpose, objectives, investment style and governance structure. Such consultations should include notice and comment periods, and the final proposal on each of these aspects of fund policy could even be put to a referendum if garnering broad public support would be helpful.

Papua New Guinea (PNG) offers an unlikely but encouraging example of such democratic control over the creation of its new SWF. Legislatively proposed in 2012 and voted into law in mid-2015, the formation of the new PNG fund involved extensive engagement and consultation with the general public, government agencies and international donors over three phases.[19] In Phase 1, public awareness forums were organized in the nation's capital, Port Moresby, to inform the public on the SWF proposal and to seek comments and suggestions from citizens on key government policies relating to the fund. Phase 2 involved the legislative drafting and parliamentary submission of a bill to establish an SWF, incorporating feedback gathered in the first phase. Public awareness forums were held across the country to inform the public on the bill and promote transparency around the fund. Following approval of the bill, a third and final phase was conducted between 2012 and 2015 involving further public consultations. These were undertaken to gain input into enabling Acts for the SWF and the structures necessary to fully establish and manage the fund, including the SWF board, investment mandate, location, and governance and accountability arrangements. While the fund is yet to become operational, the effort to ensure transparency, visibility and active citizen participation in the design and establishment phase offers a working precedent for how to practically realize some of the recommended popular control devices for SWFs.

After establishment, citizen-owners would also need opportunities to participate in fund decision-making and to monitor whether the decisions of SWF management are made exclusively on the basis of considerations that count as 'reasons of the public': that is, to ensure the government custodians are not self-serving in their administration and use of the fund.[20] The public release of information about fund performance and board decision-making, the regulation of board powers and the stipulation of certain rights for citizen-owners all seem feasible. So too does the creation of institutions to promote and facilitate robust public debate about a fund's performance. Chapter 7 considers how some sovereign funds already undertake such practices. More radical devices, not yet practised anywhere, include the option of direct elections for SWF board representatives. While conceivable, if other mechanisms for ensuring accountability of government-agents to their citizen-principals over the investment of sovereign wealth are effective, these may be preferable to full direct democratization of SWF management. In any case, it is only when some combination of these measures are implemented that a set of norms can emerge on what citizens actually want from their sovereign fund.[21]

The condominium model of control therefore offers a basic blueprint for popular power over SWFs. A closer look, though, at the peculiarities of the SWF organizational structure suggests that some control devices require further elaboration or modification. Figure 5.1 depicts the basic

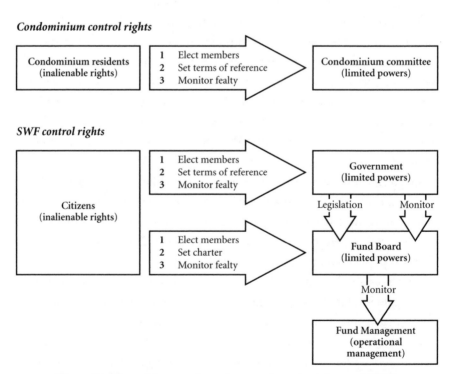

Figure 5.1 The architecture of popular control: condominium and SWF

structure of a sovereign fund, and the relationship of control between owner and institution and compares it with the control dynamic at play in a condominium. This exercise reveals an important difference in the control architecture of the condominium (and the citizen–state relationship it is meant to reflect) and an SWF. While in a condominium there are essentially two parties involved in the popular control dynamic, resident and committee (reflecting citizen and government), the SWF control dynamic involves a multitiered accountability relationship.

To satisfy an equivalent level of control to that available to the residents of the condominium, citizens must exert control over their SWF in two ways:

1   through their government, which has primary custody of the SWF; and
2   directly, through control over the fund's governing board.

Without the latter form of control, we are simply substituting accountability of the government to the citizenry for proper popular control over the SWF. In that approach, the 'state is accountable to the people, but the Fund is accountable *only* to the state',[22] and the citizens' institutional control over the SWF is incomplete. Accordingly, the devices of popular control over SWFs must be applied to the *citizen–board* relationship in addition to the regular control devices a citizenry should wield over its government.

Figure 5.1 also indicates that there is a separate entity within a sovereign fund responsible for its day-to-day operational management that reports to the board, but which is organizationally separate from both government and the board to ensure independence of the fund's financial decision-making.[23] As the figure shows, the citizenry's right of control targets three distinct aspects of fund activity:

- *election* of board representatives;
- fund governance through *objective-setting* in a founding charter; and
- *monitoring fealty of representatives'* commitment to those fund objectives.

There are good grounds for not allowing direct or indirect citizen (or government) control over the operational agency and its responsibilities, explored below. Instead, the focus of the control right should be on the dynamic between the citizenry and the board, the analogous relationship to the condominium residents and their committee. With some exceptions again detailed below, most of Pettit's condominium control devices are easily transferable to sovereign funds. They could take the form of a three-pronged control right:

1 Citizens influence the fund through *election* of SWF managers.
2 Citizens exercise directive influence through *formulating the fund's overall objectives*. These can be set down in a charter outlining the fund's purpose, mission, organizational structure and responsibilities and how these promote the objectives. This must include a clear set of terms on the government's status as fiduciary legal owner, the board's role as manager and the citizenry's role as ultimate owner, as well as the relationship between all three. Such terms should, ideally, be developed after proper public debate.
3 Citizens must be able to exert *ongoing control* over the fund by *monitoring management's fealty to those objectives*, and *compliance* with these terms. There must be frequent and detailed disclosure of SWF performance and the reporting of key decisions on issues like investment strategy, asset allocation, risk management and performance. Headline investment decisions should also be specifically reported on in order to equip the domestic constituency with a proper understanding of activities of the fund that may attract overseas attention.

Whether each of these tenets of the proposed control right is desirable and feasible is considered below. Indeed, a combination of some or all of these features might be more or less appropriate in different contexts. For instance, larger communities may face obstacles in implementing all these proposals. Certain principal-agent control mechanisms might produce sufficient accountability such that direct management of SWFs by elected lay or expert representatives is not necessary, or can be achieved far more economically.

The point here is to emphasize that, in theory, such mechanisms for enhanced democratic control over SWFs are plausible. Essential to realizing all these aspects of the control right is meaningful transparency. If an

SWF does not disclose its activities, its governing framework and the reasons for its key decisions, its citizen-owners will lack the fundamental basis for institutional power over the fund. In addition, institutional devices that promote ongoing interaction between citizen-owners and their representatives are critical to achieving the monitoring function. Options here include the use of citizen juries and citizen assemblies, explored below, to gather popular opinion on whether an SWF is managed in line with ongoing citizen expectations. But the adapted institutional power mode of control certainly suggests that a degree of democratic control over SWFs is plausible and desirable.

Objections to democratic control of SWFs

The idea of subjecting SWFs to popular control raises legitimate concerns. These worries also arise in debates over democratic control of pension fund assets and their investment. Four key objections typically surface that need consideration.

(i) Transparency objection   One of the most crucial requirements of the institutional power model is a high degree of transparency around SWF activities and decision-making. While sovereign funds are capable of publicly disclosing information on multiple aspects of their operations,[24] as some already do, even the most open funds say that there are limits to transparency.

Martin Skancke, former Director General of the Asset Management Department of the Norwegian Ministry of Finance that oversees Norway's SWF, notes that, notwithstanding the Norwegian fund's high level of transparency, 'there are certain aspects in the management of the Fund that, based on pure business considerations, are not made public'.[25] These include the 'exact timing and procedure of fund allocations in advance of the relevant actions', since the deployment of 'considerable amounts of capital into the financial markets' is involved.[26] Given the size of many sovereign funds, there is a risk of adverse pricing effects if such information is prematurely disclosed.

Those who share this concern would argue that certain aspects of the day-to-day investment operations should be exempt from the same level of disclosure, and thus democratic control, for commercial/competitive reasons. Given this legitimate worry, a delimited field of SWF activity could be granted as commercial-in-confidence without substantially diminishing citizen control, as long as much of the fund activity is still subject to transparent reporting.

A more complex consideration is whether these aspects of an SWF's business should open up to formal citizen input *prior to their determination.* That is, should citizens not just know about them retrospectively, but actively shape and inform choices made with regard to certain aspects of sovereign fund management? Pettit would argue that genuine democratic control requires active citizen input into policy questions so citizens may influence the direction of government in a manner acceptable to all. At the very least, citizens must be able to determine if there is a gap between the policy direction that the SWF management is taking a fund in and that desired by the citizens. How is this possible when SWF board representatives, whether appointed or elected, may not have regular input from the citizens?

One institutional possibility for feeding citizen's perspectives into SWF policy on a more regular basis is the use of citizen juries or citizens' assemblies. These alternatives involve small groups of randomly selected participants from the population coming together to deliberate on issues of public policy and making decisions on behalf of the citizenry at large. Random selection and deliberation are central to these devices to ensure the sample is descriptively representative. In that sense, they act as micro-publics offering a representative citizenry's perspective. Democratic theorists such as Archon Fung have shown that not only do these methods help identify and generate popular perspectives on policy issues, but they can be used to feed back into public decision-making processes.[27] Such devices can help overcome the obvious challenges for large, populous states or nations that wish to incorporate input from their vast citizenry into SWF management.

(ii) Direct election objection The proposal for direct election of members of the SWF board or governing body is also likely to meet with resistance. In the condominium scenario, the idea of elected committee members is uncontroversial. What qualifies candidates for representation is their membership of a discrete, residential community whose collective affairs they have a direct interest in administering and with which they are familiar.

The metaphor strains when applied to a sovereign fund. The status quo for selection of SWF board members is generally government appointment, with candidates appointed on the basis of board experience or financial expertise that equips them for the specialized task of sovereign wealth management. If expertise is crucial for the role of sovereign wealth management, then how appropriate is the device of popular election for SWF board representatives?

Objectors to the direct election of SWF board members have valid reservations. The logic behind the current approach of appointed experts from outside government is that it ensures independent 'arm's-length' management by specialist experts, ensuring a requisite degree of competency in and avoiding politicization of sovereign wealth investment.[28] The 'arm's-length' philosophy for SWF investment decision-making, where board members are drawn from outside government and delegate the actual task of investment to experienced fund managers, is encouraged by the Santiago Principles. Governments are *not* to 'intervene in decisions relating to particular investments', and nor presumably are their constituent citizens since such influence may compromise the purely financial basis of investment decision-making.[29] The concern is that if board management positions were opened up to electoral processes, one of the core purposes of these funds (i.e. to quarantine a particular chunk of public money from everyday political pressures and augment it through return-seeking investment) would be compromised.

Elected board members do not automatically give rise to these worries. That depends on who is eligible for election. If direct representation is important, but must be balanced with a requisite level of expertise in board directors as well as a commitment to arm's-length management, the field of eligible candidates could be appropriately restricted. For instance, some SWFs already ban former politicians or bureaucrats from appointment to their boards to guard against politicization.[30] There is no reason why similar provisions could not apply to direct elections rather than appointment of board members. Equally, because management and oversight of an SWF can require some technical competence and expertise, many sovereign funds demand substantial industry experience and technical knowledge as eligibility criteria for board appointment. With such restrictions, direct SWF elections could ensure suitably qualified candidates and uphold the arm's-length quarantining of sovereign wealth essential to its successful investment.

Even with those constraints, opposition to ordinary citizens influencing the running of SWFs through voting for suitable representatives may persist. At the other extreme, radical democrats may consider voting alone to be too weak a version of popular control and insist on the possibility of lay representatives standing for election to SWF boards. Both of these perspectives rest on conflicting views about the capability of citizens to exercise effective popular control over SWFs, the validity of which I now consider.

(iii) The 'incompetent citizen' objection   The question of ordinary citizens' competence, either as SWF board members or as voters on sovereign fund policy, is fundamental to the whole issue of popular control over sovereign wealth.

The most radical response to the 'incompetent citizen' worry is a strident defence of the intrinsic democratic value of lay members on SWF boards. While such a proposal would mark a sweeping departure from the current expert-dominated management of sovereign funds, the idea that citizens should be directly controlling the investment decisions of their own capital, whether or not they are adequately versed in investment matters, is not theoretically unprecedented. In the pension fund context, social theorist Robin Blackburn has proposed that workers eventually take over the running and investment of employee pension funds as part of the effort to cultivate 'ethical capitalism'.[31]

There are also working precedents for the election of civilian non-experts to governance and leadership roles in other areas of specialized policymaking on democratic grounds. In Germany, companies are required to appoint employee workers as members on their company boards, and in the UK, since 2012, there are now elections for lay representatives to the specialized role of Police and Crime Commissioner across England and Wales.[32] Elected PCCs do not run the local police, but simply oversee their operations, set budgets, report on progress and identify policing priorities, allowing independent operational management of the police force while reflecting community views on those issues through their electoral mandate. The main eligibility criteria for the PCC position are that a candidate be over eighteen, registered to vote in the relevant police area, a British, Commonwealth or EU citizen, and free of certain criminal records.[33] Elected PCCs are also encouraged to be independent of government insofar as there is a requirement for parliamentarians to relinquish their seats if elected to the role.[34] In other words, they must be local citizens with a connection to the community they want to represent and who are independent of government at the time of assuming the role. Their competency is judged by local electors directly affected by their work, not predetermined by Westminster. The first elections to these roles occurred in November 2012, with the second elections in May 2016. The 2012 elections were criticized for low voter turnout, averaging below 15 per cent. A review found that 80 per cent of voters did not feel they had enough information to participate. The elected PCCs have delivered mixed results, with supporters saying public engagement and police accountability has improved, while critics worry about the lack of legitimacy of elected PCCs following low voter turnout and politicization risks for the police. The example is still instructive, though, in showing the potential for directly elected lay involvement in niche areas of important public policy where an elected representative does not assume operational management, but is responsible for improving the accountability of a particular public entity to the community.[35]

These examples notwithstanding, the radical response will not convince those who insist that 'investment management is an exacting discipline and should be protected from the public because of their lack of knowledge and expertise'.[36] Consequently, one might (legitimately) worry that the issues to deliberate over in relation to sovereign wealth are too complex by nature for a layperson to grasp. Issues such as portfolio construction and exposure, performance benchmarks and risk policy might be too technical to be readily comprehended and constructively debated by non-experts.

This worry echoes a common anxiety among opponents of greater popular control over government generally. It holds that certain areas of modern life and public administration are so complex, and yet so important for the public's welfare, that they are best delegated to experts.[37] Such anxiety involves scepticism about citizens' general fitness for contributing to policy and political matters and apprehensions about the inherently complex nature of particular issues.

This concern exists in relation to popular control over investment management. For SWF governance experts Clark and Monk, 'many issues [in SWF management] are so difficult to understand and require the skills and expertise associated with domain-specific knowledge that common sense or a common commitment to the public good are not adequate bases for collective decision-making'. Research into the effectiveness of untrained civilian representatives in analogous investment decision-making contexts does cast doubt on the efficacy of this proposal.[38] As some commentators have observed, 'there are undeniable costs resulting from financial ignorance'.[39] Indeed, democratic processes may actually 'overwhelm the best interests of those who stand to benefit (or otherwise) from the collective decision-making process'.[40]

When the lessons of global finance from the past decade are factored in, it is hard to deny that investment management requires technical skill and can, in many respects, be highly complex. Capital markets can be volatile, prone to information asymmetries, dangerously interconnected and unpredictably complex. That is why the daily investment decisions of most sovereign funds are delegated to their separate operational arm and from there to internal or external fund managers. It is asset management experts who conduct the actual task of investment selection and return generation. In current practice, then, there is already extensive delegation to specialists, delegation that should *not* be disrupted.

This reduces the scope of the objection to questioning citizen's competency to influence the policy parameters within which the experts operate, and in assessing managers' fealty to those objectives. Since the most demanding, technical aspect of SWF management – the investment of assets – is already outsourced to experts and not up for grabs for direct citizen control, the real issue is whether citizens can meaningfully participate in influencing and evaluating other aspects of sovereign fund policy. These include the establishment and framing of an SWF's governance; the formulation of a fund's mission and investment mandate, and the effective monitoring and review of an SWF's performance in accordance with its investment and policy objectives.

In these areas, there is no good basis for preventing citizen influence on competency or expertise grounds. If informed popular input into other areas of SWF design and decision-making is desirable, there are several participatory democratic tools that can help equip citizens with the requisite understanding to constructively and responsibly execute their popular control of SWFs. Over the past two decades, 'people's conventions' have been held in numerous different polities, including Britain, the Netherlands, Canada, Ireland and Spain, on important national questions of institutional or constitutional design with great success.[41] Many citizen participants in these conventions revealed a change in attitude from prior to the convention, indicating a degree of reflectiveness among citizens that bodes well for such deliberative democratic techniques. On the basis of similar evidence from his own deliberative democratic experiments, Archon Fung has argued that 'if ordinary citizens generally possess or can with reasonable effort acquire the knowledge and skills necessary to make wise decisions in this area, then (other factors being equal) considered judgment favors assemblies of citizens over experts deploying their technical prowess'.[42] He goes on to give examples where citizens have, in fact, mastered complex policy issues in a citizens' assembly context, calling into doubt the idea that citizens cannot grasp technical matters. This is cause for optimism regarding the efficacy of participatory control devices over SWF management.

Another option for encouraging effective citizen input into sovereign wealth management is to use what Fung terms 'lay stakeholders . . . unpaid citizens who have a deep interest in some public concern and are thus willing to invest substantial time and energy to represent and serve those who have similar interests or perspectives but choose not to participate'.[43] Governments could engage small groups of willing lay stakeholders for education, discussion and decisions about SWF policy.

Finally, if a particular government was keen to engage a larger sample of citizens in SWF decision-making, it could undertake a deliberative poll of a sample of citizens on foundational sovereign fund policy issues. James Fishkin, the key proponent of the deliberative poll concept, explains the idea:

A deliberative poll attempts to model what the public *would* think, had it a better opportunity to consider the questions at issue. The idea is simple. Take a national random sample of the electorate and transport those people from all over the country to a single place. Immerse the sample in the issues, and with the chance to question competing experts and politicians. At the end of several days of working through the issues face to face, poll the participants in detail. The resulting survey offers a representation of the considered judgments of the public – the views the entire country would come to if it had the same experience of behaving more like those citizens immersed in the issues for an extended period.[44]

The world's first nationally televised deliberative poll occurred in Britain in 1994 with much success. It was on the interesting social question of what to do about rising crime. The poll assembled 300 participants from all around Britain for a weekend in Manchester and polling of the participants beforehand and afterwards revealed a change in many participants' thinking.[45] If such initiatives can educate and empower relatively uninformed citizens to make informed choices on difficult policy questions, doubt is cast over the power of the incompetent citizen objection.[46]

There is another, more fundamental response to the 'incompetent citizen' objection. It argues that the expertise of public administrators, tasked with regulating on behalf of the 'non-expert' citizen, is *only* properly conducted when an assessment of the public's needs and desires occurs first. That argument, attributable to John Dewey, holds that a regulator's expertise in administering state business, even highly technical matters like sovereign fund management, can only be ascertained through consultation with the public:

> For Dewey, the regulator's expertise necessarily involves the kind of engagement with the public that otherwise legitimates the assignment of value choices to the public's representatives. It issues from adoption of a 'scientific attitude of mind ... apparent whenever beliefs [are] not simply taken for granted but established as the conclusions of critical inquiry and testing'. Particularly (though not exclusively) within the realm of regulation, critical inquiry begins with an assessment of the public's needs, which are discerned through consultation with the public itself.[47]

That process is a dynamic one in which the experts help educate the public on policy choices, and the public in turn communicates a more informed set of preferences about the future direction of that policy to the experts.

Understanding the democratic control process as a 'mutually educa-tional' one[48] between citizen and expert challenges the atomistic conception of citizen and public official upon which the 'incompetent citizen' objection is grounded. The expectation that the citizens should 'arrive' at the policy-making process fully versed and competent to opine on technical matters of state arguably involves a denial of the state's responsibility to properly educate its citizens on important policy matters. Indeed, it can be argued that '[g]eneral apathy and a lack of sophistication on the part of the public are symptoms of, not justifications for, the exclusion of the public from regulatory decisionmaking'.[49] In the case of sovereign fund management, when such a significant aspect of public wealth is in the hands of expert managers outside the traditional apparatus of the state, there are strong grounds for mandating regular communication and dialogue between citizens and management to ensure this didactic exchange occurs.

(iv) The 'diminished performance' objection   Even if Dewey's idea of exchange between citizens and expert SWF managers occurs such that citizens are competent to opine on matters informing SWF policy, another objection arises concerning the costs of democratic control. Extensive consultation with, disclosure to and education of the public is costly, both in terms of resources and time. In the competitive world of investment, which often relies on opportunistic decision-making and timely application of expertise, this sort of public engagement could harm the fund's efficiency and, ultimately, returns.

There are two responses. The first acknowledges that there are aspects of an SWF that should not be subject to transparency requirements or direct citizen input on account of their potential to compromise SWF performance. As noted above, there are good grounds for keeping the actual function of investment decision-making confidential. A second response notes that some of the world's most transparent and accountable sovereign funds do not suffer from relative underperformance, nor a legitimacy crisis in the eyes of their citizen-owners. Norway's sovereign fund is not only one of the world's most transparent funds, but also lays claim to stellar invest-ment performance as the world's largest sovereign fund. Similarly, the New Zealand Superannuation Fund has boasted some of the steadiest, most impressive annual returns in the SWF community since its inception in

2003, at the same time as having one of the most demanding accountability regimes. It is the only SWF, for instance, that requires publication of monthly performance reports and public disclosure of all CEO expenses.[50]

For the sake of argument, though, assume that there is a potential cost to investment performance from enhanced public participation in SWF management. The question then becomes whether the goal of functional effectiveness is prior, equal or secondary to that of democratic legitimacy. Surely, if high management fees for external mandates are justified on the basis of augmented returns that are in the best interests of citizens, then, similarly, some expense to facilitate access to and participation in the democratic control of a fund can be accommodated on the grounds of instilling proper control rights in the true owners of sovereign funds. Securing citizen buy-in to a sovereign fund's activities may even reduce costs in the long run if it helps the fund avoid unpopular, controversial investment decisions. In other words, no accumulation without representation! Effective community control over sovereign wealth is worth the money in the long term.

6

Dirty money: generating sovereign wealth ethically

[The Future Fund] was not set up ... as a 'green bank'. It was set up to invest for future generations ... that is the investment mandate.

Peter Costello, Chairman of the Australian Future Fund, 2015[1]

The Future Fund should be at arm's-length but it is public money invested and it is a public institution. That fact alone obliges us to consider the implications of its actions ... It should seek profits only in so far as they help to balance the ledger. If we cannot do that without causing harm in other countries, how can we endorse this enterprise?

Senator Richard Di Natale, Australian Greens, 2012[2]

In 2011, Australia became a global leader in the fight against Big Tobacco. The government introduced some of the world's toughest anti-smoking laws, raising tobacco taxes by 25 per cent and announcing the first ban on brand names on cigarette packaging globally. Shortly after, it was revealed that the federal government's main sovereign investment vehicle, the Future Fund, held almost AU$150 million in global tobacco shares. A furore erupted.

The perceived contradiction in government policy led to calls for ethical restrictions on the Future Fund's investment mandate.[3] A senator from the left-leaning Greens party introduced a Private Member's Bill in 2012 to force 'the Fund to divest its unethical holdings in tobacco and nuclear investments'.[4] The bill proposed the creation of guidelines on responsible investment practices for environmental and human rights concerns, labour practices and the manufacture of war weapons.

The government and the Future Fund rejected the case for ethical investment restrictions. In its submission on the proposed bill, Future Fund senior management argued that its existing approach to responsible investment was sufficient and that the bill's impact would be detrimental on investment performance. It listed a host of potential harms to the fund if the bill were implemented, including risks of higher costs, a smaller investment universe, shortened investment horizon and reduced access to quality asset managers and strategies. In short, it was going to be a burden and one that might impair the fund's returns.

The bill was unsuccessful. But in February 2013, following public pressure that forced an internal review of the Future Fund's tobacco holdings, senior management announced that the fund would divest all tobacco holdings.[5]

Australia is not alone in experiencing debate over how its sovereign funds should generate returns on national wealth. Dilemmas over ethical investment (EI), or what is now more frequently termed responsible investment (RI), have plagued sovereign funds across the globe from the Arctic to the Antarctic. Norway made headlines in 2015 for requiring its sovereign fund to divest from companies that derive 30 per cent or more of their business from mining or burning coal. But critics were quick to point out that Norway is Europe's largest producer of other fossil fuels, having generated the world's biggest stockpile of sovereign wealth from exploiting North Sea oil and gas over four decades.[6] At the opposite pole, the New Zealand Superannuation Fund (NZSF) came under local fire for its equity investments in mining giants associated with human rights abuses and environmental damage. The New Zealand public demanded divestment of the mining stock as citizens fretted that their retirement would be funded by blood money. But the fund's management argued that its responsibility as an active shareholder, with an express commitment to improving the conduct of its portfolio companies, meant it should keep the shares and lobby the offending company's management to change behaviour. A sustained debate followed on exactly which strategy – divestment or engagement – would best ensure that New Zealand fulfilled its duty as a responsible investor and that the country ethically generated its long-term wealth.

Episodes like these suggest a need to investigate whether SWFs should be subject to responsible investment obligations and, if so, in what form. The saga over the Australian Future Fund's tobacco divestment revealed a gap between the public's expectations of appropriate investment strategies for national wealth creation and fund management's belief that its highest obligation to the public was to generate maximum returns for the future. That gap may well still exist. No audit of the Australian public's views regarding appropriate investments for its SWF has ever been undertaken. Yet even when the fund reports stellar investment returns, its performance is increasingly overshadowed by questions about how it generated that income. In 2015, despite delivering a whopping 15.4 per cent annual return, scrutiny of the reported figures focused on the fund's exposure to fossil fuels through holdings in Australian mining giants Rio Tinto and BHP Billiton.[7] The Future Fund chairman and chief investment officer were put on the defensive, interrogated about why they were not following Norway's fossil fuel divestment lead.

Dilemmas also arise even where the investment behaviour of funds is heavily circumscribed by ethical considerations. Both Norway and New Zealand are already subject to quite demanding RI obligations. Both within the sovereign wealth universe and more broadly among institutional investors, they constitute two of the world's most socially conscious investors. Each boasts an explicit responsible investment mandate and a commitment to ethically generated returns. Yet even these funds face ongoing predicaments over how to satisfy those obligations in a way that is consistent with the values and expectations of their home communities.

This chapter is about those dilemmas. If citizens are to enjoy meaningful control over their sovereign funds, this must include control over the wealth within those funds – how it is invested and augmented.[8] Exactly how to secure that control is challenging. Sovereign funds need guidance on how to determine the values of their sponsoring communities; strategies for giving effect to those values in investment behaviour; and approaches for balancing a responsibility to their citizen-owners' expectations and the obligation to generate a particular return. Was it sufficient for the Australian Future Fund to retrospectively divest its tobacco holdings after years of enjoying returns from an industry widely criticized by the public, and indeed the government? Is it acceptable that Norway divests from just one fossil fuel and not others? Is New Zealand's strategy of engaging rather than divesting in line with the community's moral compass for how to respond to ethically questionable holdings in its portfolio? For sovereign funds to be truly community funds, guidance on how to tackle these ethical conundrums to ensure a nation's wealth is generated in a manner consistent with the values of its sponsor community is long overdue. To that end, this chapter recommends a two-step reform process in which, first, a statutory responsible investment obligation must be included in the investment mandate of all sovereign funds; and second, its content is determined by citizen-owners through participatory democratic processes.

The lack of responsible investment by sovereign funds

Before proceeding, it is helpful to know the extent to which sovereign funds already address ethical considerations when investing.[9] Of the more than seventy funds in existence today, only three sovereign funds have an explicit, overarching RI mandate. Two of these funds – Norway's GPFG and New Zealand's NZSF – have been investing ethically for around a decade, and are considered world leaders in responsible investment.[10] The third SWF, not yet operational but legislatively established in early 2012 and passed into law in July 2015, is Papua New Guinea's sovereign fund for holding windfalls from the production and sale of the country's liquefied natural gas project.[11]

These three funds have what I call an 'integrated' RI mandate. This requires a portfolio-wide approach to responsible investment. The ethical impact of every allocation of portfolio assets must be evaluated. In addition to integrated RI mandates, up to another eighteen sovereign funds are subject to some form of targeted ethical investment obligation.[12] Targeted RI obligations single out particular industries or companies whose products are banned from the portfolio given certain characteristics of the industry, or because such products violate norms the investors want to uphold. As a result, responsible investors with targeted obligations lack an overarching obligation to consider ethical implications in *all* investment decisions. They do not assume a whole-of-portfolio outlook when it comes to ethical considerations. Instead, their ethical investment is limited to piecemeal exclusions by sector, instrument, entity or country.

In practice, an SWF with targeted obligations is at higher risk of ethical transgressions than a fund with an integrated RI mandate. In the latter, socially responsible considerations assume equivalent status to other components of the investment mandate. Under the circumscribed approach of a targeted mandate, a fund is still at risk of unethical investment in asset classes or products not covered by the select constraints. The fulfilment of the ethically *un*constrained investment mandate is top priority, while compliance with ad hoc obligations is given separate, subsequent consideration. Accordingly, only full incorporation of ethical obligations into the overarching investment mandate is likely to adequately shield citizens' ethical exposure from complicity in immoral return-seeking. The general absence of comprehensive RI mandates among SWFs, as well as the noticeable lack of SWFs as signatories to the United Nations Principles for Responsible Investment (UNPRI),[13] a voluntary and aspirational set of investment principles for institutional investors committed to generating returns responsibly, both reinforce the striking absence of RI practices among the sovereign fund community.[14]

Why ethical investment of sovereign wealth matters

Is this absence of ethical constraints on investment by sovereign funds particularly worrying? The dilemmas experienced by the citizenries of Australia, New Zealand and Norway do not seem unlike the sorts of dilemmas that face each of us in our daily lives. Citizens, in their individual capacity as owners and consumers, make choices constantly that may compromise their integrity. The new car I purchase may be a high polluter; the clothes I wear may have been made in a sweatshop; the interest I earn on my bank account might be generated through questionable investments; and the money I inherit from my grandparents might have been built on the proceeds of crime. My right to acquire and possess these objects is not necessarily constrained by a set of *externally* imposed ethical constraints, at least at the point of acquiring or inheriting these things. Citizens approach the market as free agents, largely at liberty to heed or disregard the ethical impact of their individual choices. So why should citizens' collective ethical integrity require particular protection or consideration when it comes to the accumulation of a nation's sovereign wealth?

One answer lies in the coercive nature of SWF investment. In the case of the acquisitions above, I have an exit option. I can reject the inheritance, move my money to an ethical bank, buy a 'green' car or wear responsibly made garments. But when it comes to the collective wealth of a nation in an SWF, there is no exit option. Law professor Lawrence Backer made this precise point when comparing the investment approaches of the Norwegian GPFG with a well-known *private* fund, TIAA-CREF, committed to socially responsible investment:

> The critical difference [between state-sponsored funds and private funds] is grounded in notions of *coercion* and in whether or not the ulti-mate investors have a choice in the manner in which they are repre-sented and their funds are invested. In both the public and the private fund, individuals are the ultimate stakeholders and investors. It is for their benefit that these funds are created and it is their interests that they ultimately serve. [However, the] Norwegian Fund's institutional holder is the state apparatus of Norway, but the ultimate beneficiaries are the citizens of Norway on whose behalf the government acts. The TIAA CREF funds are administered *directly* for the investors on whose behalf the fund managers operate. But TIAA CREF investors are *free to exit* the . . . Fund at will (or at least in accordance with procedures there-fore agreed to when they first invested their funds). Norwegian citizens have *no such right*. They are bound by the choices made for them by the state apparatus. They are *at least one critical step removed* from the Fund. As a consequence, the TIAA CREF Fund has to be more careful and conscious of the wishes of its ultimate investors than does the Norwegian Fund. The Norwegian state is accountable to the people, but the Fund is accountable *only* to the state.[15]

TIAA-CREF, like Norway's GPFG, seeks to invest responsibly, but the ulti-mate investors and stakeholders in that case are 'free to exit' if the fund departs from the expectations of those investors or transgresses their ethical prefer-ences in some unforeseen way. But citizen-owners of an SWF cannot exercise such protest against their funds. How then can citizens be considered owners of sovereign funds in the sense of controlling their property just like private fund investors, if they cannot shield themselves from exposure to the morally objectionable implications of that property? Such practices constitute a specific infraction of ethical integrity.

A second reason why it matters that sovereign wealth in particular is invested within ethical bounds concerns the nature of citizen complicity in fund activities. It may be tempting to think that even if a sovereign fund offends the ethical values of its citizen-owners through its investment activities, it is not the moral responsibility of those citizens, since on my fiduciary conception of SWFs it is the government-*agent* and its representatives managing the fund who undertook those decisions.

It is a mistake, however, to talk about ethical complicity and moral responsibility of collectives or corporate entities in a way that empties our moral system of individual culpability. Individuals play a crucial role in our system of moral responsibility. According to philosopher Christopher Kutz:

> Moral responsibility . . . is a system through which we humans attempt to regulate our behaviour towards each other and the world to minimize the amount of suffering we cause and perhaps even make some improvements here and there. This system of social control works through our individual psychologies, our motivations to avoid criticism and to receive praise – to feel that our lives have been well-lived. Given such a conception of moral responsibility, it is rather beside the point to talk in terms of corporate moral responsibility – the system of moral responsibility functions, when it functions at all, through our individual consciences.[16]

Even if the potential culpability of a collective association or corporate agent in a moral wrong is acknowledged, it is possible to simultaneously acknowledge individual complicity in that act. One type of culpable agent does not substitute for another blameworthy participant in that act. On that view, sovereign funds,[17] and/or their government sponsors, may be held morally responsible for ethical transgressions through investment decisions alongside their citizens, but on either approach citizens cannot escape individual complicity. Consequently, if moral responsibility invariably attaches to individuals, collective investment funds which coerce individuals into their investment decisions must do so within parameters that shield those *individuals* from undesired complicity.

One final observation is that the use of an agent, at least in the eyes of the civil and criminal law, typically *increases* a principal's responsibility for ugly acts, rather than diminishing it, since the principal enjoys increased powers as well by virtue of this relationship.[18] This would mean the citizens bear even greater responsibility for the acts of their sovereign fund precisely *because* they are the principal of the government-agent managing the fund. We cannot selectively choose our exposure to fund activities, hiding behind the agent of government or fund management in some areas, but demanding control and benefit privileges in other respects. That would amount to the owners' asymmetric claiming of privileges but denial of responsibilities.[19]

Given that citizens' integrity is potentially jeopardized by the coercive nature of unconstrained SWF investment and '[f]und complicity is, at root, a question of citizen complicity', SWF investment must 'answer to the full range of ethical demands'[20] that a citizenry might ask of that fund. Citizens cannot be protected from the consequences of these acts by virtue of their fiduciary relationship with government and the fund. On the contrary, it is precisely because of that relationship that governments must constrain the investment universe of sovereign funds. All these attributes differentiate SWFs from other financial market participants, constituting a special case for the imposition of an ethical investment duty on sovereign wealth.

The practical challenge of responsible investment among SWFs

Acknowledging that sovereign funds should invest responsibly to reflect their sponsor community's values is one thing. But realizing that obligation in practice is another. The experience of sovereign funds that already boast an ethical investment mandate and yet still fall foul of citizens' views over their asset holdings underscores the challenge. A closer look at New Zealand's experience over the operation of its responsible investment obligations is instructive.

The NZSF has been subject to a statutory responsible investment obligation since its inception in 2001. The fund's founding Act set outs its overarching investment mandate, which requires the Guardians 'to invest the Fund on a prudent, commercial basis . . . in a manner consistent with:

(a) best-practice portfolio management; and (b) maximizing return without undue risk to the Fund as a whole; and (c) avoiding prejudice to New Zealand's reputation as a responsible member of the world community'.[21] The legislation does not provide any guidance as to the terms' meaning or ordering, but the Guardians have interpreted the mandate to imply none of the three components of the investment mandate has precedence over the other so each must be taken into account when considering investment issues.[22] No further guidance was provided on the meaning of clause (c) as it relates to responsible investment, but it has since been interpreted by the Guardians to imply a series of ethical obligations and duties in investment decision-making.

Despite detailed policy statements on this clause, the fund has attracted significant controversy over its interpretation of the RI obligation, the sort of controversy that highlights the need for popular input into SWF ethical investment guidelines. As touched on above, a high-profile episode involved the NZSF's equity holdings in mining giants Freeport and Rio Tinto, which run gold and copper mining operations in West Papua. In 2003, serious allegations concerning human rights abuses, severe environmental destruction and damage to the local indigenous population were publicly documented in relation to Freeport and Rio Tinto's Grasberg mine.[23] Multiple institutional investors, including the Norwegian GPFG, divested their Freeport and Rio Tinto holdings in the years following.[24] Despite this information, the NZSF acquired equity holdings in both companies in 2006, and maintained those holdings amid ongoing reports of ethical transgressions at the Grasberg mine. Fund management argued that these investments were permissible under the statutory RI obligation in their investment mandate, since the board interpreted that obligation as mandating the fund to engage with offending companies to change their behaviour.[25]

In 2011, a freelance journalist published a scathing critique of New Zealand's Freeport investment, deploring the fund's continuing investment despite fresh evidence of human rights breaches, corruption and environmental harm at the Grasberg mine.[26] The journalist, Karen Abplanalp, queried whether the fund's NZSF's stated preference for *engaging* with company management rather than *excluding* the investment from its portfolio was out of step with citizens' expectations of the NZSF's responsible investment obligation. In contrast, when justifying its divestment decision,

GPFG management declared that '[t]here are no indications ... that the company's practices will be changed in future, or that measures will be taken to significantly reduce the damage to nature and the environment'. Consequently, the Norwegian Council of Ethics had deemed exclusion essential to ensuring the GPFG did not 'run an unacceptable risk of contributing to grossly unethical conduct'.[27]

In an official response to Abplanalp's article, the NZSF Guardians clarified that the holdings were passive investments gained through index investing, which meant they had not 'picked' the stock. They also challenged the equation of responsible investing with *exclusion*, arguing that their engagement approach fully recognized the failed environmental, social and governance standards in Freeport, and sought to address those failures by changing company behaviour, rather than walking away through divestment or exclusion. The NZSF CEO, Adrian Orr, argued that retaining the holding allowed the Guardians to continue influencing the company in an effort to improve the situation for West Papuans. On the Guardians' view, when compared to the alternative exclusion option, their attempts to engage with Freeport management for the past five years would have the 'biggest impact on the affected people and environments'.[28]

Whether, in the long term, engagement could achieve more than exclusion is debatable.[29] For our purposes, though, that is of less relevance than whether the Guardians' investment management approach endowed New Zealand's citizens with a meaningful sense of control over their own fund and its assets. As Abplanalp mused: 'Is the fund doing good, as Orr believes, or simply helping to prop up activities that would be illegal in this country – activities that most New Zealanders would be horrified to support let alone make money from, if they were happening here? Do we want our pensions paid for in this way?'[30]

Certainly, that was the view of some key political figures in New Zealand, including the Green Party leader, Russell Norman, who criticized the fund's lack of divestment action as being out of touch with public preferences on this issue: 'In order for engagement to be effective, it needs to carry a credible threat of divestment, which the NZSF has shown time and again it does not have. The divestments they have made in regard to tobacco, cluster munitions and nuclear weapons manufacturers have only come as a result of an enormous amount of public pressure.'[31]

In a worrying sign for New Zealanders' democratic control over their sovereign fund, the Guardians' response also highlighted that 'responsible investment is not about making New Zealanders feel good about the Guardians' investments'. The Guardians reiterated that investment decisions must make sense from a responsible investment *and* commercial perspective, underscoring that the 'Guardians cannot and do not invest to be popular'.[32]

While sovereign funds should not be populist and reactive in investment decision-making, the case at hand raises a subtler dilemma: how best to give effect to citizens' sense of influence and control over their sovereign wealth while at the same time quarantining investment decisions from political agendas so that a sovereign fund can meet its financial objectives. Moreover, it raises the question of how prescriptive ethical investment constraints must be since, in New Zealand's case, the fund had a legislatively entrenched responsible investment obligation, and yet the evidence suggests that this did not always translate into citizens feeling that they had adequate control over their national fund's behaviour. On the contrary, deep discomfort arose over some of the fund's investment decisions.

The discomfort intensified. So much so that in September 2012 the NZSF divested its NZ$1.28 million holding in Freeport on account of 'breaches of human rights standards by security forces around the Grasberg mine, and concerns over requirements for direct payments to government security forces'.[33] In defending the decision, the NZSF said it had reached a conclusion that further engagement would not be successful, and that such a consideration was a relevant factor in deciding which strategy to pursue.

The New Zealand saga underscores two points. The first is the special status of a sovereign fund's ethical activities in relation to individual citizens' integrity. Karen Abplanalp wondered whether New Zealanders wanted their pensions paid for in a morally questionable way. Australian Senator Richard Di Natale (quoted in the epigraph) questioned how Australians could endorse the enterprise of wealth accumulation through practices 'causing harm in other countries'. It is only right, then, that all citizen-owners of SWFs concerned with living ethically ask similar questions of their funds. Indeed, they must do so since a fund that invests their resources on their behalf, investments from which they and their successive generations will derive benefit, has implications for their own ethical agency. This makes the question of popular control over ethical guidelines qualitatively different from that of other aspects of a fund's governance.

The second takeaway from the Freeport example is that the desire to have control over one's ethical integrity is not simply satisfied (or compromised) by the presence (or absence) of ethical guidelines alone. The next chapter demonstrates that the early investing life of Norway's GPFG generated substantial public controversy regarding the appropriateness of its investment holdings in certain weapons industries. At this initial stage in the GPFG's history, it lacked proper ethical guidelines, prompting a radical overhaul of the fund's investment approach to ensure its investment activities were better aligned with the ethical values of Norwegians.

Yet, similar levels of controversy plagued the NZSF well into its investing life, *despite* the presence of a statutory obligation to invest responsibly. Even with extensive guidelines for interpreting that ethical investment obligation and regardless of a detailed, transparent and systematic set of procedures for handling investee companies like Freeport, the NZSF's approach to its holdings in this company appeared out of step with the preferences of New Zealand's citizens. These public controversies suggest that the imposition of ethical guidelines alone is *not* enough to secure citizens' ability to live with integrity through their fund. Those guidelines actually have to reflect the citizenry's notion of what it means to live ethically, not the government's idea of what that should mean.

What can be done?

A two-step reform process could help ensure that citizens adequately control the investment activities of their funds and are shielded from complicity in unethical investment. First, governments should apply a general statutory obligation for their SWF to invest responsibly in their fund's enabling legislation. The Santiago Principles could be amended to require that all SWFs include a clause in their legal investment mandates to the following effect: 'The Fund must be invested in a manner consistent with the domestic and international ethical obligations of the owner state.'

Second, the precise content of this obligation should then be determined by the citizens of SWF-owning communities through general participatory processes for determining SWF policy. My model of enhanced popular control over sovereign wealth already requires citizens to express (informed) preferences on a fund's investment policy framework. However, as evident in this chapter, ethical investment guidelines usher in a distinct set of moral and practical considerations relative to other aspects of investment policy. Citizens must therefore be educated on and influence various aspects of the investment mandate and strategy, including return targets, risk tolerance, portfolio design (including permissible asset classes, sectors, geographic destinations, currency composition, the desired split between domestic and overseas investment), and most essentially the ethical obligations constraining fund investment activity. This should follow public consultation and education over options for responsible investment in light of its objectives. Only then is it possible to ensure that the ethical integrity of individual citizens is properly protected.

Objections to ethical investment of sovereign wealth

Given the general absence of mandated responsible investing among SWFs, the proposal that all sovereign funds be subject to a responsible investment obligation, the precise content of which should be popularly determined by the citizens of sponsor communities, will surely invite objections. Four potential protests are considered here. The first two consider the appropriateness of SWF board members including ethical considerations in the execution of their trusteeship duties; the latter concern a given community's capabilities in and predilection for responsible national wealth accumulation.

(i) The trusteeship objection In a keynote speech to a 2011 sovereign investor roundtable, then IFSWF chairman David Murray resisted calls for sovereign funds to embrace ethical investment. He defended a particular conception of SWFs as 'first and foremost wealth preservation and augmentation vehicles, [a] purpose [which] may be jeopardized if funds are required to pursue multiple bottom lines'.[34]

Murray's view reflects a widespread understanding of SWF trusteeship in which management's fundamental task is to maximize wealth for the state-sponsor and its citizens. Intrinsic to this understanding are two assumptions. The first is a belief that prosperous and virtuous investment necessarily conflict.[35] I address that worry in a moment. The second is that wealth is the highest-order interest of domestic beneficiaries, current and future. To quote Murray:

> As SWFs are tools for preserving and augmenting wealth of their founding communities, any constraint on investment strategy impairs a fund's ability to generate an optimal return for their domestic beneficiaries. This deprives not only the fund, but most crucially its *owning community* of wealth, adversely impacting the living standards of both *current and future generations* . . . Reducing the ability of sovereign funds to maximize returns, effectively diminishes *long-term public budgets* for healthcare, pensions and critical infrastructure in savings deficient countries.[36]

SWF trustees would therefore fail to promote the best interests of future citizens if they prioritized ethical investment over wealth maximization, assuming a trade-off.

Implicit in this narrow conception of sovereign funds' purpose are two interpretations – one legal and one conceptual – about the nature of SWF trusteeship. First, those that concur with Murray's view might do so in the belief that the ultimate legal obligation of a trustee acting in an asset management capacity is to preserve and augment the beneficiaries' assets. But legal interpretation of 'trustee' derives from existing approaches to pension fund trusteeship, where the liabilities and fiduciary relationship differ vastly from those of a sovereign fund.[37] Indeed, some sovereign funds have deliberately avoided the term 'trustee' for their board members, instead employing labels such as 'Guardians', precisely to escape the common law or statutory importation of standard fiduciary duties to SWF governance.[38]

A broader notion of trustee specifically tailored to SWFs is necessary. Woods and Urwin have argued that it is precisely because SWFs are *not* subject to the same type of legal fiduciary duties that bind pension fund trustees that they are freer to pursue multiple bottom lines as part of their specialized investment missions to improve national welfare or achieve social goals.[39] If the very idea of a sovereign fund is to marry some financial purpose with a wider social goal, surely the notion of SWF trusteeship could be similarly broadened to capture duties beyond wealth maximization.[40]

Even if the legal notion of SWF trusteeship is revised, some may still philosophically believe that the primary duty of SWFs (and their trustees) to future citizens is wealth maximization. But this one-dimensional notion of current and future citizens' interests as they affect one another is out of step with scholarly thinking on intergenerational justice. Such theory recognizes that today's communities wield an asymmetric influence over multiple aspects of the world that tomorrow's citizens will inherit.[41] Indeed, present generations of citizens have been deemed to hold a responsibility to future generations in at least three equally important respects: first, a duty to 'conserve the diversity of the natural and cultural resource base so that it does not unduly restrict the options available to future generations'; second, 'each generation should be required to maintain the quality of the planet so that it is passed on in no worse condition than that in which it was received'; third, 'each generation should provide its members with equitable rights of access to the legacy of past generations'.[42]

Whether or not one endorses this view of society's obligations to future generations, it does provide a basis for challenging the idea that such interests are met solely by endowing future citizens with commercial security. If, in the quest to provide that commercial security, a sovereign fund pursues investments that diminish the 'natural and cultural resource base', 'the quality of the planet' or 'access to the legacy of past generations', sovereign fund trustees could be held responsible for harming the interests of future generations. Surely these broader non-monetary interests of future citizens (however defined) deserve consideration.

For this reason, the concept of sustainability continues to gain a foothold in the investment mandates of asset managers.[43] Although a highly contested concept, it is an increasingly prolific component of many financial actor approaches to the markets.[44] Sustainable development is 'development that meets the needs of the present without compromising the ability of future generations to meet their own needs'.[45] A sustainability constraint on SWF investment would require sovereign wealth to be deployed in the markets so that it meets the needs of the present without compromising the ability of future generations to meet their own needs.

In fulfilling this obligation, all that can be asked of trustees today is that they act reasonably; to make a judgement to the best of their ability, bearing in mind the possible consequences for the ethically minded citizen of tomorrow. There is obviously a limit to what future generations can demand of today's trustees, since present citizens cannot know what the ethical predilections of future citizens will be, but they can demand that trustees exercise their best judgement about what is ethical and sustainable.

(ii) The efficacy objection   The other idea at work in Murray's objection to ethical investment of sovereign wealth is an assumed conflict between virtuous and prosperous investing. Recall the Australian Future Fund's response to the attempt to incorporate ethical obligations into its mandate.[46] The fund's major worry was a greater risk of diminished returns.[47] Ethical investment was seen as a threat to returns in a number of ways. It would impair the fund's ability to fully diversify; reduce the universe of allowable asset managers, investments assets and strategies; and increase compliance costs and resource requirements in managing the administrative burden of screening, divesting, monitoring and targeting.[48]

There is an ongoing debate over the extent to which ethical and commercial investing conflict. A growing corpus of research shows the conflict is exaggerated or non-existent.[49] Indeed, some SWFs have made a business case for ethical investing,[50] with both Norway and New Zealand adapting their RI mandates to recognize the link between ethical investment and good returns.[51] Analysts have also pointed to the special case for sustainable development considerations enhancing returns in long-term investors like sovereign funds: 'Socially responsible investment does not necessarily entail any irresolvable trade-offs between public and private interests, or financial and ethical goals. While commercial considerations do not always coincide with ethical ones, over the very long-term they should given ecological constraints to infinite economic growth.'[52]

Hard-core ethicists might reply that even if responsible investment did involve some return diminution, this may be tolerable if wealth enhancement is considered one among many values that a community fund might wish to pursue through an SWF. The experiences of Australia, New Zealand and Norway suggest that communities do not only care about maximum return over other policy outcomes for their sovereign funds.

In any event, I argued above that the best interests of fund beneficiaries should include both a fund's goal of wealth management alongside other laudable objectives it was set up to achieve. Ultimately, sovereign funds are something more than purely financial entities whose only accountability is to the supreme value of wealth preservation, augmentation or maximization. Instead, they are new policy tools proving instrumental in securing a wider set of values for an owning community. In the name of that task, some trade-off, if it exists, is potentially justifiable.

(iii) The reasonable disagreement objection   Even if the trustees' potential objections to an ethical investment obligation for SWFs are overcome, the citizens in whose interests these recommendations are proposed may pose other hurdles. Most significantly, what if a community cannot agree on the content of ethical investment guidelines for their sovereign fund?

Accepting the fact of ethical pluralism – that citizens will embrace diverse moral doctrines and conceptions of the good – fundamental agreement may not be possible. Reasonable disagreement on what is ethically suspect may run so deep that no consensus is achievable.[53] Imposing ethical constraints on a communally owned fund, then, reintroduces a coercion problem to SWF investment.

There is an optimistic and pessimistic response to this objection. On the optimistic view, deep disagreement on serious moral issues may not indicate irreconcilable disagreement on ultimate values. If so, communities may seek to create or 'find' consensus. This is precisely the Norwegian experience. An expert committee, known as the Graver Committee, charged with developing ethical investment guidelines for Norway's sovereign fund identified evidence of an 'overlapping consensus' among Norwegians on moral values:

> Norway is a pluralistic society and there is no consensus on one particular uniform ethical perspective. The absence of a uniform perspective [however], does not mean that there is no agreement on certain ethical principles. In many instances, Norwegians will arrive at the same answer to questions of ethics from different angles of approach ... In these cases, we have what we might call *overlapping consensus.*[54]

The committee then used this moral consensus as a basis for identifying widely held ethical values to guide the Norwegian fund's investment.

An alternative method for establishing consensus is to actively cultivate that agreement. This involves opening up deliberations on ethical values to citizens (a step that Norway did not take). Deliberative democratic theorists have identified various strategies for resolving disagreement fairly among 'reasonable citizens' interested in reaching agreement.[55] Such strategies, some of which were touched on in the last chapter, such as citizen assemblies or juries, typically rely on citizens sharing at least a basic commitment to the legitimacy of fair deliberative process. Communities might be able to reach an overlapping consensus, even if one did not exist initially, sufficient to offer a basis for forming ethical investment guidelines on national wealth.

The pessimist will continue to wonder what if agreement is still not possible? What if reasonable disagreement is fundamental? Is the enterprise of ethical investment doomed? In such a scenario, one possible answer is to uphold the fact of reasonable moral disagreement. That is, we should not try to force agreement, but rather respect the presence of radical or deep disagreement within a community and design mechanisms for our sovereign fund to respond to this reasonable disagreement.

One such mechanism is described in political theorist Karl Widerquist's proposal for citizens' capital accounts. The idea of a citizen's capital account (CCA) involves giving each citizen their own account within a collectively owned sovereign fund, proportionate to a per-capita share of the fund's total value.[56] For the architects of this proposal, the main objective is to give individuals greater control over the *returns* of their community funds rather than the principal itself: 'The CCA system would personalize the [collective] fund by giving each individual an account within the larger fund. The account would accrue returns all the time, but within limits. Individuals could decide when to withdraw their returns or whether to leave their returns in the account to accrue compound interest that they can draw on later.'[57]

The CCA proposal has been criticized as an 'insufficient . . . mechanism of full democratic control' since 'it only focuses on the last decision point' regarding the use of sovereign fund returns.[58] While that criticism is fair, Widerquist briefly flags the possibility that citizens could exert some influence over their account: 'Account holders could have some control over the principal, such as the right to direct investing some or all of their assets to one or more competing funds within the CCA-fund system.'[59] This idea is not elaborated further, other than to say that any citizen control over the principal must involve regulation over risk levels, an entirely reasonable point.[60]

Individuals could indicate assets, sectors and products to which they do not want exposure and accordingly forfeit returns flowing from these assets. The fund would then offer different returns levels to each citizen based on the design of their individual account exposure. In theory, each citizen would receive a different amount of returns from their equally owned fund, since citizens would design their own mix of asset exposure. For some, this would mean forfeiting returns where their preferred assets underperformed relative to the rest of the portfolio. Other citizens might 'beat' the fund's overall performance if their preferred assets were strong performers. These unequal outcomes would be directly felt through the distribution of returns.

Whether such a system would be administratively possible is another question. It is noteworthy that some pension funds allow their members a degree of influence regarding what assets their retirement savings are directed towards.[61] If the augmented CCA proposal could work in similar ways, this mechanism would offer sovereign funds a practical response to the reasonable disagreement problem, although it does not fully shield citizens from the ethical implications of their fund investments since the overall fund may continue to invest unconstrained.

The other mediatory initiative that might lessen the extent of citizen coercion in problematic SWF investment activity would be to allow citizens the right to decline their investment returns. For this to be possible, the right to SWF income must be individualized, a point discussed in Part III of this book. For now, I note that if returns attach to individuals as part of a benefit right to investment income, citizens could decline those returns where they feel they were earned in dubious ways.[62] In doing so, they would use their benefit right to make their control rights more effective. Such a strategy offers another tool for dealing with serious ongoing disagreement, where either that disagreement cannot be resolved despite attempts to do so, or the domestic community wishes to support a diversity of moral views rather than seeking to impose a consensus.

(iv) The immoral community objection   One final worry in the democratic vein concerns the opposite problem. What if, instead of exhibiting deep

disagreement, a community displays high levels of agreement, but on dubious values? A community may agree on ethically *un*constrained investment. They may decide their highest obligation to future generations is wealth maximization, or that its own ethical values are a second-order interest to that of financial return. Just as it is entirely reasonable to assume that citizens would wish to avoid complicity in morally repugnant practices through government investment, it is equally reasonable to imagine a citizenry preferring its SWF to privilege wealth augmentation, even where this might involve ethical transgressions.

This potential control rights tension is surmountable. A trumping preference for prosperity over virtuous investment among present citizens should still be sensitive to intergenerational equity. Upholding a present-day preference for wealth maximization above all gives full and disproportionate deference to the democratic preferences of today's citizens over future people. As the Norwegian Graver Committee observed: 'We do not manage the Petroleum Fund only on our own behalf, but also on behalf of future generations. As such, the Fund carries hereditary rights and obligations. A defining characteristic of the Fund is that a substantial proportion of those on whose behalf the Fund is managed cannot choose its manager.'[63]

When it comes to sovereign wealth, the imposition of the unconstrained preferences of the present generation might have irreversible consequences for tomorrow's citizens. At a minimum, then, even the most profit-oriented citizenry of today must still curtail their investment expectations to respect a minimum obligation of sustainable investing and accept that, where possible, today's trustees should invest with a view to protecting the ethical integrity of future generations. Beyond that, the demand for ethical sovereign wealth accumulation relies to a large extent on the better angels of our nature. While seemingly utopian, examples of such behaviour in the practical world of SWF management are explored in the next chapter.

7

Role models of community control: Norway and New Zealand

Norway is regularly lauded for having the largest as well as one of the most transparent and ethically conscious sovereign wealth funds in the world. But this has not always been the case, particularly in the eyes of the Norwegian citizenry. Early on in the fund's life, at the end of the 1990s, Norwegians were deeply critical of their investment fund. In 1999, a news story revealed that the Norwegian fund was invested in a Singaporean company producing anti-personnel mines. The report caused a public backlash given Norway's high profile in the Ottawa process that led to the creation of the Mine Ban Convention prohibiting the use, development, stockpiling, production and transfer of anti-personnel mines. Norwegian citizens struggled to comprehend how Norway could be a party to this convention, and nevertheless invest public money in anti-personnel mine production.[1]

Public opinion began to shift. Norwegians started to insist that their 'sovereign wealth fund should not only be used for intergenerational justice, but should also contribute to the implementation of universally accepted values and norms'.[2] To its credit, the Norwegian government was highly responsive to the public mood and established an expert committee to clarify the fund's approach to responsible investment and develop guidelines. While the fund was subject to some ethical obligations, these were narrowly focused on environmental sustainability. It tasked the 'Graver Committee' – the expert committee chaired by philosophy professor Hans

Peter Graver to provide advice on the formulation of a 'normatively and procedurally clearer' ethical investment framework.[3] The Graver Committee's recommendations resulted in the adoption of new ethical guidelines in 2004 and the establishment of a Council on Ethics for evaluating compliance with these guidelines in 2005.

The Graver Committee consisted of ten members, who met eight times to develop their report. The committee also held meetings with non-governmental organizations (NGOs) to collect input for its work and called on various experts to achieve the soundest possible basis for the proposal. Remarkably, there were no opportunities for direct citizen input. None of these sessions were open to the public.[4] In January 2008, as part of the first evaluation of the 2004 ethical guidelines, the Ministry of Finance held a large international conference in Oslo with participation from invited NGOs, academics, financial institutions, fund managers and investment experts from Norway and abroad to discuss the challenges of responsible investing.[5] The conference was not open to the Norwegian people, although it did mark the commencement of a consultation process with the aim to 'gather feedback' on and 'maintain broad political support for' the ethical guidelines, and which included a 'public hearing'. Once again, though, the 'public' hearing was only for invited organizations.[6]

The Norwegian experience of formulating ethical investment guidelines is perhaps the most comprehensive effort by a community to identify the values of its citizens for the purpose of developing policies to guide the accumulation and management of a nation's sovereign wealth. This begs the question of how effective this rigorous, although not entirely democratic, process has been in identifying the values of Norwegians citizens for the purpose of developing ethical investment guidelines. Put another way, did such measures endow Norwegians with a sense of control over the investment and management of their national wealth?

In offering an answer, this chapter compares and contrasts Norway's governance arrangements to the world's other top-performing SWF when it comes to the potential for citizen control. Both the Norwegian and New Zealand sovereign funds are exemplary on many of the key prerequisites for popular control such as transparency, accountability and ethical investment obligations. They are role-model funds. But as this chapter shows, even their impressive institutional arrangements still fall short of my recommended approach in crucial respects. Understanding what these two exemplary funds do better than most, but also how they still fall short of the fiduciary ideal of citizen ownership, highlights the full suite of measures towards which to aspire for meaningful democratic control over sovereign wealth. At the same time, both the Norwegian and New Zealand experiences isolate general feasibility challenges for the preferred model of control. For if these two prosperous countries with small populations and progressive political cultures fail to fully satisfy our ideal in certain respects, the model may need tailoring to better accommodate the constraints of feasibility.

Current control arrangements over sovereign fund management

It is helpful to start by seeing the extent to which citizens already exert control over their sovereign funds. The institutional design and governance arrangements of SWFs vary widely. Existing assessments of SWFs have sought to rank individual funds on criteria relevant to evaluating democratic control, such as transparency, accountability, structure and behaviour, although no existing index or scoreboard directly measures *popular* control over sovereign funds.

The most comprehensive of existing assessments is the Truman scoreboard, developed by economist Ted Truman in 2007.[7] It is helpful in two ways. First, the most recent 2012 scoreboard results demonstrate how transparent and accountable SWFs currently are as a group.[8] The overall focus of the Truman scoreboard is transparency and accountability. It assesses funds in four categories: (1) structure, (2) governance, (3) transparency and accountability and (4) behaviour. The overall focus on whether SWFs are accountable to their home governments and citizens[9] means the Truman rankings bear on citizens' potential to exert democratic control, despite that attribute not being specifically evaluated.

Second, comparing Truman's systematic criteria to my proposed control architecture reveals how SWFs can still improve on enhancing community control. My proposed control right covers three areas: election of management; setting of the fund objectives; and monitoring management fealty to those objectives (see Chapter 5). Truman has gone into fine detail on SWF responsibilities within these three areas, but not always through the same lens needed to assess effective popular influence and power over sovereign wealth. I identify those aspects of fund decision-making to which greater popular control should apply.

Turning to the 2012 Truman scoreboard, overall SWFs fall short of full compliance with criteria that are noticeably weaker than my popular control ideal. Appendix 3 of this book summarizes these results, including a comparison to the 2009 Truman scoreboard results for forty-four funds scored for both years. The 2012 ranking scored a sample of forty-nine sovereign funds from over forty countries on thirty-three individual elements to do with SWFs' structure, governance, transparency, accountability and behaviour.[10] The individual elements are equally weighted and translated into a 100-point scale.

The group's average score of 54 reflects relatively weak compliance with the elements, leading some commentators to characterize SWFs as unaccountable and non-transparent relative to peer institutional investors.[11] A caveat is necessary. There is huge variation in compliance with the Truman criteria. No fund received a perfect score, although the Norwegian GPFG came close, topping the list at 98, closely followed by New Zealand's NZSF on 94, and Chile's ESSF and the Alaska Permanent Fund both on 91. Including Norway, there was a cluster of high performers (twelve funds scoring 80 and above) and a similar size cluster of poor performers (sixteen funds scoring below 40), with the majority of twenty funds scoring in the middle. Most worrying is the sizeable cluster of poor performers in which there seems little potential for meaningful democratic control. This bottom cluster is dominated by SWFs from Africa, the Gulf and South America in largely non-democratic states.

Despite this varied performance, there is a promising tendency towards greater transparency and accountability among *established* SWFs. The better-performing funds tend also to be members of the IFSWF. This suggests that this book's focus on refining the Santiago Principles holds some promise of compliance. But when it comes to adoption by the wider SWF community, expectations must be realistic. The 2012 Truman assessment revealed that 'most of the newer SWFs appear not to be following the example of the best of the older funds', and the IFSWF has 'fallen short in promoting the substantial adherence of some of its members to those principles'.[12]

Indeed, the overall performance of SWFs against criteria weaker than my ideal suggests current sovereign fund design is substantially diluted relative to what is needed for meaningful democratic control. Nearly all Truman criteria relate to public reporting requirements. While information disclosure is a crucial part of democratic control, the reforms discussed here demand more than that alone: they also require avenues for citizens to critique those decisions, feed back their views to representatives, select those representatives, and shape the desired purpose of the governing body in the first place. None of the Truman elements assess a sovereign fund's arrangements on these counts.

Other features essential for establishing popular control do not feature at all in the Truman scoreboard. The obvious missing criterion is selection of the governing body/board members (including the possibility that there should be direct elections for board members). This is a result of the overall emphasis on *government* contra *citizen* accountability in the Truman elements, a wider symptom of the conflation of government and citizen interests (as shown in Chapter 2), and which motivated the proposal of direct control devices between citizens and SWF boards.[13]

The overall message is that when judged against the weaker Truman standards, most sovereign funds lack governance arrangements that endow their sponsor community with democratic control over their activities. If most funds struggle to fully comply with lower standards of transparency and accountability, my recommended regime of control rights risks utopian infeasibility.

Role models for democratic sovereign fund management

Reassuringly, a closer look at two of Truman's top-performing funds suggests that there is not always a substantial gap between the ideal of direct popular control and current institutional practice. The respective approaches of New Zealand and Norway to the management of their sovereign funds, including the design of their investment mandates, is promising for popular control over sovereign wealth. Although both funds require amendments to fully comply with our ideal, these reforms 'would not be so distant from current arrangements as to seem utterly infeasible'.[14]

Consider the Kiwi approach. New Zealand created the NZSF in 2001 with the New Zealand Superannuation and Retirement Income Act 2001 to pre-fund the country's rising superannuation costs.[15] The NZSF commenced investing in 2003 with NZ$2.4 billion in seed cash and currently holds almost $20 billion (approximately NZ$30 billion). To prevent political interference, the fund is administered independently from government by a separate entity known as the Guardians of New Zealand Superannuation, consisting of five to seven members appointed by the Cabinet on the recommendation of the Minister of Finance, following nominations from an independent committee and consultation with political parties.[16] The candidates must be persons with 'substantial experience, training, and expertise in the management of financial investments'.[17] Such an appointment process, while transparent, lacks any popular participation by citizens.

The NZSF has been subject to a statutory responsible investment obligation in its founding legislation since inception. As noted in Chapter 6, the RI clause requires management to invest so as to avoid 'prejudice to New Zealand's reputation as a responsible member of the world community'. The Guardians' current interpretation of the overall mandate, including the RI obligation, is set out in a *Statement of Investment Policies, Standards and Procedures*.[18] The Guardians espouse an ambitious belief that 'improving ESG [economic, social and governance] factors can improve the long term financial performance of a company',[19] and have articulated how to pursue policies in accordance with this belief in their Responsible Investment framework. RI actions under the framework include investment, engagement, voting, exclusion and/or divestment from the fund. Since 2009, the fund has also pursued 'positive investment' strategies identifying investments that provide social returns such as 'tangible, measurable' ESG benefits.[20]

Of these strategies, the Guardians' preference, as illustrated earlier, is for *active* strategies of engagement rather than exclusion.[21] This involves communicating directly with investee companies or external managers where there may be a breach of ESG standards, and trying to foster better corporate governance. During 2014–15, the NZSF engaged with 133 companies, including 6 companies on human rights and safety, 76 on severe environmental damage, 43 on bribery and corruption, and 8 New Zealand companies on governance issues.[22] The majority of these engagements (119) were part of collaborative efforts, while 14 companies in the portfolio were approached directly by the Guardians, including all 8 engagements on human rights.[23] A further 6,961 were engaged with on sustainability reporting practices. As part of this active approach, the Guardians have previously described exclusions as a measure of 'last resort',[24] and 'divestment as a form of failure',[25] although more recent policy statements mollified that language,[26] most likely in the wake of criticism following the Freeport saga discussed in Chapter 6.

Despite this preference for engagement, the NZSF has an active exclusions policy that identifies five areas where entities directly involved in product manufacture will be automatically excluded or divested, including: (1) cluster munitions, (2) testing of nuclear explosive devices, (3) anti-personnel mines, (4) tobacco and (5) whale meat. Specialist screening companies are used to identify companies eligible for engagement, exclusion and divestment. As of December 2015, 168 companies had been excluded under these provisions,[27] signalling the expansion of this strategy from just 33 exclusions and divestments in June 2009.[28] This growth has largely being driven by tobacco-related entities, which dominate the current exclusions list.[29]

The NZSF has refined and expanded its RI approach over the years, partially in response to two independent reviews. These reviews were both made available to the public, although not open to public input. Both were generally positive, although each identified areas for improvement. The New Zealand Auditor-General recommended the fund expand its screening process beyond equity positions and sovereign bonds to include corporate bonds, as the current approach left the fund at risk of holding an excluded entity.[30] This report also noted the challenge of the Guardians' collaborative engagement approach, in which the fund seeks to engage with investee companies alongside other large investors to maximize influence. The Auditor-General cautioned that such an approach risked rendering the fund dependent on other companies 'making decisions that are consistent with [the NZSF's] "avoid prejudice" requirement'.[31] A review by Mercer in 2009 noted that the Guardians could go further to achieve full integration of ESG issues into their RI practices, given *internal* fund managers 'have not explicitly integrated ESG in their own investment thinking' and the fund needed to 'better monitor and encourage [external] managers' inclusion of ESG in their investment processes'.[32]

The NZSF accepted many of these recommendations and implemented changes accordingly. In October 2009, the Guardians assumed direct over-sight of RI policies, abolishing the Responsible Investment Committee charged with advising the Guardians on RI matters in an effort to more fully integrate ESG considerations into investment decision-making. This effort was advanced in 2012 with an organizational restructure that moved the Responsible Investment Team from back office to the front office Investment Analysis group to ensure that RI obligations under the invest-ment mandate are given deeper consideration in the investment process.[33] Management has also expanded its RI focus beyond traditional RI classes, creating its own specific guidelines for Private Equity and Public Markets responsible investing. The fund now conducts an annual review of managers' RI policies.[34] In 2015, the NZSF expanded its engagement capabilities through the appointment of BMO Global Asset Management to provide RI engagement services globally.[35] This aim of this appointment has been to improve the reach, transparency and effectiveness of the engagement programme. BMO provides quarterly reports on its engagement activities, available on the NZSF website, which indicate an increase in both the number and depth of engagement discussions with NZSF investee compa-nies.[36] This additional resource has also allowed the in-house NZSF invest-ment team to strengthen its focus on domestic engagements.

Norway's experience with community input into the GPFG's govern-ance and investment mandate has been different. Although the New Zealand Guardians were criticized as 'slow to fulfill their ethical mandate, being initially for two years without in-house SRI [socially responsible investment] experts and lacking a formal policy',[37] Norway's GPFG lacked *any* form of ethical investment obligation in its founding legislation or policy for its first decade of existence. Established in 1990 as the Government Petroleum Fund (GPF) by an Act of the Norwegian Parliament (the 'Storting'),[38] the first transfer to the fund did not occur until fiscal year 1995, six years after its establishment, due to recession in the first half of the 1990s.[39]

There was no referendum on whether to establish the fund and no public consultation on its design, but there was a reasonably high degree of public awareness about the proposal, given the importance of its under-lying assets.[40] The fund was created with proceeds from Norway's North Sea oil and gas discovered in 1969.[41]

In 2001, the GPF became the Government Pension Fund Global (GPFG), better reflecting both the renewed focus on 'global justice', as well as the fund's role as a government savings vehicle that could provide a buffer for any shortfalls in pension liabilities.[42] Initially, the GPF's purpose was twofold: to 'decouple government spending from oil revenues in the short term', and to act 'as a long-term savings vehicle . . . to help cope with expenditures associated with the ageing of the population'.[43] The GPFG is housed within Norway's central bank, the Norges Bank. As with other 'internal' sovereign funds residing within government,[44] the GPFG is a deposit account in the central bank managed by public servants (rather than an 'arm's-length' board of trustees and independently hired manage-ment). Operational management rests with a special team within the central bank called Norges Bank Investment Management (NBIM). NBIM may appoint external asset managers and exercise ownership rights in investee companies. It also formulates strategy advice for the Ministry of Finance and Parliament regarding fund investment.

The extent of the Ministry of Finance's 'owner' responsibilities is notable. It is responsible for the overall management of the fund, including framing and performance of the investment strategy, identification of permissible asset classes, allocations and geographic exposure, implementa-tion of ethical investment decisions and risk control. All these tasks are undertaken *without* public consultation, but with a high degree of government oversight and involvement.[45] According to SWF analysts Clark and Monk, the extent of the government owner's power over the GPFG is unusually high, a contrast to typical 'arm's-length' governance arrangements in which governments delegate core tasks to a designated expert board.[46]

Entirely unique to the Norwegian fund is the use of a government-appointed Council on Ethics. The council provides advice on compliance with the ethical investment guidelines, including the exclusion of compa-nies. It is made up of five government-appointed members, expected to be independent experts in the theory and practice of ethics, as well as in Norway's international commitments in treaties and conventions. For some, this structure, along with the high profile ethical investment mandate, means the fund is worryingly 'enmeshed in the machinery of government' and consequently 'not "protected" from parliament and public opinion through statutory powers invested in its trustees'.[47] If that is true, then, conversely, the GPFG is promisingly open to public scrutiny and parliamentary oversight from a popular control perspective.

Indeed, transparency and accountability are considered essential elements of the GPFG's governance framework. According to Martin Skancke, the former Director General of Asset Management at the Norwegian Ministry of Finance, professionalism, accountability and transparency were the three key priorities in the design phase of the fund.[48] To secure these ends, policymakers pursued a rule-based approach to the management of Norway's sovereign wealth. The first steps were full integration of the fund with the national budget, and the adoption of a rule-based approach for transfers to and from the fund to ensure transparency around the use of petroleum revenues. As for withdrawals from the fund, a spending rule adopted in 2001 restricts the government from spending more than 4 per cent of the fund's total capital in the annual national budget. Clark and Monk have characterized this rule-based approach to short-term government spending as 'an implicit contract between political elites on behalf of the national best interest'.[49] Though citizens did not participate in the design of these rules, their interests were at the heart of the system's design. Crucially, the extensive rule-based system controlling flows in and out of the fund bestows on Norwegians a form of permanent control over the government's use of the GPFG.

Accountability was achieved through checks and balances, with 'a clear division of responsibilities between Ministry of Finance and Norges Bank',[50] while transparency was deemed essential for building consensus around the Petroleum Fund and imposing a disciplinary effect on the fund management.[51] With visible fund assets exceeding 100 per cent of GDP in value, sufficient disclosure of GPFG performance to allow policymakers to 'tell the public exactly how they are going to invest the money, and what the returns on investments are' was and is considered critical.[52]

For these reasons, the GPFG is subject to extensive reporting requirements. Norges Bank presents quarterly financial reports to its government owner containing valuations and measurements of returns, *which are publicly released*, with a full list of every single asset held by the fund published yearly in the annual report. The annual reports also contain detailed figures on the total return, benchmark return, management costs and attribution of the excess returns, as well as articles on investment philosophy and the process for selecting external managements. The reports are presented to the Norwegian Parliament, with most information in both Norwegian and English. It is one of the most impressive annual reports in the SWF community in terms of disclosure.[53]

Norges Bank also provides extensive information on assessment, measurement and reporting of investments, as per its obligations under its own regulations and under the Santiago Principles.[54] From 2007 onwards it has published a full list of how it voted on every issue in every company in which it invests where it exercised its ownership rights.[55] As the manager, Norges Bank also reports to an independent company hired by the Norwegian government which checks the fund's calculation of the difference between actual and benchmark performance. These reports are publicly released. Finally, there is an independent audit by the office of the Auditor-General, which is reported directly to Parliament.

While many of these policies were determined without public consultation by Ministry of Finance bureaucrats, they are considered effective in fostering a culture of accountable, transparent fund management, and thus equipping citizens with an ability to monitor the fund properly.[56] The Storting also exerts control over the fund on citizens' behalf. Skancke has observed that 'all significant changes to the Fund's investment strategy are in practice presented to Parliament before implementation as a way of ensuring broad political support for important strategic choices'.[57] As well as changes to the investment strategy, the Ministry of Finance typically communicates updates to Parliament on all important matters affecting fund management, including the size of the petroleum revenues, the size of the fund, and the outlook for fiscal sustainability, as well as specific fund performance data, giving Parliament an extensive oversight of the GPFG.[58] Apart from some elements of the GPFG's management that are not deemed appropriate for public disclosure on commercial grounds (for instance, the fund does not disclose the 'exact timing and procedure of fund allocations in advance of the relevant actions' on the basis this could have adverse pricing effects),[59] the GPFG is highly transparent.

The only area in which the GPFG is lacking public influence and over-sight is investment strategy. The fund's initial investment strategy was determined by civil servants in consultation with expert economists.[60] Its ethical investment guidelines, including updates, were also determined by experts without public input. That said, the Graver Committee was very committed to ensuring the fund's EI guidelines would enjoy 'legiti-macy in the political community' and properly represent Norwegian values.[61] Acknowledging an inherent pluralism in ethical outlook among Norwegians, the committee still observed an 'overlapping consensus' on certain ethical principles among citizens.[62] On this basis, it argued that the fund's ethical guidelines must be 'firmly rooted in the values underlying Norwegian policy'. To discover these, the committee argued that it must search for the 'main normative characteristics that are consistent over time'.[63] Only then could 'lasting support from the Norwegian public for the ethical foundation of the Petroleum Fund' be ensured, including from future generations whose values present generations could never know, but whose interests they could do their best to represent by extrapolating from existing values.[64]

In developing strategies for the fund to give practical effect to these values, the Graver Committee concluded that the GPFG must conduct its ethical investment so as to *avoid complicity* in gross or systematic breaches of ethical norms relating to human rights and the environment[65] and to comply with sustainable development, considered 'a precondition for return on the Petroleum Fund's financial investments in the long term'.[66]

Following the 2008 review of the EI guidelines, new guidelines were adopted in 2010. These were further updated in December 2014.[67] The 2008 review consisted of two external reports commissioned by the Ministry of Finance, which also conducted its own evaluation process, consulting with stakeholders and the public.[68] One of the external reports co-authored by the Albright Group and American law professor Simon Chesterman[69] recommended more engagement with companies, more attention to climate change, *more opportunities for public submissions*[70] and dialogue with companies, improved disclosure of implementation of the ethical guidelines, and the addition of tobacco companies as a specific criterion for exclusion. In response, the fund's exclusion policy was slightly expanded allowing the GPFG to exclude companies for 'serious', not just 'gross', violations of human rights or war crimes.[71] The 2010 updates required negative screening of companies that produce tobacco, produce weapons that violate fundamental humanitarian principles, or sell weapons or military material to pariah states. They also *explicitly link* long-term financial returns to the maintenance of healthy social and environmental returns, qualifying Norges Bank's objective to achieve the 'highest possible return' as 'dependent on sustainable development in economic, environmental and social terms [and] well-functioning, legitimate and effective markets'. Norges Bank aims to vote at all annual general meetings, which amounts to about 10,000 general meetings and more than 85,000 resolutions annually.[72] However, commentators have noted that, in practice, 'as with the Council, the NBIM has limited institutional capacity and has elected to engage mainly with the largest (but not necessarily the most problematic) companies'.[73]

The overall effect of the 2010 revisions to the GPFG's governance is to put 'more emphasis on the economic case for ethical investing'.[74] Today, the GPFG has a more comprehensive approach to EI as a result of these changes with the updated approach attracting praise for the GPFG as an investor pursuing responsible investment on 'a portfolio-wide basis' that helps the fund 'act as an ethical, universal owner'.[75] Additional amendments to the guidelines in 2014 further strengthened the environmental reach of the Council on Ethics. Two new criteria for exclusion were added, on climate and coal.[76] From 2016, companies may be excluded on the basis of unacceptable climate-gas emissions or if more than 30 per cent of their operations are based on thermal coal.

Comparing the role models on democratic control

Comparing governance and investment approaches of the funds of New Zealand and Norway, I argue that the Norwegian model proves more effective at endowing citizens with control over their sovereign wealth and in particular their ethical exposure through their SWF's investment activities. I contrast the funds in three areas crucial for democratic control: transparency, accountability and responsible investment policy.

Transparency

Both funds are exemplary in their public disclosure, creating the preconditions for genuine popular control through substantial reporting on fund performance, investment, size of assets, risk procedures, fund structure and so on. As evident from heated debates in both countries over the ethical footprint of their funds, both SWFs foster the circumstances for informed, open debate on their policies, a prerequisite for citizens to exercise influence over fund management towards ends that the community desires. While neither fund gives citizens direct opportunities to influence its decisions, the fact that so much of each fund's behaviour is made public allows for sufficient awareness and debate on these matters. New Zealand is especially impressive on this front. The NZSF has always embraced highly transparent practices, in the belief that doing so enhances domestic and international legitimacy and that, in turn, is to the fund's commercial advantage. From inception, it has published detailed annual reports. In contrast to many of its peers, it releases a full and complete list of all current holdings and the value of their position. Remarkably, it is the only SWF in the world required to publish monthly performance and portfolio figures. It also publishes the expenses of its CEO. At the start of each year, the fund publishes a 'statement of intent' that sets out the fund's objectives and plans for the coming financial year. The fund then assesses its performance against those objectives in its annual report and both documents are tabled in Parliament.

Accountability

Another positive attribute of both funds is their overall emphasis on popular accountability. The GPFG outperforms New Zealand on this front. Indeed, the GPFG goes well beyond the Truman criteria, which simply require *clarity* on fund structure. Instead, the Norwegians actively incorporate a citizen-centred conception into their fund purpose and structure. Consider that the GPFG defines the relationship of Norwegian citizens to the fund and explicitly declares equity between current and future citizens as one of its central purposes. Indeed, the GPFG shows potential to adopt an even more citizen-oriented understanding of its ownership that could translate into explicit and direct popular control rights over the fund.

While neither Norwegian nor New Zealand citizens influence the appointment or selection of those running their funds, both funds still exemplify a highly accountable management framework. Clark and Monk observe that the governance of the GPFG 'places a premium on public accountability, represented by the minister of finance and the accountability of the minister to government, and ultimately, parliament'.[77] These governance arrangements derive their legitimacy from the processes used to represent the public interest. As a result, the fund enjoys bipartisan support for its commitment to global and intergenerational justice, even if this commitment places a burden on fund performance on some occasions. It would have been preferable if the Norwegian people themselves had helped identify that purpose through participatory mechanisms and enjoyed the chance to choose the fund's objectives in line with that shared purpose, but in the absence of a fully democratized control process, the Norwegian fund still appears to pursue a purpose broadly acceptable to the Norwegian citizenry.

The absence of channels for Norwegian citizens to *directly* participate in the formulation of fund objectives and policy is disappointing, though. As Richardson observes: 'While the [GPFG] functions under a legal framework that reflects a "public commitment to procedural democracy", the general public itself has few opportunities to participate directly in the fund's governance except circuitously through their elected Storting representatives.'[78] As law professor Lawrence Backer, already cited in Chapter 6, cautions: 'The Norwegian state is accountable to the people, but the Fund is accountable only to the state.'[79] This absence of direct input from Norwegian citizens into the operation of the GPFG's ethical investment activities led the co-authors of a 2008 external review of the ethical guidelines to observe that 'the Government and people of Norway have a role as stakeholders that reaches well beyond their role as shareholders. Accordingly, the broader Norwegian interests in promoting sustainable, ethical governance will require resources beyond NBIM and the Council.'[80]

This substitution of direct citizen control with government accountability is what motivates the need for more popular control. Even in those aspects of the GPFG's governance that are more citizen-oriented, such as the Graver Committee's attempt to identify a 'broad, democratic basis' for ethical investment decisions, the process for formulating that basis was not open to the public. Instead, the expert committee heard only from select NGOs and chosen civil society representatives, resembling a sort of 'professional stakeholders' approach to direct citizen involvement in collective decision-making.[81] Norwegians' ability to properly monitor management fealty to fund objectives and policies is somewhat stunted as a result. While the GPFG's extensive disclosure practices mean more information is disclosed about fund practices and policies relative to most sovereign funds, retrospective disclosure is not sufficient for genuine institutional power. Norwegians need more opportunity to directly influence the ongoing direction of the fund in response to reported information.

Responsible investment

Although Norway was slower than New Zealand to develop its RI approach, its mandate and RI strategies ensure stronger shielding of citizens' ethical agency. The Graver Committee and its report also constituted a more thorough effort to find a 'democratic basis' for exercising the GPFG's EI obligations than any equivalent attempt by the NZSF to do so.[82]

In terms of RI mandates, Norway offers a much stronger commitment to ethical investment than the indirect reputational formulation of the NZSF mandate. When it was first set out in its 2004 guidelines, Norway's EI mandate contained two principles: the first stipulated that the fund's pursuit of a 'high return' was 'dependent on sustainable development in an economic, ecological and social sense'; the second required the fund to 'avoid investments that represent an unacceptable risk of the Fund contributing to grossly unethical activities'.[83] The updated 2010 guidelines, and 2014 amendments, have expanded and clarified the reach of these principles, improving the coverage of the mandate. The inclusion of a sustainable development obligation will help Norway meet its intergenerational obligations.

The New Zealand RI mandate, by contrast, is couched in far weaker terms, asking the fund to 'avoid prejudicing New Zealand's reputation internationally'. There are several problems with this 'world reputation' formulation. Commentators have noted that this mandate, unlike the

Norwegian approach, does not explicitly require 'active consideration of social and environmental issues, and promotion of improved corporate behaviour',[84] leaving the Guardians free to interpret its meaning. This gives rise to the possibility of conflict between the mandate priorities since the Guardians are also required to 'maximize return' and employ 'best-practice portfolio management'. As Richardson has observed: 'the [NZSF] ethical investment duty is commingled with other legislative goals relating to financial considerations. By contrast, Norway's ethical screening Guidelines are placed in a separate instrument to which compliance is not constrained by or conditional on the [GPFG] adhering to other legal norms.'[85]

As the New Zealand legislation provides no guidance on how to resolve conflicts between these goals, nor any clarity on what should happen if the NZSF's reputational and ethical concerns do not coincide, the Guardians are bestowed with substantial discretion to interpret this obligation as they please. This leaves New Zealand's citizens dependent on the judgement of a few board members to decipher and uphold their ethical preferences.

The New Zealand mandate has also been criticized for vagueness and ambiguity in its language. This has manifested in a failure to prevent the fund's investment in 'companies with unacceptable or questionable human rights behaviour or environmental impacts, such as Nike, Walmart, BJ Services (operating in Myanmar), and Exxon Mobil',[86] most of which have been excluded from the Norwegian investment portfolio. On the whole, the NZSF mandate compares less favourably to the more strident and explicitly ethical formulation of the Norwegian fund's mandate.

When it comes to the ability of citizens to monitor and influence the direction of the fund's ethical investment programme, both funds are deficient relative to our ideal, but the NZSF falls shorter. Consider that the initial development of the New Zealand ethical mandate was led by the Guardians, who continue to enjoy broad discretion over the interpretation and implementation of their RI mandate. Similar criticism can be levelled at the GPFG, given its use of an independent expert committee to develop ethical guidelines (a committee that was only open to select experts and civil society organizations and not to the broader public). However, given the high profile nature of the Graver Committee and its report, mandated by the Storting, there was at least some link to the domestic community through Parliament, which had, after all, been responding to public opinion when it demanded the creation of those ethical guidelines. Moreover, the experts on the Graver Committee operated from the standpoint that 'the ethics of the Petroleum Fund must be rooted in democratic values'.[87]

While the Graver Committee (or the Storting, in drawing up its terms of reference) could have improved its democratic legitimacy by seeking out citizen input to test the committee's identification of an 'overlapping consensus' in Norwegian ethical values, it did at least conduct multiple hearings with various civil society organizations, and was subject to extensive public debate.[88] By contrast, the evolution of the NZSF's RI policy has been less transparent, more piecemeal, and dominated by the Guardians. The NZSF's approach has also suffered from a lack of proper direction from the New Zealand government on the appropriate parameters of the RI mandate.

On the whole, if Norway's citizens are capable of exercising a degree of influence through less direct means than our ideal model proposes, then the Norwegian approach holds substantial promise for the feasibility of basic reforms towards more comprehensive popular control initiatives.

Towards full democratic control

What do the Norwegian and New Zealand approaches teach us about institutionalizing genuine popular control? First, accountability to Parliament or government agencies alone is not sufficient. Given that the core demand of popular control is that citizens should be endowed with an independent ability to influence the objectives and governance arrangements of a sovereign fund, as well as to exert ongoing control over the management team and monitor their fealty to these objectives, governments should establish mechanisms such as deliberative polls or regular citizen assemblies to allow citizens to hear updates on the fund's progress from management, and then provide input on any proposed changes to strategy and operations.

Second, participation by *civil society* on behalf of citizens, while desirable, is not a substitute for direct citizen participation. These organizations come with their own agendas and represent their own views. There must be mechanisms for direct citizen input to SWF management regarding popular preferences on investment strategy and objectives.

Finally, the opportunities for public participation should not be limited to the establishment phase, but must apply to the ongoing activity of a sovereign fund, especially given the likely evolution of a fund's investment strategy as it matures. The public fury over the Norwegian fund's unethical investment practices several years into its investing life shows that public awareness takes time to grow, and that attitudes can shift over time. New Zealand's experience over its Freeport mining controversy also showed that its RI strategies were not fully supported by the New Zealand public, even though its overall commitment to ethical investment was popular. Constant review is therefore essential to ensure sovereign funds continue to respect and promote the values of their sponsor communities.

PART III

DISTRIBUTING SOVEREIGN WEALTH

Show me the money! Citizen benefit from sovereign wealth

The highly developed East Asian city-state of Singapore and the low-income West African nation of Namibia share something in common: political leaders in both countries want their citizens to benefit more from their nations' sovereign wealth. Singapore has a sovereign fund, GIC Private Ltd, seeded with excess foreign reserves. With around US$344 billion under management, it is one of the world's largest SWFs. Namibia lacks a sovereign fund, but is rich in natural resources. With exportable volumes of uranium, petroleum, copper, lead, zinc and diamonds generating healthy returns for the country, some have called for an SWF to help preserve these mineral windfalls. Singapore is rich. Namibia is poor. Despite their differences, both are subject to demands for their citizens to benefit more directly from their respective pools of national wealth.

During Singapore's 2015 general election, one of the newer political parties, SingFirst (Singaporeans First), demanded that the returns from Singapore's main sovereign fund be allocated directly to the people. The party campaigned on a platform of generous public spending, advocating S$300 monthly cash handouts to elderly citizens and larger education subsidies. According to SingFirst's senior leaders, funding for these initiatives should come from GIC returns. The party's Secretary-General Tan Jee Say accused the government of monopolizing the fund's income at the expense of citizens: 'GIC attained 6 per cent ... but gives us only 2.5 per cent. This

3.5 per cent difference is kept by the Government and amounts to as much as S\$8.75 billion. This is our money and must be returned to us.' Party Treasurer David Foo echoed this theme: 'What we're [questioning] is how you allocate the S\$8 billion NIRC [Net Investment Returns Contribution]. If we stabilize the population growth, we need [only] to maintain the infrastructure, but the rest of the money can be invested in people.'[1]

At the same time, across the Indian Ocean, another secretary-general was making similar demands of his nation's sovereign wealth. Mahongora Kavihuha of Namibia's Trade Union Congress (Tucna) called for the establishment of a sovereign wealth fund to manage Namibia's mineral resources for the benefit of citizens. 'Since the time of colonialism, Namibia's natural resources and national wealth have benefited exclusively a small minority of the population, as well as foreign corporations that control these resources.' Instead, what Namibia needs, according to Kavihuha, is a transparent, special-purpose fund to act as a vehicle of redistribution: '[Our] sovereign wealth fund must be distinct from the government budget and must serve to ensure that the country's wealth benefits impoverished and marginalized groups in society.' Only then, in Kavihuha's eyes, could Namibia ensure that the majority of citizens receive direct benefits from their resource wealth through the provision of essential services and poverty-alleviation measures such as a basic income grant.[2]

The idea that citizens should directly benefit from their sovereign wealth is not peculiar to these countries. Nor is the belief that a sovereign wealth fund can help create and share the benefits of national wealth among citizens. But, as Singapore's experience shows, the existence of an SWF per se is no guarantee that a community will feel it is benefiting sufficiently from its sovereign wealth. Even when that sovereign fund distributes part of its returns to the community through public spending and investment, as happens in Singapore, debate may persist on whether that counts as adequate benefit distribution to citizens.

That is the issue to which Part III now turns: a citizen's right to benefit from sovereign wealth and the different ways a community may realize that right. The next chapter compares collective and individual modes of benefit distribution, drawing on Alaska's experience in fighting for the implementation of its individualized benefit right. Chapter 10 looks at how the benefit of both SWFs and their returns might be used to tackle inequality.

This chapter lays the foundation for those discussions by demonstrating why benefit from property is the other crucial component of ownership, alongside control rights. The right to benefit, understood as the right to a property's income, can be exercised over shared property like sovereign wealth. This requires an understanding of the ways in which SWF investment income can be used and the distinct distributive implications of those options for a community's welfare. Only with that understanding can a community determine which of the alternative uses of SWF income best transforms an SWF into a community fund. I argue that the best option is direct dividends to citizens, which not only effectively satisfies a citizen's right to benefit from sovereign wealth, but also reinforces their democratic control rights over these assets.

Benefit from property

The first step is to understand how the idea of benefit relates to sovereign funds. Part II examined how control rights associated with ownership apply to collective assets like sovereign wealth. Now the focus shifts to the other conceptual component of ownership. What does it mean to benefit from property, let alone collective property?

In ownership theory, the majority of property rights concern an owner's ability to control their property (the right to use, possess and manage property and the right to the capital).[3] But ownership privileges also include a right to income from an owned asset. It is this right to income that property theorists classify as a 'benefit' rather than 'control' right.[4]

Some have questioned the benefit/control conceptual distinction. Surely, an owner's ability to receive the income a property generates means they *control* the income stream. A right to income from property might therefore be just another control right. Yet it is only when an owner forfeits their control privileges over an asset (whether forfeiture through sale, lease, loan or investment) that the benefit of income from property is realizable. The difference lies in the 'structure and value' of the two types of rights, more precisely on the 'use value' of an owned object.[5] For this reason, leading ownership scholar Honore has described the right to income as 'a benefit derived from forgoing personal use of a thing'.[6] Similarly, contemporary property theorist John Christman argues that income from property offers '*increased* benefit [from] relinquishing the ownership' of one's property: 'the idea here is that a right to gain *extra* benefits from a holding – benefits different from the use value of the object – is captured by the right to income'.[7] The right to income, then, is benefit at its most literal: a gain, a profit, a reward, contingent on the surrendering of some other property right(s). Advantages conferred by control rights primarily involve an owner *using* their property. Conversely, benefit from income results from an owner 'forgoing personal use' of their asset.[8] I must generally give up my right to unrestricted use of my house if I want to rent it out to a tenant for income.

In some respects, this income-based idea of benefit from ownership is narrow. There are many ways in which owners benefit from property beyond any income stream it yields. I benefit from the house I own even if I do not rent it out just by living in it. It offers me shelter, refuge, security, protection and privacy, all of which enhance my welfare. Similarly, there are numerous ways in which citizens may benefit from sovereign funds. Since SWFs are typically set up for a purpose that, by definition, is welfare enhancing, citizens are advantaged by the sheer existence of a sovereign fund, even when they do not directly receive a portion of its income. Whether a development fund for community investment, a savings fund for future generations, a currency stabilization mechanism to prevent economic instability, or a reserve management tool that controls inflation, SWFs are, by their nature, intended to benefit the citizenry and state of their founding government. In the case of SWFs, then, the restriction of 'benefit' to the single concept of income seems misleading. Should a citizen's right to benefit from their sovereign fund extend beyond the income stream generated by SWF investment activities?

Applying benefit rights to sovereign funds

The control/benefit distinction, although 'admittedly rough',[9] persists in property theory. Its drawbacks notwithstanding, it does enjoy a natural intelligibility in the sovereign fund context. By definition, an SWF is an income-seeking vehicle. Its fundamental task is to augment public wealth by pursuing financial returns through market investment. To do so, citizen-owners (and their governments) relinquish their 'use' rights to this portion of public capital in two senses. First, at the SWF creation stage, they surrender their 'use' rights to the capital by supporting its removal from the annual budget cycle and quarantining it in a sovereign fund. Since this public capital would otherwise be available for redistribution to (and use by) citizens through the annual state budget, there is a relinquishment of control when this revenue is converted from flow to stock; from public revenue to sovereign wealth.

After establishment, the citizenry further surrenders its use rights by entrusting this capital to skilled managers for return-seeking investment. Inevitably, then, the investment of sovereign wealth amounts to citizen-owners deriving benefits 'from forgoing personal use of [sovereign wealth] and allowing others to use it'.[10] This is the case irrespective of the investment management approach adopted. Whether a fund outsources to external managers, uses in-house management by government officials, or embraces a more democratic process involving initiatives recommended in previous chapters that feed citizen preferences into SWF investment decision-making, under all such approaches, citizens forgo personal use of their SWF property. They do so in order that others may use it for investment that (ideally) generates a reward in the form of financial returns. Investing sovereign wealth therefore satisfies the basic concept of an income right in which an owner 'allow[s] others to use [their property] for reward'.[11]

Whether there is a reward is, of course, contingent on the investment performance of a fund. Forgoing personal use of sovereign wealth is not a *guaranteed* realization of this income right since there is no certainty that the SWF will perform financially. An SWF may invest a community's wealth and generate a negative return (as was especially common in the financial crisis years of 2008–10), and *not* be in breach of any enforceable income right since risk and uncertainty are inherent to financial investing. Compare this to more conventional cases of deriving income from property, where income is comparatively secure. Contracts for renting out property to tenants or lending money to a creditor typically protect the owner's right to income by deeming a default on payment as a legal breach of income rights.[12] A relative degree of certainty of income flow is therefore built into the contractual terms of the trade.

The volatility risk regarding SWF income notwithstanding, the manner in which sovereign funds generate investment returns satisfies the idea of an income right to property: citizen-owners forfeit personal use of their sovereign wealth for reward, aware that the reward is variable and cannot be guaranteed or legally enforced. A benefit right to sovereign fund returns should therefore form part of a citizen's suite of ownership rights to SWFs.

Models of benefit distribution from SWFs

If an owner's benefit right is satisfied as long as they receive the earnings from their property, in what form should citizen-owners receive their SWF income? Existing practice suggests there are multiple ways of conveying SWF returns to citizens. These can be distinguished by the different type and degree of benefit they bestow on communities and their citizens.

(i) Cash dividend The most intuitive realization of an income right to property is for the owner to directly receive all income generated in its original monetary form. Given that SWFs produce monetary returns, and there are multiple co-owners, the most straightforward means of realizing a shared income right is to transfer the investment returns as equal per capita cash payments directly to each citizen-owner.[13] On this approach, a sovereign fund acts as a temporary repository for investment income before directly transferring any earnings in cash to the ultimate citizen-owners.

The benefit conveyed by cash dividends is direct and individualized. It is *direct* since the citizen-owner receives the income in the original state in which it was derived, as a pure financial return. Cash dividends are also a highly *individualized* benefit since payment can go to every single member of an SWF-owning community in their individual capacity.

There is already a working model of the cash dividend approach – the Permanent Fund Dividend in Alaska. The PFD is given to every eligible member of the population who applies based on a portion of the Alaska Permanent Fund's realized earnings.[14] In doing so, it provides a direct, individualized benefit to every Alaska citizen. Both of these attributes – its directness and individualization – are consistently emphasized as central to the PFD's longevity and widespread support. Only two years into its operation, in 1984, Jay Hammond, the former Governor of Alaska primarily responsible for the PFD's introduction, praised the dividend's directness: 'Alaska's dividend program . . . takes money, *undistilled*, away from the government, and rains it equitably and in *full force and value*, upon the public.'[15]

Hammond's comments echoed the views of PFD advocates, who argued that direct cash distributions 'would deliver benefits more efficiently' than other ways of distributing Alaska's resource wealth.[16] Despite Alaska's massive influx of oil wealth since 1969, and the sevenfold increase in government spending that resulted, dividend advocates pointed out that Alaskans were not seven times better off.[17]

Whether true or not, this was the perception of Alaska's citizens. Although much of the money had been spent on beneficial public programmes such as the construction of schools, the financing of generous college loans, and monthly cash payments to Alaskans aged over sixty-five, polls at the time showed 'a substantial majority of Alaskans believed the money was wasted, and many had no understanding of what the money brought'.[18] Such findings led Governor Hammond and dividend supporters to conclude that 'private allocation of oil money would result in more efficiency and utility than the government's use of it'.[19] In other words, cash payments to citizens would be far more effective at ensuring individual citizens *did* benefit and *perceived* that they benefited from their sovereign fund. Less direct forms of distribution risked opaqueness, with Hammond describing selective loan subsidies as 'hidden dividends'.[20] Once operative, the PFD programme assumed a highly direct format of annual cash deposits from government to citizen every October.

The PFD is also celebrated for its highly individualized character. Its genesis resulted in part from the belief that 'individuals have a right to decide how to use a portion of their oil wealth'.[21] Although the final 1982 PFD bill removed language to this effect, 'a review by legislators of the preliminary bill characterized the dividend payments as individual compensation for each state resident['s] ... equitable ownership of the state's natural resources.'[22] In addition to its justification, the format of the PFD is also strongly individualized. All residents of Alaska are eligible as long as they have been resident in the state for twelve months prior to the year of their first PFD payment. Even children are entitled to their own dividend, with parents receiving the payment on their child's behalf until maturity. As a result, every single PFD payment attaches to an individual, as opposed to a family, employee, partnership, household or any other economic agent.

To determine each Alaskan's portion of fund earnings, the PFD is calculated as 10.5 per cent of the APF's realized net income for the past five fiscal years after deduction of programme costs. This figure is divided by the number of eligible residents in a given year to produce the individual dividend amount.[23] Erickson and Groh explain that this 'formula was designed as a smoothing mechanism and insures that dividends are not interrupted in the occasional years when the fund loses money on its investments'.[24] As noted earlier, an Alaskan who has received all thirty-four annual PFD payments since the first distribution in 1982 to the most recent payment in October 2015 received just below $40,000.[25]

The effectiveness of the rolling five-year formula, from the perspective of security of income, is evident when the reliability of dividend payments is considered against the volatility of the APF's historical returns. As Figure 8.1 shows, the APF has occasionally experienced negative returns from investment activities (2001–2, 2008–9, 2012). Yet, the dividend payment has been made without exception, every year. A negative return impacts the amount of the dividend, but the smoothing formula for its calculation ensures that an annual payment is always made. As a result, Alaskans' income right to their SWF earnings is respected, irrespective of fund performance. Even now, as Alaska faces a fiscal crisis and considers how to redesign the management and distribution of its resource revenues to ensure a more sustainable budget, the dividend looks set to be preserved, albeit potentially capped, as a key feature of the Alaska model.

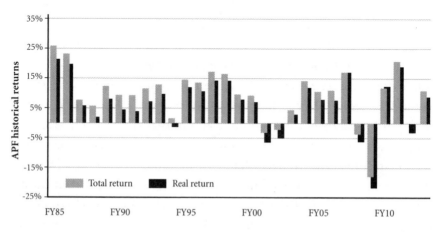

Source: Alaska Permanent Fund Corporation, see APFC (2014).

Figure 8.1 Alaska Permanent Fund historical returns, 1985–2013

There are criticisms of the Alaska approach, but on balance the PFD delivers secure benefit to individual Alaskans from their sovereign fund earnings, offering a unique model for how sovereign wealth can be used 'to *directly* and equally benefit ... *individuals* ... while largely bypassing tribal chiefs, kings and sovereign governments'.[26]

(ii) In-kind benefits   An alternative form of individually distributing SWF income is to use sovereign returns for targeted public provision or tax relief. Like cash dividends, these payments are linked to individuals and paid to everyone, but rather than direct cash transfers, the distribution may take a variety of cashless, in-kind and thus less direct forms. Classic in-kind benefits to individuals include 'unemployment compensation, disability benefits, retirement pensions, child care support, health care, aid to dependent children, food stamps, free school lunches and so forth. Also included are many kinds of educational support, including public universities, subsidized student loans [and] publicly financed scholarships'.[27] We could add to this list subsidies for essential goods such as water, transport, energy and housing. Alternatively, SWF income could be used for tax relief. Presumably, every citizen's tax liability could be reduced in proportion to their per capita share of SWF returns, ensuring all individuals benefit through a reduced tax burden.

The essential idea behind 'cashless' payments, whether in the form of public provision or tax relief, is that although citizens would not receive their share of SWF returns as a lump sum, they would still benefit individually from the returns in the form of reduced expenditure. To apply the observations of philosophers Murphy and Nagel to SWFs, '[a]ll these measures leave ... individuals with more resources at their private disposal than they would have if the distribution' of SWF income had not occurred.[28]

Since both the in-kind benefit and cash dividend approaches target individuals, the models only differ in terms of directness. The in-kind approach conveys a less direct benefit in two senses. First, if SWF returns are used to reduce individual liability for public goods and services, the sense of immediate benefit from SWF earnings to the individual citizen may be less palpable than through a cash dividend.

Second, the indirectness of this model also inheres in its implicit conditionality. The realization of cashless benefits like subsidies and tax cuts are contingent on citizens undertaking some act to receive the payment. For subsidies, they must access a particular public service, such as an education facility or a medical centre, to trigger payment. If a tax cut, a citizen must generate a tax liability against which to claim a rebate. In that sense, the instantaneousness of the benefit, both actual and perceived, relative to cash dividends, is reduced. Recipients have far greater discretion over a physical lump-sum payment of money than over an in-kind benefit, making the benefit more tangible. For this reason, the in-kind benefit model is best classified as an indirect individual benefit.

The SWF world has an embryonic and controversial precedent of cashless benefit distribution in Mongolia. In 2009, Mongolia created the Human Development Fund (HDF), a general government vehicle for accumulating and redistributing mining wealth from its vast gold and copper deposits.[29] Established as a sovereign fund,[30] with a mission to raise Mongolia's human development status to that of a developed country by 2020,[31] the HDF was tasked with disbursing direct cash payments to Mongolian citizens as well as payments linked to pensions, health insurance, medical care, education and housing.[32]

In this respect, the HDF resembles an 'Alaska plus' model, offering a combination of cash transfers and in-kind benefits for other public services. Like Alaska, it emulates the individualized notion of benefit endowed by Alaska's dividend scheme, with every Mongolian issued a Human Development record book used to receive HDF payments. Leading supporters of the HDF praise its operations as making 'it legally possible for every citizen of Mongolia, for the first time in its history, to be equally eligible to own a share of the nation's minerals'.[33] On the day the HDF received parliamentary assent, a senior Mongolian civil servant described the fund as 'the greatest investment . . . in the Mongolian people' because it allowed the people to 'own shares [in their SWF] in the form of residential and tuition payments, withdrawals of health and social insurance'.[34] While Mongolia had previously distributed mining proceeds through a popular targeted and then universal Child Money Programme,[35] the HDF distributions marked the beginning of universal cash transfers to every Mongolian. Unlike Alaska, though, the law regulating the HDF does not contain a formula for determining the size of payments or subsidies from the fund. Instead, they are approved annually in the government's budget process, a feature which proved problematic for the sustainability and legitimacy of the system.[36]

The first distributions occurred in February 2010, with every citizen receiving a cash handout of 70,000 Mongolian Tugriks (MNT), equivalent to about US$50, followed by smaller payments totalling MNT 50,000 by the end of 2010.[37] In 2011, the payments became more regular, amounting to monthly cash handouts of MNT 21,000 (about US$15). In August of that year, the Mongolian Cabinet decided that each student regardless of age would receive MNT 500,000 for tuition fees.[38] In total, the HDF distributed approximately US$580 million in 2011 through discretionary handouts,[39] attracting both criticism and praise.[40] A recent study found that inequality and poverty were significantly lower because of the HDF than they would have been otherwise.[41] However, the programme became unsustainable as HDF revenues from mining royalties and dividends were substantially lower than expenditures. The initial HDF legislation did not set out any limits on the accumulation or distribution of funds, and expenditure of mining revenues became a political football and subject to lavish election promises. Whenever delays occurred over payments, protests resulted and new promises were made.

By June 2012, universal cash transfers ceased and a targeted version of the Child Money Programme was reintroduced, still financed by the HDF. This programme entails a benefit of MNT 20,000 (US$14.72) per month per child under eighteen and enjoys bipartisan support. While it pales into insignificance relative to the MNT 1 million in in-kind benefits for student tuition fees, disability and retirement pensions and house deposit purchases, on top of average cash transfers of MNT 252,000 per person, made between February 2010 and June 2012, the child distributions are likely to continue until at least the next election in 2016.[42]

Looking ahead, the future of Mongolia's distribution of sovereign wealth, whether cash or in-kind, is in doubt. In October 2014, a draft law released by the Office of the President of Mongolia announced the abolition of the HDF and the creation of a traditional sovereign wealth fund, the Future Heritage Fund, from 2018. This fund will be dedicated to savings and investment and, at this stage, is not earmarked at all for cash transfers.[43] For some this spells the end of the Mongolian model of resource revenue distribution: 'Although Mongolia retains universal child transfers, it has effectively moved away from the resources-to-cash model by announcing that it will delink their payment from resources revenue.'[44]

The success or failure of the Mongolian distributions is instructive, but not the key point for our purposes. The scheme is credited with reducing poverty and inequality, but also increasing debt, possibly inflation and losing political and public support through poor design and implementation. At points, cash transfers actually exceeded mineral revenue, and the gap had to be met by borrowing. What is revealing, though, is the lack of broad support for direct disbursements of Mongolia's mining revenues. Direct disbursement went from a peak of 25 per cent support when the idea was first publicized to under 10 per cent as the scheme came to be seen as wasteful and irresponsible. As Figure 8.2 shows, direct disbursement never received as much support as other possible uses of funds such as 'invested by state' or for 'long-term social development', and these gaps have widened over time.

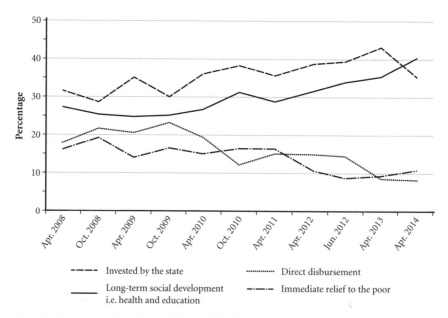

Source: Sant Maral Foundation, in Yueng and Howes (2015a), figure 9.

Figure 8.2 Public support for different uses of mineral wealth in Mongolia, 2008–14

These results are revealing in that they suggest that in some communities, in-kind benefits may better satisfy the preferences of a recipient population when it comes to sovereign wealth distribution. In Mongolia, direct distribution of resource revenues seems never to have been the public's favoured policy option. A 2010 opinion poll of Mongolian citizens on the preferred ways of delivering HDF benefits revealed that more than 87 per cent of Mongolian citizens wished to see their benefit in *cashless* form.[45] According to the poll, 22.1 per cent preferred to receive the money in the form of compensation for pension and health insurance, 14.6 per cent for health services, 18.5 per cent for education costs, 18.1 per cent for apartment leasing and rebates on loan interest, with the largest group of 31.4 per cent preferring compensation in livestock loans and other loans.[46] Similar findings were evident in 'workshops, community groups, environmental protests and in the vibrant Mongolian press', pointing to:

> a national consensus that the government should utilize mining revenues
> to focus on improving access to basic services and housing conditions,
> reducing inequality in life expectancy and material standards of living,
> and maintaining environmentally sustainable income flows to transform
> mineral wealth into renewable assets for sustainable and broad-based
> growth to meet Mongolia's most significant development challenges.[47]

The *indirectness* of in-kind benefit distribution may then prove a virtue of this model, but that depends on ascertaining popular preferences on benefit distribution and on implementing an effective system of cashless transfers.

(iii) Budget transfer The focus now shifts to *collective* modes of benefit distribution. The first and more common of these options is the 'general budget transfer' approach. This involves a non-earmarked transfer of SWF income to the sovereign sponsor's budget. In doing so, sovereign wealth is converted from *stock* to *flow* – that is, from public wealth to revenue, available for government expenditure.

This method of distribution conveys a *collective* and relatively direct benefit to the community. The transfer is bestowed upon the citizenry as a *collective* and the preservation of SWF earnings in monetary form within the budget makes this a more *direct* type of benefit than the other collective distribution model of government investment discussed below. But the degree of directness enjoyed here depends on how the funds are ultimately spent by the government. In theory, the citizenry as a group benefit since the transfer of SWF returns from a quarantined sovereign fund to the government's purse immediately boosts available resources for current spending or investment. On the assumption that the government's budget is then managed in the citizens' interests, the community benefits.

One might wonder about the practical difference between the in-kind approach discussed above and the budget transfer model, since both use SWF returns for spending on essential services and public programmes through government budgets that ultimately impact on individuals. The main distinction lies in the *individual claimability* of the benefit. Under the Mongolian system, payments were linked to individuals. Each citizen possessed a book linked to their sovereign fund and used it to claim their individual share of the fund's returns. While the ways in which Mongolian citizens can then use those funds is delimited by the state, the system is still individualized. Each citizen has a claim to a per capita share of the fund and may use that revenue on certain, stipulated expenses.

With a budget transfer, the primary distribution and benefit occurs at the collective level, since SWF returns are transferred first to the general government budget and then (ideally) allocated to certain expenditure which will directly benefit citizens. The key point to register is that this spending is not allocated to, or claimable by *individual citizens*. While the collective benefit provided by the budget transfer *may* ultimately benefit individuals, the benefit is *not* allocated to those individuals. Instead, it is entirely contingent on the effective spending of these returns by the sovereign sponsor.[48]

A budget transfer approach is in operation in several sovereign funds. In Singapore, investment earnings by the two Singaporean sovereign funds, the GIC Private Ltd and Temasek, may be transferred to the annual budget through the Net Investment Returns Contribution (NIRC).[49] In the 2015 financial year, the NIRC amounted to S$8.9 billion, equivalent to 13 per cent of the budget. The NIRC is comprised of two components: the Net Investment Income (NII) and Net Investment Return (NIR) from the investment of Singapore's reserves. The NII is income received from investments managed by GIC and Temasek, while the NIR is the long-term *expected* real return on certain assets in Temasek and GIC's portfolios. The NII is cash flow from realized SWF investments, while the NIR is a paper profit, based on unrealized gains that Temasek and GIC (as well as the Monetary Authority of Singapore) *estimate* they will deliver for the long term.

The Singaporean government is allowed to channel up to 50 per cent of NII and NIR annually into the government budget. This, the Singaporean government argues, means citizens directly benefit from the investment returns of their sovereign funds: 'The investment returns from our reserves give us resources for Government spending to benefit Singaporeans. This includes Government investments through the Budget in education, healthcare, transport infrastructure, improving our living environment and R&D to grow our future economic capacity.'[50]

But the NII and NIR provide benefit to citizens in different ways. The NII, in the words of Temasek's CEO Ho Ching, is 'real cashflow into the government kitty', while the NIR is a 'spending licence' based on long-term expected real returns.[51] Consequently, the NIR contributes to the annual budget less tangibly and immediately than the NII, although both reflect as a boost to government inflows as a percentage of GDP. The NII/NIR contributions are estimated to have topped up the government's operating revenues by 14–15 per cent in recent years.[52] The government can therefore commit to more generous, long-term spending on the basis of anticipated future returns from their sovereign funds.

While Singapore's budget transfer of sovereign wealth is constitutionally enshrined, it is discretionary. It is entirely up to the government of the day as to whether it exercises the NIRC transfer option, rendering Singaporeans' benefit rights to sovereign returns vulnerable to governmental whim. The government also has discretion over how the returns are ultimately allocated within the budget. Past allocations have included a mix of expenditures, some likely to benefit present citizens (for example, education and healthcare) as well as investments associated with long-term benefits, such as R&D, and 'physical environment' improvements that tend to privilege future citizens.[53] The fact that 50 per cent of the NII is also returned to the principal of the funds and not available for present spending ensures a balance between future and present citizens' benefit rights.

An alternative budget transfer approach is practised by Norway's SWF, the GPFG. The GPFG employs a rules based framework to govern transfers from the fund to the general budget. The Fiscal Policy Rule holds that an annual transfer from the GPFG, capped at 4 per cent of total fund capital (the fund's anticipated average long-term real return of the fund), may be transferred back to the budget to help cover the non-oil deficit in any budget cycle. Given the current size of the fund at around $850 billion, this permits a substantial transfer of around $33.5 billion. While actual fund returns may be quite volatile, spending in line with this expected average helps preserve the real value of the fund and imposes fiscal discipline on the use of fund earnings, while still allowing a generous injection of fiscal revenues back to the government. The only deviation from this rule-governed approach occurred in January 2016 when, for the first time, the Norwegian government made an additional withdrawal from the fund to cover emergency budget needs amid declining oil revenues.

For Martin Skancke, this rule-governed transfer ensures current generations of Norwegians enjoy direct benefit from their SWF's income:

> Current citizens benefit *directly* from the fund because we take money from the fund annually to finance the budget. We have set up a Fiscal Policy rule that says we will spend every year on average an amount corresponding to the real return on the fund. We are paying dividends in the sense that we are transferring money into the budget. That is how [current] Norwegian citizens enjoy the returns.[54]

While fair in spirit, there are two aspects of Skancke's view that need qualification. First, if Norway is providing dividends to citizens by transferring SWF returns to its budget, this distribution is a collective rather than individual dividend in the vein of Alaska's or Mongolia's disbursements. This is because the benefit within the budget transfer model lacks the same degree of individual claimability as those cash or in-kind benefit models. The returns in the general budget are not referable to individual citizens (who have no claim to them). This is not to deny that budget transfers convey benefit, but just to challenge its characterization as *individual* benefit akin to a dividend distribution.

Second, while the act of transferring fund returns to the government-sponsor's budget maintains SWF earnings in their original monetary form, and is in that sense a 'direct' benefit to citizens, whether this approach ultimately confers benefit upon citizens is entirely dependent on how a given government uses this revenue. In Norway's case, the transfer is used to cover the country's non-oil deficit, so the idea of benefit is inbuilt into the purpose of the transfer (insofar as offsetting a deficit is considered beneficial).

However, there is no guarantee that a transfer of SWF returns to a general budget is automatically beneficial to citizens. If SWF income injected into a budget helps fund generous public provision, this would, as Skancke believes, benefit citizens. This is more likely on a Norwegian approach, which governs the flows between its national accounts and sovereign fund in a disciplined manner. The Norwegian government must first form the national budget *without* including any resource revenues. This budget, known as the 'structural non-oil budget', is allowed to contain a deficit of up to 4 per cent of the size of the sovereign fund. That, of course, is the same amount that can be transferred back annually to the budget from the fund to help cover the non-oil deficit. If the deficit is generated by generous social spending commitments, then we can conclude that Norwegian citizens collectively benefit from their SWF returns.

On the other hand, the non-oil budget deficit may result from other spending decisions besides generous public goods provision. Perhaps the Norwegian Parliament increases the salaries and benefits of its Members of Parliament. Perhaps funding is used for overseas humanitarian intervention or is hoarded to help deliver a surplus in an election year for the government's own political advantage at the polls. Such policies may or may not be deemed beneficial for Norwegians – that is a matter for their polity. The crucial point is that transfer of SWF earnings to government budgets without further stipulation as to what expenditure the government should direct those returns to means there is no guarantee that citizens benefit from their sovereign fund income. Put differently, the dependence of the benefit's realization on government's good will to spend the returns in advantageous ways for the citizenry arguably jeopardizes the security of citizens' benefit rights to SWF income.

(iv) Government investment   The final distributive model also conveys collective benefit, but of an indirect kind. Rather than a straight budget transfer, some sovereign funds deploy SWF earnings to investment spending in projects that create shared benefit for a community. Examples of such investment include spending on infrastructure, socioeconomic development, community enhancement and growth stimulating initiatives. Such initiatives must involve the commitment of capital to a particular policy end that promotes the general welfare.

The main difference between this model and the budget transfer approach is that, under the latter, the citizenry in each generation receives its SWF returns through expenditure in the general budget. Such funds are then theoretically consumed by citizens through the allocation of these revenues to public goods and services, and the expenditure is accountable through their elected representatives.

Under a government investment approach, SWF returns are *converted* from a monetary reward into a non-pecuniary benefit in the form of infrastructure or some community-enhancing initiative that typically does not pass through the government's annual budget. The benefit conveyed is still of the collective kind, because individuals have no ability to claim the returns, but it is even less direct than the budget transfer approach since such investments are typically long term, locking up SWF returns in projects that may not deliver benefits for years or decades, privileging future citizens over present people.

Abu Dhabi's development fund, Mubadala, is a working example of the government investment model. Mubadala is a strategic fund tasked with the twofold mission of delivering socioeconomic benefits to Abu Dhabi citizens, and accelerating the Emirate's economic development. It does so by pursuing an investment strategy with a double mandate of delivering 'both financial and social benefits to Abu Dhabi and creating value for our shareholder, our partners, and the people of the UAE'.[55] This mandate relates to both the principal and earnings of the fund, such that investment returns are not treated in isolation, but redirected back to the fund to help fulfil this mandate.[56] In effect, then, fund income is directed towards socioeconomically beneficial investments in the Emirate.

There is no guidance on what constitutes 'benefit' for the purposes of Mubadala investments. Accordingly, fund personnel interpret the 'benefit' mandate in light of the fund's broader mission to be 'a catalyst that facilitat[es] Abu Dhabi's ambition to diversify and transform its economy, develop a new generation of business leaders, and build a prosperous future for its people'.[57] To achieve this objective, Mubadala focuses on outcomes such as job creation and construction of social infrastructure. Collective benefits resulting from the fund's local investments to date include job creation in the aerospace and semiconductor sectors, establishment of educational infrastructure such as a university campus affiliated with Sorbonne University in central Abu Dhabi, and a more diversified economy that is less dependent on oil as a source of national income.[58]

Despite these extensive domestic investments, according to fund personnel 'there is not necessarily a high degree of awareness [of Mubadala] among the citizens'.[59] This does not alter the fact that its investments may confer actual benefits upon the citizenry. For one fund official, Mubadala certainly provides 'indirect benefit to the local population' sufficient to dismiss the need for direct dividend distribution: 'The development of Abu Dhabi through social infrastructure and job creation is a tangible benefit to the people . . . We don't need a [cash] dividend as well because helping the prosperity of the state is enough to help the people'.[60] Such a statement underscores the idea that all these forms of distribution ultimately advantage citizens, but the individual claimability of the benefit is what separates the models.

The approaches are also distinguished by their intergenerational implications. Present citizens are unlikely to experience the advantageous impact of government investment spending as fully as future citizens. If government *investment* is, by definition, meant to foster future benefits, then it is questionable as to whether such an approach sufficiently realizes the income rights of both present and future citizens. In Mubadala's case, there was scepticism as to whether the very citizens whom the fund is meant to benefit through local investment and social infrastructure actually knew that it was the fund, and thus *their* public money, that was financing these local ventures. Beyond those citizens directly involved in the construction and development of such long-term projects, it is dubious that present citizens on the whole can be said to benefit sufficiently from SWF investment income under the 'indirect collective' approach.

Choosing a distribution model for SWF income

The typology above outlines four broad ways in which benefit from SWF returns may be conferred upon citizens, illustrated through practical examples. The list is not exhaustive. There are numerous ways a state could distribute such returns, and various purposes to which they may be directed.[61] But this typology captures the main types of benefit, summarized in Table 8.1.

The question is which, if any, of these is more desirable in light of the model of fiduciary citizen-ownership defended in this book? That is, does one of these disbursement modes better facilitate a citizenry's control over and benefit from sovereign wealth in its capacity as principal over government agents managing SWFs? Ideally, the preferred model of benefit distribution should reinforce the accountability and transparency encouraged by the suite of control measures proposed in Part II.

At this point, one might (fairly) wonder whether this exercise of delineating benefit types and adjudicating among the alternatives is in keeping with the spirit of popular control over sovereign funds. If truly committed to democratic control of SWFs, then why bother setting out options for citizens' benefit rights at all? Surely the appropriate response is just to identify that citizens have the right, and then defer to the democratic process in each community over what form that benefit should take.

These questions reflect a wider concern about political theorists 'seeking to supplant or short circuit the democratic process' through their prescriptive contributions.[62] While a valid worry, the purpose of this exercise is simply to offer resources for, rather than displace, public debate. As Swift and White observe, the political theorist occupies a 'fundamental' yet

Table 8.1 Models of benefit distribution for SWF returns

Distribution type	Individual	Collective
Direct	Cash dividend	Budget transfer
Indirect	In-kind benefit	Government investment

'modest' place in the political and policymaking process as a 'democratic underlabourer'.[63] In this role, the theorist can use her analytical tools to offer both clarification, through identifying the values at stake in a particular policy debate, and persuasion, through advancing informed arguments about why certain principles imply particular policies.[64] Rather than usurping the democratic process, this contribution may be seen as enhancing democratic legitimacy where one considers that democratic legitimacy is not just about the people ruling, but ruling in an informed and reflective manner, whether or not they ultimately heed the political theorists' advice. And there is the crucial point: that this analysis is simply an offering, one that fellow citizens may decide to accept or not.[65]

In recommending a preferred model of benefit distribution to a community, a primary consideration is the impact of each distribution mechanism on SWF governance. Since citizens must be able to influence their fund's management and ensure the fund's returns are generated in a way that at the very least respects, and ideally promotes, their collective values as a community, distribution of SWF returns should help foster interest in the activities of a sovereign fund and promote transparency around its investments and performance.

On these grounds, a slight preference emerges for the individual modes of benefit distribution (dividends or in-kind benefits). Both of these distribution models better equip citizens to be effective principals over their government-fiduciary. The major concern with the *collective* approaches (budget transfer and government investment) is that the government (at least in the working models examined here) retains ultimate discretion over the spending of SWF returns. With a budget transfer approach, governments typically determine how these returns will be spent within the budget, inevitably privileging some citizens' interests over others. Equally, under the government investment approach, some sectors will benefit over others, depending on what future needs governments identify and choose to finance. That said, with decent levels of public engagement on SWF investment policy in line with the recommendations in Part II, it would be possible to stipulate constraints on collective distribution options that ensure they align with citizen preferences and sufficiently transfer the benefit of SWF earnings to the community. But on current working examples, both collective models endow citizens with less initial power and influence over their sovereign funds than governments over whom they need to retain control.

Of the individual models, the cash dividend approach may be marginally preferable given its neutral character. Giving individuals cash avoids any imposition of government will on citizens regarding how they should use their benefit right. Instead, discretion is left entirely to the individual, who may use their cash dividend as they please. It offers the most impartial form of distribution since such a payment is indifferent as between citizens' various priorities and values (up to a point, at least: it clearly privileges the preferences of citizens whose desire is for more money). Generally, handing citizens their SWF returns in the fungible form of cash minimizes the likelihood of privileging the priorities or preferences of some citizens over those of others. Cash dividends also offer greater potential security of benefit rights since the claimability of the cash dividends is most easily linked to individuals. That permanent, tangible link between citizen and sovereign fund in turn promises enhanced potential for citizen oversight of their SWF. Direct dividends can therefore act as both a benefit distribution *and* accountability tool.

The ability of cash dividends to link control and benefit rights is unique. The distribution of direct, individual benefits can be used as a mechanism for enhancing awareness among, and therefore accountability to, citizens regarding their sovereign fund. When a dividend payment is due, citizens have extra reason to monitor a fund's performance, in turn improving their effectiveness as a principal over their government.

Evidence of this accountability-enhancing effect of cash dividends exists in the Alaska dividend scheme, where the annual distribution of returns to citizens helps heighten interest in the management and health of the underlying sovereign fund (discussed next in Chapter 9). The Mongolian approach to in-kind benefits, though, reminds us that any accountability-enhancing effect of dividends only exists when dividends form part of a well-designed, disciplined system of transfers that the public understands and supports.

The accountability-augmenting potential of direct benefit distribution is in contrast to the absence of this effect under the collective benefit models. The observation by the Mubadala official who lamented that the Abu Dhabi fund's extensive social investments and explicit effort to produce domestic social returns have not resulted in a strong awareness of the fund among the local population underscores this point. When it comes to linking the goals of the benefit and control rights, the individual models of distribution emerge as preferable. Further research must be carried out on whether the budget transfer approaches of Norway and Singapore encourage sufficient interest in their sovereign funds to support effective fund governance.

Turning finally to one more aspect of the fiduciary model of ownership – the intergenerational aspect. Since governments must act as fiduciaries for present and future generations, models of benefit distribution that promote, or at least do not obstruct, intergenerational equity are essential. Yet all four models potentially compromise intergenerational equity in some respect.

Consider the individual benefit models of cash dividends and in-kind benefits. Both threaten the ability of SWFs to be intergenerationally just, since they contain no obligation to consider how their respective return distributions affect an SWF's underlying objective to amass intergenerational savings. In this respect, they lack mechanisms through which to ensure the interests of present *and future* citizens are given equal consideration.

This is easily fixed, however, through the articulation of an appropriate pay-out rate. This rate must ensure that the principal is grown sufficiently to meet any future savings and transfer obligations *before* returns are distributed. One way of achieving this is to first transfer some portion of investment returns to the fund principal for inflation proofing, or inflation proofing plus principal augmentation, after which returns are distributed to present citizens. This is the approach adopted by Norway. In contrast, Alaska was more concerned to ensure that the rights of present citizens were privileged over future beneficiaries who would receive the windfall savings in the Permanent Fund. Accordingly, the Alaska model gives legislative priority to dividend payment, although this is currently under review. An appropriation is first made for payment of individual dividends, after which the remainder of SWF earnings is used for inflation proofing.[66] Different measures can be used depending on whether a state needs to give more weight to the interests of future or current generations, but the rights of both groups of citizens must be considered in the overall design to ensure that SWFs promote intergenerational equity.

The collective benefit options also risk violating intergenerational justice requirements, but for the opposite reason of neglecting *present* citizens' benefit rights. Budget transfers should benefit today's citizens, but they are contingent on the governments' proposed expenditure of those returns in any given year. If transfers were used to endlessly accumulate large surpluses, this would almost certainly privilege future generations at the expense of today's citizens. Again, the devil may be in the design detail. The Norwegian approach offered its citizens slightly more security than the entirely discretionary transfer approach of Singapore. Still, both of these models are deficient insofar as they do not stipulate what these returns should be spent on, once they are back in the budget coffers. Without such a stipulation, present citizens lack assurance about whether their income rights *will* be realized.

Similarly, government investment of SWF returns risks neglecting the benefit rights of today's citizenry, since government investment, by definition, is geared towards securing longer-term benefits. Of course, much depends on the life span of the relevant projects and initiatives a government chooses to support under this model. Once again, a population might have to stipulate the sorts of projects a government could invest SWF returns in to ensure an acceptable allocation of benefits as between current and future citizens. Without such stipulations, there is a high risk that under this approach present-day citizens miss out entirely on their returns.

Are dividends desirable?

In terms of enhancing citizens' control over their government fiduciaries and ensuring equality between citizen-owners of sovereign wealth over time, there is a modest preference for direct dividends distribution of SWF returns to citizen-owners.

This begs the question of whether SWF dividends are desirable in practice? There are certainly objections regarding dividends from the perspective of sovereign funds. But these are secondary too. One concern that regularly attends a per capita cash distribution needs addressing. A sceptic might worry that cash payments are possibly more vulnerable to individual frittering, waste or misuse than in-kind benefits. Some communities might therefore approve of the sort of restrictions that in-kind benefits impose, in wishing to protect against irrationality, or weakness of will in recipients.

It seems possible, though, that citizens, reflecting on what is really conducive to their own individual good, would wish to retain the maximum influence over this one aspect of their sovereign fund property, given that the greater bulk remains in the principal. Cash dividend distributions allow citizens unconstrained control over one small part of their SWF property, only fully possible under a cash distribution approach. Moreover, if the benefit right is meant to resemble compensation for the control owners forfeit over their property, citizens might prefer maximum control through dividends as compensation for this forfeiture.

All this ultimately hinges on a given community's preferences regarding the realization of their SWF benefit right. This reinforces the need for participatory democratic devices on many aspects of SWF policy, including the issue of how citizen-owners should benefit from sovereign fund earnings. Such preferences may be informed by lessons from the world's only working model of SWF dividend distribution, including how that emerged in Alaska and the attitude of Alaskans to their dividend programme. These are the themes to which we now turn in Chapter 9.

9

Owner-state or owner-people:
lessons from Alaska

Alaskans did not receive 103 million acres from the federal government as individuals; we received the land *as a state*. True, the people in a constitutional democracy are the ultimate owners, but their ownership did not mean that they could pocket the state's resource earnings.

Walter J. Hickel, second and eighth Governor of Alaska[1]

Wally Hickel likes to refer to Alaska as an 'Owner State'... I prefer to term Alaskans as an '*Owner People*' to reflect our constitutionally mandated public, rather than state, resource ownership.

Jay Hammond, fifth Governor of Alaska[2]

Cast back to Alaska, 1974. The race for the infant state's third governor is on. It's a showdown between Republican rivals Walter (Wally) J. Hickel, a self-made millionaire and former Governor of Alaska, and Jay Hammond, bush pilot, hunting guide and professional trapper. Both were vying for control of the state during its economic boom years, touting distinct ideas about who should benefit from Alaska's recently discovered oil wealth, and how.

This was not just a battle of gubernatorial candidates, but of rival political philosophies. For Wally Hickel, Alaska's resources were collective property, owned by Alaska's community. Any returns earned from their exploitation must be invested in *common* goods to benefit all Alaskans. On

Jay Hammond's view, the state's natural resources belonged to Alaska's citizens. Proceeds from their sale and exploitation should be divided up and allocated directly to *individual* Alaskans to reflect their equal ownership. Both Hickel and Hammond supported public ownership of Alaska's resources. Yet their distinct ideas of how public property is owned by the community implied radically different distributions of the state's sovereign wealth: community investment for Hickel and individual spending for Hammond. Or, in the words of Hammond above, an 'owner-state' versus an 'owner-people' approach.

Jay Hammond defeated Wally Hickel in the 1974 gubernatorial race, marking the ascendancy of the 'owner-people' conception of resource ownership in Alaska. This laid the foundation for Alaska to become the first and only state in the world to distribute its sovereign fund returns through a cash dividend programme.

While Alaska has been enjoying over three decades of its dividend programme, similar competing ideas of how a community co-owns their resources and in what way they should reap the reward have plagued other sovereign wealth funds. Communities disagree over whether the proceeds of state windfalls should remain in their custodian sovereign funds, at the government's behest for community investment and spending, or be divided up and distributed to individual citizens reflecting a more people-centred idea of public ownership.

In response, this chapter takes a closer look at Alaska's experience in adopting one approach over the other – dividend distribution as opposed to community investment of SWF returns – and how that decision has been received in practice by Alaskans. As Alaska is the only working model of cash distributions of SWF income globally, understanding its novel experience is vital. It can offer a blueprint for communities who also wish to embrace dividends, or a cautionary tale for those who prefer other options.

The birth of the Permanent Fund and Dividend

The Alaska Permanent Fund was established in 1976 by amendment to the Alaska Constitution, a year before oil production started in Alaska's Prudhoe Bay, North America's largest oilfield. The oil's location on state lands meant that significant royalty revenues on top of production and property taxes would start to flow to Alaska's government (which was then in its relative infancy following the grant of independent statehood in 1959). Since the oilfield's first discovery in 1967, an initial windfall of $900 million from exploration licences alone, then more than five times the entire budget of Alaska, had already flowed into *and out of* state coffers in less than a decade.

Cognizant of the oil's finite nature and nervous about wasteful misuse of the substantial anticipated future revenues once the oil started to flow, Alaska amended its constitution to require that a portion of the oil revenues be set aside in a savings fund for future generations. The combined desire to convert the state's finite resources into permanent financial assets and to quarantine these revenues from political misuse drove the APF's establishment as a future savings fund.[3]

It was another four years before Alaska's legislature decided how to manage the investment of the APF, and consequently its earnings. Direct cash distributions of resource revenues had been briefly mooted following the first discovery of oil in the late 1960s, but it was not until the creation of a return-generating APF and the sense of security that it created regarding protection of the oil wealth principal that the prospect of direct distributions received serious attention.[4]

Historical recollections of the impetus for citizen dividends from the APF point to several motivations. Some favoured direct distribution of a portion of Alaska's new oil revenues as a check on government growth and state greed. Others saw it as protection against savings raids on the APF, on the basis that it would give citizens greater interest in the underlying source of their payment. Some supported the proposal on equity grounds, since elites were already perceived to benefit disproportionately through special interest appropriations of oil wealth, while another group preferred cash dividends on efficiency grounds, considering individuals better able to utilize the oil revenues than government.[5] Others made arguments for the dividend on equality and fairness grounds, given the huge benefit it would provide to low-income and subsistence Alaskans.[6]

For the main instigator of the dividend concept from its inception to its legislative creation, then Governor Jay Hammond, these arguments boosted the case for dividends,[7] but they were *not* the driving force.

According to Cliff Groh, the principal legislative assistant working on the 1982 Permanent Fund Dividend legislation, and Gregg Erickson, economics consultant to the Alaska state legislature at the time of the dividend debate:

> For Hammond and the small group of Alaska legislators, aides and ordinary citizens who worked with him when he was governor to achieve a resource-based investment dividend, the shared core idea was neither charity, nor leveling, nor an attempt to build an income floor. Their shared commitment was to the notion of *collective ownership* and the fundamental fairness of *sharing the returns in equal proportion to their equal ownership*.[8]

This account of the dividend's original conception as an ownership right is supported by the former Director of Policy Development and Planning in the Governor's Office at the time, Fran Ulmer, who described Hammond's vision of the dividend as 'ownership income', not 'taxation income or a Basic Income or any sort of handout'.[9] While there were also strategic motivations for the dividend ('it was a defensive posture to help keep the Permanent Fund alive'),[10] Hammond's fundamental belief was that a dividend would give each citizen an individual stake in Alaska's collectively owned state wealth.

The importance of ownership in Hammond's vision for the PFD owed much to the intellectual scaffolding of the 'owner-state'[11] idea already in place within the state. Prior to Hammond's governorship, the idea that the community of Alaska collectively owned the state's resources had been expounded by the second (and later eighth) Governor of Alaska, Wally Hickel. Taking office in 1966, just a decade after Alaska gained statehood and finalized its constitution, Hickel took the antecedents of the 'owner state' concept in Alaska's Constitution and the Alaska Statehood Act, and sought to entrench this philosophy throughout the bureaucracy and the community. Article VIII of Alaska's Constitution had already achieved the critical first step in creating an owner-state – constitutional enshrinement of local collective ownership over resources: 'The legislature shall provide for the utilization, development and conservation of all natural resources belonging to the State, including land and waters, for the maximum benefit of its people.'

Significantly, Article VIII also clearly stipulated the public's right to benefit from this collective ownership, a goal which Hickel, as 'governor of [the] young Owner State', sought to translate into reality by 'build[ing] an organization of public servants who thought as owners'.[12] The goal was to create a bureaucracy that could help reap the rewards of Alaska's shared ownership of resources by ensuring that resource revenues went back into public goods and services to benefit all citizens.[13]

For Hickel, though, translating popular constitutional control of the commons into a reality did *not* involve individualizing this right of ownership. On the contrary, Hickel was explicit that the intent of the 'successful Owner State' was 'not to generate cash payments for the people'.[14] Based on competing readings of Article VIII of the Constitution, Hammond argued for an 'Owner People' concept and its policy implication of an individual share of Alaska's resource earnings for every citizen in the form of a dividend, while Hickel rejected this reading and advocated an 'Owner State' ideal of collectivized ownership. In Hammond's words: 'Wally Hickel likes to refer to Alaska as an "Owner State" . . . I prefer to term Alaskans as an "Owner People" to reflect our constitutionally mandated public, rather than state, resource ownership.'[15]

The Hickel–Hammond disagreement echoes the sort of contestation over SWF ownership discussed in Chapter 3. Ultimately, Hammond triumphed, both electorally over Hickel in the race for re-election as governor in 1978, and in his quest for an individualized dividend model of shared resource ownership. Legislative wrangling combined with 'serendipity', and a 'triumph of strategy' led to the ultimate passage of the PFD as an additional feature of the APF.[16]

The crucial point of this tale is that the PFD's genesis is steeped in ideas of public ownership (whether based on state or citizen). These debates show that Hammond, the PFD's author, saw the dividend as a means to *individualize* the benefit owed to citizens from their shared resources, a move that Hickel resisted on the basis of his purely collectivized notion of ownership. As economist Scott Goldsmith argues, the 'dividend is not designed to provide a "basic income" to all Alaskans', and is far better understood as an 'equitable redistribution of the earnings from the natural resources owned by the citizens of the state collectively'.[17]

The successful passage of the PFD legislation meant that since 1982 every eligible Alaska resident who has applied has received an equal annual dividend from the APF. The payment fluctuates in size depending on the level of investment returns made by the APF in a given period. Since the principal of the APF is legislatively protected as 'non-spendable', the dividends must be funded entirely from returns. While returns vary, the dividend is calculated based on a five-year average of returns in order to smooth out the short-term effects of market fluctuations. The PFD is universal, with no age limit, means testing or use restriction. The only significant eligibility requirement is that the recipient must have been resident in Alaska for a full calendar year before they are entitled to receive the dividend.[18] It is paid by direct deposit into individual residents' bank accounts on the same day each year.

For PFD supporters, this is a highly egalitarian scheme in form and effect. Advocates claim that the dividend is 'a strong egalitarian policy, for it grants each citizen an equal share of a natural resource that is held in common ownership',[19] it amounts to a sizeable annual public expenditure of state funds,[20] and has significant equalizing effects. Some have argued that it helped make Alaska the most equal state in the US.[21] On one measure, Alaska has the most equal distribution of income among all US states as well as the smallest proportion of households with incomes under $10,000.[22] Goldsmith observes that, although these outcomes cannot be entirely attributed to the dividend, studies have shown that Alaska's equality of income distribution and poverty alleviation improved dramatically after the dividend's introduction.[23]

Given its endurance, and its success as an equality-promoting programme, especially in an era of welfare conditionality and retrenchment,[24] advocates of various redistribution schemes are quick to claim the PFD as exemplary of their own preferred policies, often with little reference to the dividend's intended purpose. It has been held up as the inspiration for a variety of policies, including basic income programmes,[25] poverty reduction,[26] resource dividends,[27] stakeholding grants,[28] a green tax[29] and a stake in the commons.[30]

While the PFD is synonymous with different elements of all of these programmes,[31] none of these characterizations is consistent with the rationale for Alaska's dividend. The PFD's birth reveals that it shares more in common, at least in initial conception and objectives, with an ownership right to state wealth realized through cash dividends.[32] This is significant for communities that wish to adopt the cash dividend model of benefit distribution discussed in the last chapter. The historical record shows that Alaska intended to implement precisely such a scheme, making the US state a role model for this policy of ownership dividends from public assets.

Alaska's attitudes today

What do Alaskans make of their dividend payment today? Despite the PFD's exceptionalism, little systematic analysis has been devoted to popular attitudes fostered towards the dividend, let alone its political, social and economic impact.[33] Of the limited analyses that exist, most focus on the macroeconomic effect of the PFD, especially job creation and the amount of personal income generated from consumer spending.[34]

In the absence of robust data, Scott Goldsmith has attempted to profile the impact of and popular attitude towards the dividend using '[personal] observations', 'interpretation of anecdotal information, and a limited number of surveys and other analyses of specific effects'.[35] Goldsmith's analysis produced three salient observations on perceptions of the PFD as a right flowing from ownership of state wealth.

First, Goldsmith speculates that the very absence of rigorous data on the PFD's impact is itself an affirmation that Alaskans view this money as *their* share of a publicly owned resource, not a distributive programme worthy of social scientific or policy study. As Goldsmith suggests, 'since most Alaskans view the dividends as a distribution of their wealth, they see no reason to study it as a phenomenon'.[36]

Second, the absence of an explicit link between the dividend and a particular policy or social justice objective is precisely because it *is* considered citizen-owners' property over which they should exercise full discretion. In practical terms, this means recipients receive the dividend with a 'minimum of background notices' accompanying the payment.[37] While this leaves the PFD vulnerable to characterization by retailers, the media, and special interests wishing to encourage certain uses of the dividend, for Goldsmith, the non-directive delivery of the PFD is 'consistent with the notion that the dividend is a distribution of the wealth of a publicly owned resource'.[38]

Finally, in a 2005 review of the dividend, Goldsmith argued that Alaska residents view the PFD as an 'entitlement that all Alaskans share', not a public expenditure.[39] However, Goldsmith's view of the PFD as an 'entitlement' in popular eyes is not substantiated with any survey or polling data. His conclusion is based on anecdotal observation that in Alaska's politics, it is 'political suicide' to suggest any change that might jeopardize the dividend's size or certainty.[40] It is further suggested that 'a portion of the population' feels the 'state-owned oil resources belong to them as individuals rather than to all citizens collectively'.[41] But again, no evidence is produced to substantiate that claim.

On first glance, the word 'entitlement' seems pejorative, used to conjure up the idea of greedy individuals demanding their slice of state assets, divorced from any sense of the dividend's intended purpose. A less pessimistic depiction of the PFD as 'entitlement' draws on the citizenship-ownership idea. As Goldsmith later notes, the PFD becomes an entitlement when viewed 'not as a government appropriation, but rather as a distribution of earnings from an asset owned by each Alaskan. Since each resident owns a share of the Permanent Fund, each resident is entitled to an equal share of its earnings.'[42] Here, the notion of entitlement evoked is of something that is owed, and which the citizen is *entitled* to demand. In other words, the 'PFD as entitlement' concept may derive from a deeper perception of it as an ownership right to SWF income.

These impressions of Alaskans' attitudes to the PFD have now been tested against original data. In 2011, I undertook original, qualitative research on citizens' attitudes towards the dividend. Using a combination of qualitative survey and focus group research conducted in the cities of Juneau and Anchorage, I aimed to discover if there were different interpretations of the PFD's purpose and benefit among Alaskans.[43] Qualitative surveys consist of a corpus of between ten and fifty written questionnaires or semi-structured interviews that seek to gauge the diversity of views within a given population.[44] Focus groups are moderated small group discussions between five to twelve selected participants which seek to identify a range of opinions within and across groups and explore ideas in depth. Using this combination of methods was important since each method offered distinct advantages for the data collation process. The findings supported Goldsmith's ultimate conclusion that the PFD is viewed by Alaskans as an individual share of the state's collective wealth, rather than a welfare or public expenditure.

Survey findings

Given the lack of research on perceptions of the PFD, it was appropriate to commence with a qualitative survey to discover the range of views within Alaska's population. The qualitative survey asked a sample of fifty Alaskans across three pre-formed groups about their views on the dividend and the Permanent Fund. The largest sample of thirty surveys was collected on an Alaska Airlines flight between Anchorage and Seattle.[45] A further two surveys, with ten respondents each, were conducted, one at the University of Anchorage with an undergraduate economics class and the second at a gathering of middle-class Anchorage residents living in Alaska's wealthy suburbs. These different settings ensured that a cross-section of ages and income levels were represented in the results. The findings revealed citizens' views on the PFD's popularity, conception, form and link to the Permanent Fund.

Popularity of the dividend

Virtually all those surveyed received and liked the dividend. Some responses were superficial, describing the payment as 'free money' or retorting 'who doesn't like money'. However, a significant number of participants were more reflective about their support for the dividend, indicating a range of benefits offered by the payment. Participants listed diverse reasons for their support, such as 'appreciate it for saving', '[like it as] extra spending money', '[offers] relief from the hardship of living in Alaska', 'believe in sharing state's resource wealth among residents' and '[is a] responsible way to invest in Alaskans and Alaska'. Roughly 20 per cent of respondents in each of the three groups either disliked, or were indifferent to, the dividend, confirming its widespread although not universal popularity. The main source of opposition was a belief that it was 'abused' by some citizens, and that the government could use the money more effectively, underscoring Chapter 8's observation that cash dividends are not always a consensus mode of distributing financial benefit within a community.

Competing conceptions of the dividend

The survey answers revealed competing conceptions of the PFD. In explaining their attitudes to the dividend, respondents revealed several distinct ideas about the purpose and nature of the PFD, summarized in Table 9.1. The predominant conception of the dividend was as a *stake* in the *collective resources of the state*, attached to citizenship of Alaska. Respondents' ideas of what counted as satisfactory citizenship for the purposes of justifying the dividend varied. Some highlighted sheer presence in Alaska, while others demanded contribution to and participation in the community. On the whole, though, respondents linked the idea of the dividend to participatory membership in Alaska. In that sense, the overarching conception of the dividend was not as an individual but as a *citizenship* right, contingent on certain reciprocal contributions to the state by citizens.

Form of dividend

There was almost universal support for the current form of the dividend as an annual payment. When respondents were asked whether they would prefer a one-off large payment (for example at birth or maturity) or the smaller annual payment that they receive under the current system, there was little support for a lump-sum payment.[46] Many said that the current regular payment was fairer, since it rewarded those who 'spent time' and 'invested in Alaska'. Otherwise, people could 'cut and run' with the money, rather than reinvesting it in Alaska and contributing to the future of the state and its people. Most opposition to this proposal was based on the belief that a one-off payment would *dilute the connection* the dividend encourages between citizen and state. Respondents worried that a one-off payment would mean recipients could leave the state after they received their once-in-a-lifetime dividend, or that young people would be more likely to 'blow their stake'. In contrast, an annual payment requires

Table 9.1 Summary of 2011 original survey results on public conceptions of the Alaska Permanent Fund Dividend

Conception	Discussion of original data
Collective resource ownership entitlement	The majority of responses conceptualized the dividend as a 'share' in the 'state's resource wealth' and thought of the dividend as 'a shareholder's right'. Some saw this as 'compensation' for selling off the state's resources. A few respondents pointed to the 'entitlement' culture this created, and the risk of dependency on the dividend. On the whole, though, most respondents saw this as a 'fair way to share the revenues of Alaska with its citizens'.
Reward of citizenship	A large number of responses offered a related, yet distinct, conception of the dividend grounded in notions of citizenship. Rather than highlighting an individual right to a share of the natural resources they own, these responses emphasized 'community', evoking images of a common state project of which they formed a part. For instance, respondents described the dividend as 'recognition' of their 'membership in Alaska's community', and 'participation in the state through work and investment'. One respondent described the dividend as a 'good, continuous connection to the state'. These answers suggest a rather elastic concept of citizenship linked to the simple requirement of state membership or presence in Alaska, while others emphasized active participation and contribution to the state.
Hardship relief	A number of participants indicated that the dividend was good because it compensated citizens for the 'hardship of living in Alaska', and made an otherwise 'difficult life in the north' easier. This response was based on a perception of 'high living costs' in Alaska relative to other states. Implicit in the response was a sense of a frontier community in which Alaskans were taking part. In that sense, it overlapped partially with the conception of the dividend as recognition of *participatory* citizenship. But the central concept at work here was one of suffering and compensation rather than community and membership in a collective project.
Accountability mechanism	A noticeable minority thought of the PFD as an accountability device, explaining that the dividend makes politicians 'more observant of voter's needs' and 'prevents the legislature from uncontrolled spending'. Interestingly, this 'accountability' conception was *not* present at all among the university students.[a] It was prevalent among responses from the flight survey and the wealthier, older response group. This may be explained by older generations' familiarity with the history of the APF's establishment, Governor Hammond's strong rhetoric on the dividend as an accountability mechanism,[b] and the controversy surrounding the earlier expenditure of the first tranche of oil revenues in the 1970s.

Conception	Discussion of original data
Redistribution tool	A minority of respondents explained the desirability of the dividend in redistributive terms. Some observed that it 'helps poorer families', others emphasized the assistance that it provided to poor regions in rural areas of Alaska, and some specifically described it as a redistribution mechanism.

[a] Goldsmith (2005) found that young Alaskans 'have very little understanding of the source and rationale for the dividend. When asked, a class of middle-school children felt that the dividend either was compensation for the high cost of living in the state, the hardships associated with life on the "last frontier" as it is sometimes called, or for the high taxes paid by their parents' (p. 562).
[b] Speaking in 1984, when concerned about threats to the dividend, Hammond argued that 'some things should be done to increase prospective dividend benefits, to maintain public support for them, and ultimately, to protect the Permanent Fund itself – *for the dividend is the best protection for the Fund*, even while it is the most equitable distribution of its earnings.' Hammond (1984), p. 19, emphasis added.

Source: Results of qualitative and quantitative surveys conducted by the author in April 2011 in Juneau and Anchorage, Alaska.

'continued presence' in the state (with some limited exceptions) to receive the PFD. In that sense, preferences on the dividend format further affirm the predominant conception of the PFD identified above: as a stake in the collective resources of the state contingent on *participatory* membership in the community.

Permanent Fund awareness

Awareness of the APF and how it related to the dividend was mixed. There was a relatively sophisticated understanding of the APF among the university student and wealthier professional respondents compared to the random aeroplane sample. Two themes emerged. First, all respondents in the former two groups knew of the APF and understood its purpose distinctly from the dividend. Second, despite this high degree of awareness, there were very different understandings of the *purpose* of the Permanent Fund. The three main ideas to emerge were that is was (a) a *distributive mechanism*, either from state to citizen, or intergenerationally among citizens across time; (b) a *savings mechanism* to help Alaska and its residents in the future; and (c) a *government finance mechanism* to help fund the operating costs of government when oil revenues eventually decline.

Among the aeroplane passengers, explanations were less nuanced. Awareness of the APF was high, as was support for it, but many answers did not distinguish between the purpose of the dividend and the APF. For many, the APF was about 'sharing part of the state's wealth [with] the people of Alaska'. This echoed the language used to describe the dividend, suggesting that respondents do connect the two, again supporting the idea of the APF as a collectively owned asset, and the dividend as recognition of an individual's share in that asset. Additional or discrete purposes for the APF were not identified, and respondents tended not to explain in detail *why* or *how* the wealth should be shared.

Focus group findings

As the survey revealed an array of views about the PFD among Alaskans, these attitudes were tested further in focus groups. Focus groups deliberately use communication among research participants as part of the method for determining not just what people think, but *why* they think that way. As focus group research aims at the 'explicit use of group interaction' to generate data',[47] the small-group discussion can also reveal patterns across demographics.

Three focus groups were conducted in Anchorage, Alaska during April 2011, comprising twenty-five Alaska residents. Research suggests that three to four focus groups are sufficient for determining whether data collation has hit 'saturation' point – 'the point where you have the range of ideas and aren't getting new information'.[48] The focus groups were based around eight to ten pre-prepared questions that teased out themes from the qualitative survey findings. The criterion for participation was residence in Alaska and receipt of the PFD. The focus group sample was constructed to achieve intergroup diversity and intragroup homogeneity, and included:

- Group 1: ten undergraduate economic students at the University of Alaska;
- Group 2: ten middle-class professional Anchorage residents; and
- Group 3: five low-income individuals, comprised of three female assisted care home workers and two homeless men.

Creating groups of participants with similar profiles helped isolate differences in opinion that could be explained by identity attributes. If one particular group displayed a certain attitude more so than another, then that attitude might be associated with the particular demographic represented in that focus group. I could also test certain suppositions. The university group, where no one was older than thirty, tested awareness and understanding of the APF and dividend among those who did not witness their establishment. The group of middle-class Alaskans included a variety of ages and professions, although on the whole the group had witnessed the establishment of the PFD and APF. As educated professionals, this group was expected to display awareness of the politics and policy around the fund and dividend. The group with low socioeconomic status was arranged to test for obvious class differences in dividend perception. Low-income Alaskans are often held to benefit the most from this programme so it is useful to see whether needier Alaskans view the dividend differently, given its potentially greater contribution to overall income in this demographic. Two key themes emerged in the focus groups:

The PFD as a 'citizen' contra 'individual' entitlement   Existing research observed that many Alaskans view the PFD 'as a distribution of earnings from an asset owned by each Alaskan'.[49] The qualitative survey confirmed that observation, but with subtly different implications. For some citizens, this sense of entitlement stems from greed, resulting in a dividend entitlement culture at all costs. According to Goldsmith: 'There is a strong feeling among a portion of the population that the state-owned oil resource belongs to them as individuals rather than to all citizens collectively.'[50] They would want their dividend no matter what. For others, the sense of entitlement derives from the idea of the dividend as an individualized monetary benefit that reflects each citizen's share of the APF assets: it is an owner's entitlement related directly to shared property.

To test whether one or other of these views was dominant in the surveys, participants were asked to consider the option of dissolving and 'cashing out' the fund. A likely extension of the 'greedy entitlement' view is that the APF should be cashed out equally among all its citizen shareholders. If the APF is nothing more than the aggregate of the shares of *individuals* in Alaska's resource wealth, then surely Alaskans would support a one-off distribution of their entire share through the dissolution of the APF.

There has been a concrete proposal in Alaska along these lines, which at the time would have resulted in an individual 'cash-out' of $40,000. The proposal was almost universally rejected, suggesting a triumph of civic concern over individual greed, or at least a balancing of individual want with a sense of responsibility to future generations. That said, the defeat of the 'cash-out' proposal is still seen by some as evidence for the individual entitlement thesis since its failure may be explained by the attachment of a specific condition to cash-out requiring the cessation of dividends and the use of all future oil revenues for funding government.[51]

A similar proposal was put to the focus groups, but using an individual cash-out figure of $67,000 reflecting the per capita worth of the APF in 2011. Interestingly, there was almost unanimous *opposition* to this proposal. Participants explained that this betrayed the purpose of the APF to save for future generations, as well as to share resources with present citizens. One concern that was widely shared was that if the fund was cashed out, 'the money would go everywhere, it would go out of the state'. Cashing out the fund was seen as tantamount to 'cut and run', which violated the spirit of the APF and the dividend as recognition of citizen participation in the state. The fact that these views spanned age groups and income brackets was also revealing. These explanations suggest that the individual entitlement thesis may be too simplistic a characterization of Alaskans' attitudes.

Evidence for the 'citizen entitlement' interpretation also emerged through participants' anger towards receipt of the dividend by temporary military personnel, and possible immigration to Alaska for dividend-seeking. Any type of recipient who did not appear to be 'invested' in Alaska, either as a resident or a patriot, and who just saw the dividend as a cash-cow was seen as 'undeserving'. Interestingly, this did not lead participants to support active participation in Alaska's society. When asked if a citizen could take their money and 'go bush', not using it to participate in mainstream society, on the whole participants accepted this as long as the citizen remained in Alaska and continued to live off the land. Such findings suggest that the entitlement conception that emerged from the survey is best understood in a 'positive ownership' sense, rather than in an 'unconstrained entitlement' sense.

Anti-welfare sentiment affirms ownership right All three focus groups showed almost unanimous rejection of the PFD as a tool for egalitarian redistribution or welfare-related goals. There was a total absence of language associated with such schemes. For instance, words like 'freedom', 'equality', 'basic needs', 'poverty' and 'fairness' hardly feature in the transcript. Equality appears only when participants discuss their 'right' to an equal share of Alaska's resources. However, language that does occur frequently includes words like 'citizenship', 'community', 'membership' and 'accountability'.

This suggests that the dominant conceptions of the dividend, when the focus group results were taken together with the survey, were the dividend as an accountability mechanism, and as a reward for community membership that attached to individual citizens *qua citizens*. That is, there was a sense of the *embedded* individual and a concept of desert grounded in citizenship. These findings challenge earlier analyses that cast Alaskans' attitudes as mere individual entitlement. The idea of ownership also came through strongly in the rejection by most participants of both the proposal for 'use' restrictions on the dividend and the proposal for means testing or other measures to ensure needier Alaskans could benefit.

Implications for SWF returns

The combined findings of the survey and focus groups suggest that Alaskans' attitudes towards the PFD reflect a more nuanced understanding of their right to a share of resource wealth than previous studies imply. If these findings are indicative of wider public sentiment in Alaska, three salient 'takeaways' emerge.

First, previous characterizations of popular attitudes to the dividend as an individual entitlement are only partially accurate. My research suggests that while many citizens consider the dividend *their* share of Alaska's collective resources, this view is grounded in and qualified by notions of citizenship and collective ownership of state resources. The PFD is not simply viewed as an unqualified entitlement, as Goldsmith speculated, or the result of individual greed as Hickel had feared. Alaskans' strong hostility towards 'cashing out' the fund or converting the dividend into a one-off lump-sum payment challenges these claims.

Moreover, alternative characterizations of the PFD as a basic income, an egalitarian redistribution or a needs payment cannot explain popular resistance to more generous distributions of this wealth. Rather, such findings are better explained by the popular view that it is the *citizen* of Alaska, rather than the individual, who should receive the PFD benefit. Put another way, it is not the idea of 'entitlement' that does the work in explaining popular attitudes to the PFD; rather, it is notions of citizenship and collective ownership of the Permanent Fund that best characterize Alaskans' understanding of the PFD. This finding helps explain their support of the dividend's current format and resistance to changing its means of distribution. If correct, this bolsters the case for characterizing the PFD as an income right attached to collective ownership.

Second, while popular perceptions of the PFD were intrinsically linked to the idea of citizenship, the notion of citizenship employed was elastic. What counted as citizenship for participants varied. Some required sheer presence in the state; others articulated more demanding notions of active participation and contribution. The desire of some for the PFD to be reinvested in the state and for recipients not to 'cut and run' with their dividend suggests a stronger sense of active citizenship, underscored by a love of community, akin to that of an owner protective of their communal property.

Evidence of latent notions of patriotism and state pride in responses provides further support for the conception of the APF as collective property for which community members must be responsible and which they should protect. But on either conception of citizenship, whether just membership in the state or a thicker idea of participation, as long as Alaskans link the idea of the PFD to a sense of belonging in their community, then it is possible to view the dividend programme as recognition of every single co-owner's equal right to their communal property's benefits.

Finally, the clear distinction drawn in respondents' minds between the idea of the APF and the PFD as the 'people's money' and not the 'government's' supports the observations in Chapter 3 about the perceived difference between state and citizen property in the eyes of the people. For many respondents, the PFD was the one clear mechanism that recognized *their* claim to these collective resources: distribution to government coffers was not considered a distribution to citizens. On the contrary, citizens felt they had to protect the APF and their dividend from government greed and frittering. This suggests that Hammond's idea of the owner-people triumphs over Hickel's idea of the owner-state among present-day Alaskans. If this conception of collective ownership over sovereign wealth presents in other communities, this should sway citizens towards a cash dividend allocation of SWF returns over collective distribution options such as government investment or budget transfers of SWF income discussed in Chapter 8.

To the extent the dividend was viewed as an accountability tool, there is further support for recommending dividend distribution of SWF returns as a means of improving citizens' sense of ownership over sovereign wealth. Alaskans display a strong desire to maintain the principal of the APF as collective property, rejecting proposals to cash it out or dissolve it, *at the same time* as they are committed to receiving their individual dividend payment. In other words, there is support for protecting both present and future generations' income property rights to this sovereign wealth as well as an individualized right to community property.

Overall, then, even though the extent to which these findings are generalizable is limited given the small sample size, they do suggest that dividend-recipient citizens value the distribution of their SWF earnings in this form, as well as seeing such a payment as attaching to membership in a particular community, rather than to an individual. This offers hope for transforming SWFs into community funds, if the people are likely to receive the earnings of their sovereign fund in that spirit. The understanding of a dividend as a right of ownership for citizens embedded in a community also bodes well for their use as accountability mechanisms. On the whole, the Alaska model offers a practical precedent for any community wishing to realize benefit rights to SWF income through cash dividends.

Criticism of the Alaskan approach

If the PFD is to serve as a precedent for SWF dividend distribution, it would be remiss to overlook some criticisms of the programme. This is particularly true now, as the scheme faces a radical overhaul in the context of Alaska's current fiscal crisis. The rapid crash in the price of oil combined with declining oil production ended a winning streak of fifty-six years in which Alaska spent, saved and distributed billions of dollars in oil revenues. In the last decade alone, between 2005 and 2014 oil revenues paid for almost 90 per cent of Alaskan state government.[52] Today, Alaska faces a budget deficit of \$3.6 billion and an uncertain long-term economic and fiscal outlook. With North Slope oil production down to one-quarter of what it was twenty-five years ago and projected to decline further, combined with little belief in a sustained oil price recovery, the state is intensely debating how to raise public revenues. Several proposals are on the table, including suggestions to cut or cap the dividend, diverting a greater share of Permanent Fund earnings to finance government instead. If that happens, the world may lose or see a dramatically altered version of its only working role model of SWF dividend distribution.

The fact that Alaska has reached this point speaks to several criticisms of the dividend programme. A long-noted concern is that while the PFD and Permanent Fund are both commendable and responsible financial initiatives, they were implemented in an irresponsible fiscal policy environment. Chiefly, Alaska has no sales or income tax. This makes it unique within the US where every other state has either an income or sales tax or both. Alaskans have grown used to receiving public goods and services without having to foot the bill. Now the state government finds itself fighting a fiscal crisis without the basic levers available to most governments for generating revenue. While many Alaskans accept that reforms are needed to address the crisis, there is little support for the introduction of a sales or income tax. For a start, even if these taxes were introduced in Alaska at comparable levels to other American states, experts have suggested that this would only raise around $700 million in income taxes and $400 million in sales taxes, not enough to cover the deficit.[53] Even more significant, the property ownership conception of the dividend hinders the ability of government to introduce other revenue-raising measures. Among many Alaskans, there is a belief that they do not pay standard taxes because they do not receive full royalties on their natural resources, which in effect is viewed as a tax.[54] Militant support for the dividend has morphed into an anti-tax position. For this reason, economists have long worried that Alaska's combination of generous resource dividends in an essentially tax-free environment is a time bomb. The lesson is that SWF-financed dividends must only be considered within a wider fiscal policy context that is committed to sustainability and discipline in the management of the public finances.

Another long-running reservation about the Alaska Permanent Fund under review is that it is too heavily skewed towards the needs of citizens, both current and future generations, at the expense of government. Under Alaska's Constitution, the principal of the Permanent Fund cannot be spent, but the fund's income can.[55] At present, the majority of fund earnings are either saved for the future or spent on dividends for present citizens. The earnings are placed in an account called the Permanent Fund Earnings Reserve. This reserve account holds money that will be deposited back into the principal of the Permanent Fund for inflation-proofing purposes and money that will be paid out as Permanent Fund dividends. While the earnings reserve account is subject to legislative appropriation, the APF principal is 'locked up', protected from drawdowns for future generations. Indeed, the Alaska state legislature can legally spend all the money in the Permanent Fund Earnings Reserve. In fact, over the three decades from 1982–2012, 'the state of Alaska extracted more than $2 billion in Permanent Fund money for uses other than dividends or inflation-proofing'.[56] This money was instead spent on various government operations, which ordinarily could be funded from the state general budget, reducing the potential pool of funding available for dividends.

As of 2012, the APF had generated $40.8 billion in fund income since inception.[57] Of this, the amount distributed in dividends to citizens since the PFD's commencement in 1982 was $20.2 billion, constituting 49.5 per cent of the APF's total income.[58] The other 50.5 per cent, or $20.6 billion, in investment returns has been deposited back into the principal of the APF for inflation-proofing or saved in the earnings reserve. The Alaska Constitution does not require the state of Alaska to either pay Permanent Fund dividends or inflation-proof the APF.

APF management conceptualizes this split allocation of fund income to both dividends and the fund principal as a recognition of the claims of both current and future generations to this capital.[59] Indeed, the APF has described the cumulative distribution of fund earnings since inception as resulting in a 49 per cent allocation to current generations, with the remaining 51 per cent directed to future generations, given its redirection back to the APF principal and earnings reserve for future needs.[60] In theory, this appears as if 100 per cent of APF investment returns are allocated to citizens, although only half of the APF's earnings to date have been used to finance a *direct, individual* income right to sovereign wealth returns. But in fact, around $2 billion (equal to about 6 per cent of the then $38.4 billion in APF earnings through to 30 June 2010) was extracted to finance government. While not a huge amount, the income diverted in that year alone, if added to the PFD instead, would have boosted the 2010 payment by 25 per cent (or $316).[61]

Two aspects of this arrangement are under fire at present. The first is that government itself has little access to the APF's returns. In the state versus citizen tussle for benefit from the sovereign wealth, citizens of today and tomorrow have won the bulk of Alaska's SWF income. Yet earnings from the Permanent Fund now constitute one of the state's most substantial sources of income. At around $2–3 billion annually, the APF earnings generate more for Alaska each year than oil revenues. In the past, this division between citizen and government use of the fund earnings has been sacrosanct. Dividends have been untouchable, since fund earnings are seen as entirely citizens' property (although in practice, as we saw, government still managed to divert a non-trivial amount of these earnings away from citizens). With other sources of revenue drying up, the idea that APF earnings are *largely* citizens' property has damaged government's ability to finance itself. Such a position ultimately hurts citizens. There must be a balanced use of SWF earnings for both government and citizen.

Today, there is growing sympathy for some government use of fund earnings. A range of reform proposals are on the table, including diverting a portion of APF earnings directly to the government or rolling all resource revenues together into one enormous sovereign fund which could pay a royalty to government each year to help finance the state. Proposals for co-opting the Permanent Fund earnings include reducing dividend payments by permanently cutting, temporarily capping or changing the funding formulation of the dividend. For instance, proposals by Alaska Governor Bill Walker and Anchorage Republican Senator Lesil McGuire maintain dividend payments to Alaska's citizens but sever the link between the dividend's calculation and the size of the fund or its performance by introducing a fixed royalty payment. This raises governance concerns. Citizens' ability to democratically participate in the management and use of their sovereign wealth, particularly in the way this book recommends, would be curtailed if there was no link between the size of the dividend and the fund.

Other proposals suggest preserving the dividend but reducing the amount of fund earnings that are saved in the earnings reserve or reinvested in the principal. That is, they would take from future citizens rather more so than present ones. This touches on the second reservation about the PFD scheme. There has always been debate as to whether this split of investment returns between the PFD (present citizens) and augmenting the APF (future citizens) is just. Sequestering and transferring returns to the principal of a sovereign fund may be sufficient to guarantee future citizens' rights to sovereign wealth. Additional allocation of present income flows to SWF stock risks over-privileging future generations at the expense of present citizens' needs. As of 2010, up to $4.3 billion of the total $40.8 billion generated has been legislatively appropriated from the earnings reserve back into the principal.[62] Such an allocation could potentially violate the income rights of present-day Alaskans to fund returns. That is, it may be too generous. That is a question for a different analysis. For this reason, there is an ongoing debate about the fairness of using present-day returns for inflation-proofing the fund.

Interestingly, the design of the APF attempts to achieve this – despite allocating less than 100 per cent of returns to the PFD – by giving dividend payments legal priority above inflation-proofing.[63] If there is not enough money in the earnings reserve to pay out dividends and inflation-proof the fund, dividends have priority. Fortunately, reserves have always been sufficient to meet the annual inflation-proofing requirement.[64]

There are also concerns, though, that the needs of present citizens are over-privileged relative to future citizens. Present citizens enjoy around half of the Permanent Fund's returns in addition to not paying any sales or income tax. But if this arrangement continues such that the government is unable to fund itself, then today's citizens will also start to suffer. Alaska will be at risk of having favoured a few generations over the past three decades with a generous (and unsustainable) combination of bountiful dividends in a tax-free environment, at the expense of present and future citizens, who will receive lower dividends and the fiscal challenges of the post-oil era.

It is too early to tell how Alaska's fiscal crisis will play out for its sovereign fund and dividend programme. With a state election due at the end of 2016, and parliamentary hearings into the proposed reforms ongoing, Alaska has a way to go before agreeing a more lasting solution to its fiscal challenges. The end of the oil bonanza also raises deeper questions about the economy.[65] Alaska has lost the market for its major source of income. Even if government manages to sort out its fiscal challenges in the short term, longer-term questions remain as to the future of growth and economic make-up of the state. Any emulation of the Alaska dividend scheme must bear these local challenges in mind, balancing appreciation of the programme's success with awareness of its clear design and implementation failings.

10

Fighting inequality with sovereign wealth

Anthony Atkinson, the 'godfather of inequality research', wants a sovereign wealth fund for Britain.[1] In fact, he wants a sovereign fund for any country that wishes to halt the steady rise of economic inequality that plagues developed and developing nations alike. His proposal forms part of a fifteen-point manifesto to reduce inequality published in his latest book *Inequality: What Can Be Done?*,[2] in which he argues that a sovereign fund is an equality-promoting vehicle both within present-day communities *and* between generations. A sovereign fund promotes equality by improving a nation's current net worth, which helps citizens of today by boosting the government's coffers. And it transfers wealth intergenerationally, benefiting citizens of tomorrow.

Of these two contributions to tackling inequality, the ways in which SWFs improve intergenerational equity is most intelligible. Sovereign funds help convert a finite asset, like a natural resource windfall or trade surplus, into a permanent financial asset, the benefits of which can be shared across generations. With successful management, a once-temporary asset is both preserved and augmented.

Less obvious is how a sovereign fund helps fight inequality *within* rather than across generations. Yet a growing number of inequality analysts describe sovereign funds as a tool to help achieve greater equality between today's compatriots. They identify two ways, one pre-emptory and the other corrective, in which sovereign funds can help. The pre-emptory approach views SWFs as vehicles that spread the ownership of capital in an era where private ownership has become a leading driver of inequality. By allowing governments to invest in a range of assets on their citizens' behalf, sovereign funds redirect a portion of an economy's assets into collective hands. As SWFs grow over time, so too does a community's share of private capital growth, stemming the inequality-amplifying effects of private ownership.

On the corrective view of SWFs, their returns are identified as a potential financing source for a range of inequality-ameliorating initiatives. Proposals for funding by SWFs include targeted schemes that benefit the disadvantaged, such as social mobility programmes, long-term unemployment relief or social housing; or universal programmes associated with general improvements in equality, such as a regular Citizen's Income (CI), a one-off Basic Capital (BC) grant or an annual social dividend paid either to citizens or into government budgets to cover vital public services. Of these three, CI, also known as Basic Income, has gained substantial traction in recent times. While BC involves giving a one-time capital grant to every individual at an early stage of life, large enough to offer the potential of reasonable wealth accumulation in adult life,[3] CI gives all citizens, as of right, a tax-free, guaranteed basic weekly income, unconditionally. The payment should be sufficiently high to provide a standard of living above the poverty line.[4]

These proposals for SWFs to help finance a citizen's income, capital endowment or social dividend invite a different perspective on how to distribute the benefit of sovereign fund income than that assumed in the previous two chapters. The Alaska model of cash dividends for all citizens is a highly individualized, direct form of benefit right to SWF income. It is analogous to a shareholder receiving a dividend from an individually owned equity. And, as we saw, that is how most Alaskans conceive of the PFD: as their individual share in the state's collectively owned resources, not an equality-promoting measure (even though it may have that effect).

But for some societies, the greatest challenges facing their individual members require community-level solutions. Those communities might prefer their SWF earnings be deployed to schemes that tackle society-wide problems. Under this approach, citizens would still receive their benefit rights to SWF income, but the motivation for and format of return distribution would be distinct from individual dividends. To assist communities that prefer this option, this chapter considers the case for deploying SWF returns to what US President Barack Obama has called 'the defining challenge of our time': economic inequality.[5] It examines why a growing number of advocates have identified sovereign funds as part of the solution to inequality, and how this might be compatible with my community fund vision of SWFs.

The inequality crisis

If pushed to pick a major policy challenge common to most twenty-first-century nations which sovereign wealth could help redress, a top contender is the inexorable rise of economic inequality. It is touted as one of today's most urgent social and economic policy challenges: a 2014 Pew research poll found that people around the globe rank inequality as their greatest policy concern.[6]

This is not surprising. Multiple inequality metrics demonstrate that within-country income and wealth inequality is extremely high across the world, and in some cases at levels not seen since the 1920s.[7] Acceleration in inequality of earnings, income and wealth across the OECD and within Anglo-Saxon countries in particular has risen steadily since the 1980s.[8] On current trends, the OECD predicts that the inequality gap within its rich member nations will widen further over the next three decades.[9] Atkinson calls this the 'inequality turn', marshalling ample evidence of income inequality increasing since 1980 in most OECD countries and particularly in Britain and the US.[10] The increasingly high level of the wealth–income ratio has also attracted attention.[11] In the past, these ratios have indicated recessions. The periods just before the 1929 Great Depression and the financial crisis in 2008 were accompanied by expanding wealth–income ratios.[12]

Of the two core components of economic inequality – income and wealth – wealth differences are more extreme. Yet, inequality research in the previous thirty years tended to frame differences in terms of income.[13] This neglect of wealth inequality relative to income inequality by economists and social scientists alike was partly a function of data availability. Until recently, consistent measurements of national wealth have been scarce and unsystematic. In the eighteenth and nineteenth centuries, there was a strong tradition of national wealth accounting, particularly in the economies of Britain, France, Germany and the United States. But this was largely abandoned during the interwar period and replaced with a new focus on national income and output. Economists Piketty and Zucman explain that 'the shock of World War I, the Great Depression and the coming of Keynesian economics led to attention being switched from stocks to flows, with balance sheets being neglected'.[14] Systematic attempts to collect historical balance sheets and to develop a granular picture of public wealth only began in the 1980s.[15] Piketty's work, both in his book *Capital in the Twenty-First Century* and related studies, is a significant contribution to our historical understanding of the composition of national capital and its relationship to income.

Building on this work, leading inequality scholars have begun shifting our gaze back to wealth distribution. Much recent work highlights the increase in aggregate wealth–income ratios and top-wealth fractiles over the past few decades in several countries and its overall contribution to inequality. An oft-cited inequality measure is the Gini coefficient, a ratio that indicates the relative level of income or wealth inequality within a domestic economy with absolute inequality represented by 1 and complete equality by zero. The global Gini wealth index, measured by purchasing power parity, is currently 0.802, very close to complete inequality. If measured with official exchange rates, the share of wealth of the top decile rises to 85 per cent and the Gini coefficient hits 0.892.[16] Credit Suisse's *Global Wealth Report 2014* captures the gravity of the situation in tangible terms: the top 0.7 per cent of the world's population own 44 per cent of global wealth, whereas those with a net worth of less than $10,000 (69.8 per cent of the total population) own less than 3 per cent.[17]

When compared to income inequality, the greater magnitude of wealth inequality is striking. Gini coefficients in wealth data for individual countries lie between 0.65 and 0.75, compared to a mid-range of 0.35–0.45 for income.[18] In fact, concentrations of wealth within countries are *always* more concentrated than income from labour (for all countries in all periods for which data is available).[19] Consider the US. The share of the top 10 per cent in total labour income in 2010 was 35 per cent, with the bottom 50 per cent seeing only 25 per cent of the total pot. When it comes to wealth distribution in the US in the same year, 70 per cent of total wealth is owned by the top 10 per cent, while just 5 per cent is owned by the bottom 50 per cent. The US is the worst offender on unequal wealth ownership, but the broad trend of wealth inequality outpacing labour income inequality repeats across most countries. This pattern has only worsened over time.

Given the disproportionate impact that wealth is believed to have on household well-being and economic success,[20] action is increasingly urged. Consider the effect of wealth inequality on income inequality when wealth is invested. Piketty and Atkinson have both demonstrated that large wealth holdings have access to substantially higher financial returns than smaller ones, which serves to amplify wealth inequalities over time. This problem compounds given that a growing fraction of household net wealth is inherited rather than self-made and that inheritances are very unequally distributed. All of these dynamics have spillover effects on the political process. Greater wealth concentration increases the incentive and the ability of the wealthy to buy political influence, which in turn is used to further increase the concentration of economic power. For economist Stewart Lansley, this has the deleterious effect of gearing 'a growing share of economic activity . . . to the upward extraction of existing wealth rather the creation of new products, companies and jobs', further exacerbating economic inequality.[21] For all these reasons, several international bodies have called on policymakers to act imminently to stem worsening wealth inequality.[22]

Other less direct measures of inequality, such as poverty, social mobility and social cohesion, also suggest a deterioration of egalitarianism within capitalist polities.[23] Without revisiting well-established matters, I simply note that recent poverty measures indicate that the Anglo-Saxon states with 'liberal' welfare regimes experience poverty rates twice as high as the 'socially democratic' Scandinavian countries.[24] At the same time as the US enjoyed the status of the second richest country in the world on income per capita after Norway, it also boasted the highest poverty levels in the industrialized world, meaning precious little of the vast national income of the US reached the lower end of the income distribution.[25]

Critics of this state of socioeconomic affairs also point to high levels of unemployment and non-employment plaguing prosperous nations in recent decades, as well as a rising concern with 'social exclusion'.[26] Such data can go behind aggregate growth rates in GDP to reveal long-term unemployment and entrenched exclusion of certain groups. Despite Europe's overall GDP growth rates between the 1960s and early 1990s, the continent experienced an increase in unemployment by a factor of nearly five.[27] One consequence of this is increasing dysfunctional behaviour in communities suffering entrenched socioeconomic disadvantage. Multiple governments have responded by giving high priority to the issue of social inclusion, a policy concept aimed at promoting greater equality to ensure more cohesive societies.[28]

How can SWFs help?

If economic inequality is an intractable feature of advanced capitalist democracies, what can SWFs do to help? Analysts wishing to enlist sovereign funds in the fight against inequality envisage SWFs 'tackl[ing] inequality from both ends'[29] – on the one hand, improving the balance between private and collectively owned wealth, and on the other, by using SWF returns to finance a range of beneficial public projects that promote equality.

The first strategy of equalizing wealth ownership within societies through SWFs works as follows. The essential idea is that sovereign funds provide a vehicle through which governments can acquire a greater share of the national wealth pie on behalf of citizens. In today's economic circumstances, this requires the state to capture a bigger share of profits by becoming a capital owner. Returns on wealth measured as a fraction of national income are increasing and will continue to do so. In the UK, for instance, profits have been growing faster than GDP since the 1980s. At the same time, governments cannot just rely on economic growth or existing revenue sources to keep up with public expenditure. Holtham offers three reasons for this.[30] First, as our societies grow richer, older and more technically advanced, governments face rising demand for prized services like health and education. Yet, second, productivity gains in these sectors have not materialized and governments increasingly struggle to raise revenues to cover rising costs in a world of mobile capital. Third, growth policies as the traditional response to this problem have failed and will continue to fail to deliver the needed capital. UK economic growth over more than a century has averaged 2.5 per cent, irrespective of the political orthodoxy in vogue at any given point. As costs have been growing at a faster rate than this, governments must look to capturing those parts of GDP that outstrip average growth: profits.

The idea that states should capture profits rather than rely on growth for crucial revenue would surely win Thomas Piketty's support. The central Piketty thesis that the rate of return on investments consistently outperforms the rate of growth encourages both governments and individuals to become wealth owners. Holtham, along with Meade,[31] thinks that the best way for governments to capture a larger share of profits is to own capital through a public fund that invests in foreign and domestic equities, generating a return for the state: 'if you can't tax capital in a mobile world, you have to own it'.[32]

Another way that SWFs can help equalize wealth ownership is by generating a fund's start-up capital through taxation on wealth and profits. Stewart Lansley argues that governments can claim a greater share of national wealth either by applying a levy to existing shareholdings or requiring firms to issue new shares annually to a public fund. While both would help convert the private gain of individuals into shared gains held in a central pool, the latter constitutes a more aggressive assault on inequality through its dilution of existing capital ownership.[33]

This idea of SWFs as wealth redistributors gains more strength if my proposal for sovereign wealth to be understood as citizens' rather than government property is heeded. If sovereign wealth is transformed into citizens' wealth, then there truly is a rebalancing between private and collective ownership, and not just a reallocation of state assets within government coffers. Indeed, Anthony Atkinson and James Meade both stress that sovereign funds allow governments to exert 'beneficial ownership' over companies and property, as distinct from full nationalization of these assets. Such an idea is highly compatible with my proposed principal–agent model of SWF ownership in which governments merely hold and manage these assets on behalf of their constituents and ultimately for their benefit.

At this point, the second inequality-fighting property of SWFs becomes crucial: the fair distribution of their gains. The return generated by the fund could be hypothecated for a whole range of equality-promoting initiatives. For Atkinson, these include a universal capital endowment paid to all adults on maturity (known as Basic Capital); increased social protection in the form of a 'participation income'; or more generous benefits for all those contributing to society (whether through employment or public service).[34] In the UK, Atkinson believes that such a fund could help address the looming pension crisis.

Another way of fairly distributing an SWF's return is to earmark the income of an SWF to fund a social dividend. Such a scheme resembles aspects of the cash dividend model discussed in the last two chapters, although the focus of the social dividend is more explicitly on equalizing wealth ownership rather than recognizing individual ownership rights over collective property. Giacomo Corneo, Chair of Public Finance at the Free University of Berlin, explains how his model of a social dividend financed by an SWF could work:

> This social dividend would be a monthly or quarterly universal transfer payment received by every citizen. It is the novel redistributive tool to be employed by the polity. The income of the fund consists of its returns, net of administration costs and a reinvestment quota to stabilize in the long run the ratio of fund size to GDP. Because of the opportunities for diversification and the fact that it would not pay taxes, the SWF would over the long term yield an above-average return on capital for the citizens. This means that even those who have no private means of their own would share in the highest capital returns, since every citizen would be an equal shareholder, through the state, in the investments of the SWF.[35]

For Corneo, although one must be realistic regarding the level of funding the social dividend could reach, it would still help reduce inequality, both of outcomes and opportunities. To quote him again:

> assume for example that over a time lapse of twenty years the polity gradually builds up a SWF that eventually amounts to 50% of GDP and that such a level is maintained forever. If the rate of return delivered to the public budget is 8%, total expenditures for the social dividend will equal four percentage points of GDP. For the U.S. this would imply today a social dividend of about 2,300 dollars per person per year. This is far from being sufficient to make a living but, especially for earners at the bottom of the distribution and large families, it would substantially contribute to improve their living conditions. Furthermore, the social dividend would reduce inequality by strengthening the bargaining

power of low-skilled workers vis-à-vis their employers. Since the social dividend especially improves the fall-back option of the working poor, they can be expected to strike better wage bargains.

A social dividend, just like a cash dividend, does not have to carry with it the risk of volatile income for recipients. A community may follow the Alaska model and calculate a dividend based on the average performance of the fund over a longer period of time to help smooth out uneven performance. Alternatively, I have suggested elsewhere that adjustable dividends may prove a useful economic policy tool for governments coping with cyclical business environments.[36] In a cyclical economy, there are times of contraction when a higher rate of spending from government fiscal sources (like an SWF) may be appropriate. These are interspersed with boom times when there is greater pressure on government to retrench to avoid aggravating an overheated, inflationary economy. During such times, government should save through a higher tax intake and lower spending to build up a buffer for the next inevitable downturn. It follows, then, that in times of contraction, government spending through sovereign wealth-funded dividends may be an entirely appropriate Keynesian policy tool to help stimulate demand. Equally, when the economy is booming and private sector demand is sufficient, spending schemes such as dividends may need to be curtailed. The latter could be achieved by suspending the dividend programme and preserving that year's dividend capital in the SWF until conditions are ripe for recommencement, similar to the responsive management of interest rate levels by central banks.

There are other options for income smoothing through SWF pay-outs to the citizens, if adjustable dividends prove intolerable. Corneo argues that supernormal returns could be used to buy back a country's public debt and build a reserve that would be used to ensure that a stable social dividend is paid in periods of subnormal returns. Another creative solution is to formulate the SWF's risk-adjusted return targets factoring in the likely impact of GDP fluctuations on a representative household or the economy more generally. In other words, a country may mandate its SWF to invest in a way that is uncorrelated with other aspects of its national economy. Norway does this to some extent. While the underlying assets of its sovereign fund are dependent on the performance of international energy markets, in particular oil and gas, its sovereign fund is required to divest from sectors and companies whose earnings are too dependent on those industries. In this respect, its sovereign fund performance is negatively correlated with its national economic performance. Citizens can benefit from such an arrangement if their SWF is used to finance a regular payment to individuals. Corneo argues that a social dividend may reduce the volatility of private households' incomes when an SWF invests in stocks whose returns are negatively correlated with a country's national income.[37]

The novel potential of SWFs to fight inequality

Using sovereign fund returns to finance any of these schemes within communities would constitute a novel way to ameliorate growing inequality. No sovereign fund in the world currently deploys its earnings towards such ends, although some commentators have characterized the Alaska dividend distribution as a Citizen's Income, a view which I challenged in the last chapter. But the worsening state of economic inequality makes its redress pressing. The ascent of high-profile advocates of economic equality to senior political leadership – such as Bernie Sanders in the race for the Democratic nomination for US President and Jeremy Corbyn as leader of the UK Labour Party – is not enough. These figures need a workable plan of action to put to the voters. This plan needs to help spread wealth, but not in a way that signals a return to past failed efforts at wealth redistribution.

SWFs offer a unique solution. Unique insofar as the funds present a radical yet simultaneously conservative tool for tackling inequality, one that is deeply compatible with capitalist institutions. As investors, SWFs are key participants in global capital markets, ones which recognize and harness the increasing role of capital as a share of national income on behalf of governments. They allow the state to become a capital owner without returning to the days of full nationalization. They limit the scale of private ownership of capital without being anti-market or private sector. Best-practice SWF governance embraces arm's-length investment management of sovereign wealth by industry experts. In this respect, the proposal to use SWFs to tackle inequality is compatible with a reformist stance on capitalism, aiming to make fairer the operations of the market economy, rather than agitate for its replacement.

PART IV

WHAT NEXT?

11

Past the peak? The future of sovereign wealth accumulation

In 2014, global oil prices halved. For most of the previous five years, they hovered around $110 per barrel. But in June 2014, they started a precipitous downward fall, hitting a post-financial crisis low of less than $30 a barrel in January 2016. Where oil went, other commodities followed. Dramatic falls were recorded across nearly all commodity prices in 2015.[1] With around 60 per cent of SWF assets domiciled in oil- and gas-producing countries, tanking commodity prices equals dwindling revenues for energy-exporting governments and a new era of sustained budget deficits. And that means two things for commodity-based SWFs: cash injections stop and drawdowns start.

Some sovereign funds have already been tapped. Russia announced that its Reserve Fund, designed to help plug gaps in the national budget, was likely be depleted by 2016. Even optimistic estimates forecast the Russian fund plummeting to $5 billion in 2018 from an impressive buffer of $77 billion. Saudi Arabia, the world's largest oil exporter, is estimated to have pulled out between $50 billion and $70 billion from various asset managers in response to around $73 billion being wiped off its foreign reserve assets since the start of the oil price slide. Those assets will be redirected back into the budget to help cover the country's enormous public expenditure commitments, the highest in the Gulf region. Many of the other Middle East oil exporters are also feeling the pinch. The IMF predicts that the majority of countries in the region will wipe out their national savings within the next decade.[2] Only the fiscal buffers of the United Arab Emirates (UAE), Qatar and Kuwait are substantial enough to last for more than a quarter of a century, based on current fiscal plans and oil price projections. The rest of the Gulf exporters will exhaust their national savings within four to seven years, with Bahrain and Yemen running out of reserves in just two years. Even financially disciplined Norway, superstar of the sovereign wealth fund world, drew down on the principal of its fund for the first time in its history in 2016.

Crashing commodity prices aren't the only headache for sovereign funds. Of the $7.3 trillion in SWF assets, it is estimated that $4.2 trillion are oil and gas related.[3] But that leaves a sizeable chunk of sovereign funds dependent on trade-generated foreign reserves or buoyant domestic economies producing fiscal surpluses. Here, too, the news is not good. Growth in global trade has fallen. The World Trade Organization has decreased its trade growth estimates for 2016.[4] A critical factor behind the global slowdown is China's economic cooling. Opinion is divided over whether the data coming out of China represent a necessary correction, a temporary setback or the end of a twenty-five-year era of extraordinary growth never to be seen again. Whichever proves correct, the bursting of China's stock-market bubble, its huge private debt burden and slowing growth are all major economic policy challenges for Beijing, the effects of which reverberate around the world. Labelled China's Black Monday, 24 August 2015 saw 8.5 per cent of the Shanghai share index wiped and the loss of millions of dollars in international stock markets, prompting comparisons to the Wall Street Crash of 1929. This immediately reflected in the 2015 third quarter performance of many sovereign funds. Norway reported its largest loss in four years and the third weakest result since its launch in 1990, largely attributing this result to the Chinese stock-market crash and the concomitant volatility in global equities.

Despite these vicissitudes, Norway maintains its lead in global SWF rankings. Even with the GPFG's assets under management scaled back to approximately $825 billion (from a peak of nearly $900 billion earlier in 2015) the sovereign fund is well placed to ride out this market turbulence as it did during the financial crisis. Although the era of quarterly cash injections into the Norwegian fund averaging 60 billion kroner is on hold, the GPFG will not have to sell any assets to meet the government's financial needs. Instead, GPFG management announced in 2015 that it would use interest generated in the fixed income portion of its portfolio to cover Norway's projected budget deficit for FY2016. Sticking with this plan, the Norwegian government withdrew $780 million from the fund in January 2016, the first withdrawal from the GPFG since its initial deposit twenty years earlier.

Norway's rainy day has come. It is using its sovereign fund umbrella wisely and sustainably to weather the storm. Russia is also facing stormy conditions. But it is exhausting all its protections at once. Norway has a plan to manage its diminished portfolio through the tough times without having to sell off any assets. Russia is not sure whether its sovereign fund will still exist in a year, despite specifically establishing the fund to act as a permanent buffer in tough economic times.

What about the rest of the SWF community? Is Norway uniquely positioned to withstand the current market upheavals and survive the new era of non-oil budgeting? And what do these new economic conditions mean for countries which are yet to establish a sovereign fund but wish to do so?

For communities planning to create a sovereign fund with future windfalls from new resource discoveries, the immediate future looks gloomy. So too for countries which might have looked to other sources of national wealth, such as privatization or excess foreign reserves, to create a sovereign fund. A general weakening in global trade, a sustained, historically low interest rate environment, China's economic slowdown, and a cooling off in commodities all might lead us to worry that the peak of sovereign wealth accumulation has passed. If nations failed to sock away impressive savings during the past decades, is there any hope that they can still do so in the decade ahead? If not, where does that leave our demands for communities to create community funds through transforming sovereign wealth into citizens' wealth? The real worry, then, is whether there is a future for sovereign wealth accumulation?

Economic doom and gloom

For the short to medium term, the global economic outlook is tepid. The world still waits for a return to the pre-crisis boom years, or at least a sustained recovery. And the wait looks set to continue. For while advanced economies have begun to slowly pick up, growth estimates for many emerging economies are forecast to decrease.

In the short term – in 2016 – the OECD estimates that the major economies will experience modest growth, but that global growth will 'flat-line'. While the major economies are forecast to experience modest growth (the US by 2 per cent, the eurozone by 1.4 per cent, Japan by 0.8 per cent and the UK by 2.1 per cent),[5] these figures were all downgraded from the previous economic outlook at the close of 2015. The overarching message is that 'strong global growth remains elusive', with 2016 growth rates predicted to be the same as 2015 while GDP global growth over the next few years has been revised down.

World Bank estimates support this modest outlook, predicting that global economic growth will not surpass 3 per cent until 2017, rising at an even slower pace than predicted in 2015.[6] The US, notwithstanding its recovery, has not been able to achieve its potential GDP growth.[7] Emerging markets' growth will also slow considerably, averaging 5.2 per cent between 2015 and 2020.[8] To put these figures in context, with nominal GDP growth in most developed economies slowing to below 4 per cent a year, and below 2 per cent when looking at real GDP growth, these levels are at their lowest point since the 1960s postwar golden era of growth.

Over the medium and longer term, the outlook continues to be moderate. According to the OECD's interim economic outlook, positive yet timid growth in the US is driven by rising employment and household consumption. But global demand cannot be sustained solely by the US recovery. The eurozone's recovery is also expected to continue, albeit with urgent action needed on investment and productivity.[9] Several reports also underline the recent crisis in China and the concomitant slowdown in Chinese exports, which has had profound repercussions on the global economy and on existing trade patterns. Many commodity-exporting countries and emerging markets with a considerable stake in the Chinese domestic market will suffer as a result.[10] Recent data from the Federal Reserve are less optimistic for the US economy and expect it to grow at a much slower pace in the medium term than previously expected.[11]

In the longer term the OECD expects global average growth rates to decrease from 3.6 per cent in 2010–20 to 2.4 per cent in 2050–60, mainly caused by a deceleration in emerging markets, an ageing population and lower total factor productivity growth, measured as the ratio of output to all input.[12] Making matters worse, the negative output gap of many OECD countries, in particular of vulnerable eurozone countries such as Ireland, Italy and Spain, which the OECD estimates have an output gap between 2 per cent and 8 per cent, is expected to continue.[13]

In emerging economies, the picture is even less encouraging. Although advanced economies were declining before the financial crisis, emerging markets' growth has taken a real beating following the crisis and in 2015 in particular. This looks set to continue over the medium term, mainly as a result of plummeting commodity prices which show little sign of fully recovering.[14] Moreover, growth theory posits that emerging countries' growth patterns are set to decrease as these countries reach the technological frontier.[15]

Secular stagnation

This gloomy short- and medium-term outlook for global economic growth has led to talk of secular stagnation. The term, first coined by economist Alvin Hansen in the 1930s, describes a situation in which low interest rates and low inflation become part of an environment with low growth and excessive economic slack. The idea was recently revived, thanks largely to former US Treasury Secretary Larry Summers, to help account for the disappointing recovery witnessed by many economies after the financial crisis, despite historically low interest rates.[16] In an effort to boost demand and encourage borrowing, very low interest rates have been introduced across advanced economies in the aftermath of the financial crisis. Yet sustained growth has not set in.

Much discussion on contemporary secular stagnation pivots around these unprecedentedly low interest rates. The rate of natural interest, the rate which is low enough to allow for growth while still being high enough to keep inflation under control, has never been this low in OECD countries.[17] In other words, at a rate of interest at which we should see considerably more growth, the economy has remained anaemic as even low rates have failed to encourage people to invest.

But there is another side to the secular stagnation story: the supply side. Slower growth in labour and productivity coupled with the current demographic trends across the world (an ageing population and low fertility rates) are also to blame for secular stagnation.[18] Diminished labour productivity and aggregate hours of work across the world also help explain this persistent economic slack.[19]

The classic example of secular stagnation is Japan.[20] Despite years of negative interest rates to boost demand, Japan has witnessed low growth for two decades. The eurozone is also dangerously close to deflation and has experimented with extremely low interest rates to little avail. Analyses have shown that the current lack of aggregate demand in the eurozone is likely to continue.[21] The US's very low interest rates have also failed to bring the country back to the sustained growth it experienced before the financial crisis.[22] Labour productivity, participation and aggregate hours have all decreased in the US.[23]

Secular stagnation is not only affecting advanced economies but also emerging markets. Whereas many trends that characterize secular stagnation in advanced countries are also present in emerging markets, the latter possess their own characteristics. The recent IMF economic outlook has shown that total factor productivity has decreased in these countries as well, as has demographic growth. The level of demand has also decreased; investment to capital ratios should dwindle most noticeably in China as the Chinese economy will become more domestic-driven and consumption-focused.[24]

Finally, in the absence of sustained growth and demand, and in an effort to boost employment and GDP growth, secular stagnation theory holds that we have become increasingly reliant on financial bubbles. Under this interpretation the tech and real estate bubbles constituted nothing but short respites in a sick economy.[25] Taken together, this broad malaise affecting the global economy may well indicate that we have entered a phase of secular stagnation.

Sovereign wealth accumulation amid secular stagnation

What hope is there for sovereign wealth accumulation in an age of secular stagnation? Worryingly, the signs all point towards lower inflows of public wealth in the future. Certainly, the immediate to medium-term economic picture sketched above offers little cause for optimism. Given the commodity market falls and slow growth in global trade, sovereign wealth accumulation is likely to decrease in the short term. Countries that are commodity or trade dependent, and thus overly reliant on global demand, will suffer from a mismatch between savings and investments.

That said, the future of sovereign wealth accumulation is a more mixed picture. The same supply-side pressures driving secular stagnation will also drive the need for greater national savings. Current demographic trends and the concomitant looming pensions crisis in many countries will only intensify the need for national funds tasked with offsetting pension liabilities. Ageing populations, low fertility rates and a decrease in the labour force mean that pensions will increasingly consume a large proportion of state budgets and the case for creating SWFs will remain strong. At the same time, countries that have been dependent on substantial commodity earnings will be forced to look for new sources of sovereign wealth to help meet public expenditure liabilities. Saudi Arabia provides a case in point. In April 2016, Deputy Crown Prince Mohammed bin Salman announced plans to list 5 per cent of Aramco, the world's largest oil company, on the Saudi market by 2017. The proceeds would be used to turn the kingdom's existing government investment vehicle, the Public Investment Fund, into a sovereign wealth fund estimated to be worth as much as $2 trillion.[26] The new SWF would be tasked with diversifying Saudi Arabia's sources of national income away from oil revenues, which currently account for more than 80 per cent of Saudi exports, towards investments to become the major source of Saudi government revenue.

Growth of new SWFs

But the need for, as opposed to the actual ability to accumulate, sovereign wealth are of course two different things. Although secular stagnation has depressed demand, an increased focus on savings does not mean that countries will automatically save more. And most countries are not in the unique position of Saudi Arabia, boasting a world-leading commodity production and export business. Governments will have to get more creative about possible sources of sovereign wealth to help tackle savings deficits.

Encouragingly, there is already evidence of such SWF policy initiative. Consider the numerous innovative proposals surfacing in the UK regarding the sorts of assets Britain could use to seed a new SWF. Former London Mayor Boris Johnson has suggested combining the UK's 39,000 public pension funds into one large government investment fund to help reduce the UK's dependence on other sovereign investors, primarily China, for infrastructure financing. Another proposal advanced by a group of Labour Members of Parliament involves turning Britain's £8.6 billion Crown Estate into a fund for productive state investment by freeing it up to invest in up-and-coming foreign property markets, promising businesses and UK infrastructure. At present, the Estate fund is restricted to investing in commercial property and land in Britain and must pay its surplus income to the Treasury to help cover the cost of maintaining the royal family. That income is sizeable. In 2012, the royal property portfolio generated a surplus of £253 million, with an 11.9 per cent annual return. But, if freed up to invest in foreign property markets and permitted to allocate some of its income towards national savings, the Crown Estate could transform into a UK sovereign wealth fund. Others have suggested tapping the wealth of the UK's financial sector by hypothecating revenue from specific financial transactions. The existing banking levy could be used towards this end, as could another small levy applied to mergers and acquisitions. Chancellor of the Exchequer George Osborne and others have also touted the possibility of a shale gas fund based on reserving a proportion of taxation revenues from the sale of natural resources and the rights to explore those resources.

But few countries are in the UK's position, with the potential to exploit one of the best performing financial sectors in the world, extensive holdings of an affluent monarchy or a new natural resource discovery. Promisingly, more general proposals for seeding future sovereign funds have also entered the public debate. Political economist Dani Rodrik has suggested that governments issue government bonds in international financial markets as a means of generating underlying assets for SWFs in countries that are not resource rich.[27] In this vein, Giacomo Corneo has argued that the state can accumulate public capital by purchasing equities, financed by issuing government bonds.[28] Financing costs are generally low in the current low-interest-rate environment, but particularly for solvent countries like Germany and other prosperous eurozone nations such that only a small part of the income from the acquired stocks would be needed to cover the cost of borrowing.

Others have argued for using a share of tax revenues from a range of new and existing taxes on wealth, property and other assets. Swedish economists Dag Detter and Stefan Fölster argue for states to monetize public commercial assets such as real estate and public land and combine these proceeds with revenues earned on state-owned enterprises and other income-generating state assets to form national wealth funds (NWFs). These NWFs would in many respects model themselves on the design and governance of sovereign wealth funds. But they would ultimately be an *asset* manager, actively managing the operational and commercial assets of a state's asset portfolio. In contrast, SWFs are *fund* managers, tasked with managing a tranche of liquid, financial assets of the government allocated to higher return strategies. It should be up to individual countries whether they wish to establish NWFs or use the proceeds of public asset sales to seed SWFs. In any case, if Detter and Fölster are right, public commercial assets offer a vast, untapped source of national wealth. The authors estimate that, globally, these assets are worth up to $75 trillion, equal to global GDP.[29] They conservatively estimate that total worldwide public wealth in government hands is so vast that a return of just 1 per cent would add some $750 billion annually to public revenues.[30]

In the UK, such wealth could be raised from the sale of state-owned commercial assets such as the electromagnetic spectrum or the remaining government share of the Royal Bank of Scotland. It is too late, though, to use revenues from the privatization of Royal Mail, the last government share of which was sold in October 2015, generating a further £591 million for the Treasury. Total proceeds from the privatization amounted to £3.3 billion from its commencement in December 2013, all of which has been earmarked to pay down national debt. As social wealth fund advocate Stewart Lansley warned: 'Sales offer a one-off windfall – the family silver can only be sold once … Although such sales can reduce the cash debt at a given moment, they aggravate the problem of public indebtedness as the asset base which helps to balance the debt shrinks away.'[31] For this reason, American activist and writer on the commons David Bollier has argued that governments should be more effective guardians and stewards of digital and intellectual collective resources, such as the airwaves, the internet commons and intellectual property. If a fair economic return was applied to these public assets, the revenues could be managed through a community fund (or what Bollier terms 'stakeholder trusts') to give ordinary citizens an equity interest in public assets.[32]

In many countries, though, it is not always clear exactly where and what public commercial assets there are in the government's portfolio. Detter and

Fölster point out that more than two-thirds of public wealth remains opaque. Many countries have not properly valued their assets. Most states lack land registries to value their land holdings or have only valued a small portion of the government-owned real estate. So, while public commercial assets are a promising potential source of sovereign wealth, there are a number of steps to conquer before they become reliable underlying finance for future SWFs.

Growth of traditional SWFs

Some of these innovative proposals may help seed new SWFs. But what hope is there for expansion of SWFs based on traditional commodities or foreign reserves? Pre-crisis estimates forecast that SWFs would have as much as $12 trillion in assets under management by 2015.[33] This has not materialized. Castelli and Tagliapietra estimated that SWFs might reach $10 trillion in 2016, though according to others this will only occur in 2018.[34] While SWF growth estimates have decreased, they still compare favourably with the prospects of other financial investors. This is partly because SWFs have weathered the financial crisis relatively well and partly because of their long-term investment horizons, which free them from present-day liabilities. For the most part, they have repeatedly shown positive growth, making it reasonable to forecast that existing SWFs will expand, albeit more modestly, in the foreseeable future.

If so, where will that occur? In the past, countries that created SWFs were those with the highest ratio of reserves to GDP, such as China, Singapore, Korea and Norway. Previous statistical analysis emphasized that countries with current account surpluses and which obtain a considerable proportion of their revenue through oil exports are more likely to set up an SWF.[35] For some years, that prediction was borne out. In the past decade, economies with current account surpluses and extensive commodity export sectors tended to be found in Asia and Africa.[36] So too are the majority of the world's new SWFs. Indeed, some of the most recently operational SWFs are African (Ghana, Angola, Nigeria, Senegal and, in the eyes of some, Rwanda).[37] Zimbabwe and Egypt formalized plans to create sovereign funds in 2014 and 2015 respectively, while another nine African countries have flagged the possibility of an SWF (Kenya, Liberia, Mozambique, Namibia, Sierra Leone, South Sudan, Tanzania, Uganda and Zambia).

However, current troubles in the commodity markets are bound to stem the growth and creation of commodity-based sovereign funds.[38]

That said, the case for new or expanding commodity-based sovereign funds cannot be fully dismissed. In their latest review of SWFs, investment industry analysts Preqin identify numerous countries establishing or looking to establish state-owned investors. One such country is Israel, which has created the Israeli Citizen Fund to safeguard revenues from windfall natural gas and expects to start operating in 2016 or 2017.[39] Moreover, although commodity prices have decreased, the number of commodity-dependent countries has risen.[40] If the current crash in commodity prices eases, and there is some recovery, we may well see a resurgence in resource-rich economies creating funds.

What of new non-commodity/reserve-surplus sovereign funds? The creation of these funds depends on the unique macroeconomic and political circumstances facing the governments and communities considering this policy move. For advanced economies such as the UK which do not enjoy a current account surplus, a more modest SWF created with one of the abovementioned sources of capital may be an appropriate vehicle for boosting investment and demand.[41] Creating an SWF could also replace quantitative easing as a strategy for avoiding secular stagnation, since the latter tends to boost consumption rather than investment.[42] In Europe, there have been calls for Germany to reduce its current account balance and alleviate the problems of the eurozone's periphery by setting up an SWF.[43] Ben Bernanke has argued that Germany's trade surplus could be reduced by investing in infrastructure through an SWF.[44] All of this suggests advanced economies with current account surpluses or which suffer from a lack of demand and domestic investment opportunities might well consider this option as a tool for helping trigger growth.

Domestic political legitimacy of SWFs

Even if the economic possibility for future SWFs endures despite the elusive growth environment, will communities want such funds under present conditions? Indeed, the domestic political legitimacy of sovereign funds is under pressure on several fronts in the changing economic environment. Sovereign funds have been accused of generating volatility, destabilizing markets as they sell off assets in response to commodity price fluctuations, and equity market shakiness.[45] At the same time, some communities are questioning why vast chunks of public wealth are quarantined in savings vehicles for the future when present coffers are so tightly squeezed. Norway has had to draw down on its vast sovereign wealth savings, but this process has been transparent, disciplined and well explained to the public. Others, like the Australia Future Fund, have been criticized for and defended against accusations of inadequately investing in domestic markets, accused of exporting vast amounts of capital offshore at a time when governments face critical infrastructure financing deficits.[46]

Such challenges will persist and increase as SWFs play increasingly important roles within their home economies, as this book encourages. This makes the democratization of SWFs even more urgent. Again, as the experience of Alaska shows, education of the public is vital. Proposals to change the use of Alaska's sovereign fund earnings have met with substantial opposition, despite the public wanting a lasting solution to their fiscal challenges *and* acceptance of the key role that the Permanent Fund's income could play in providing such a solution. More transparent SWF governance is also likely to help make earnings fluctuations easier to accept. Contrast the communication challenge facing funds in the previous decade when they sought to explain their poor returns during the global financial crisis. Comprehensive education on an SWF's role, financing and performance is even more vital in such an environment.

On the whole, there is reason to think that SWFs will expand in size, number and geographic location in the medium to long term, although not at the same dramatic pace witnessed over the past decade given the likely decrease in national wealth inflows and the effects of secular stagnation in the short term. But the macro global financial trends are all conducive to creating SWFs: the growing need for national savings in light of demographic challenges and the eroding tax base of many states; the critical need across the globe for infrastructure financing; and the increasingly volatile state of financial and commodity markets heightens the case for stabilization funds to smooth government spending in deficit years. These same challenges that motivate the necessity for sovereign funds also pose some of the biggest obstacles to raising SWF seed capital. More than ever, it is time to evolve beyond Adam Smith's eighteenth-century vision of a sovereign fund based on land and stock and innovate regarding new sources of national wealth to create community funds for the twenty-first century.

12

Transforming sovereign funds into community funds

At the heart of this book is a long-established idea whose time has come. Governments should establish wealth funds to provide an additional source of state revenue. Thinkers from Adam Smith to present-day philosophers and economists have imagined such funds with different names and in diverse forms. But too few have acknowledged that such funds already exist in the form of sovereign wealth funds, or that the money in these funds is ultimately the property of citizens, not their governments, which simply manage these funds on the citizens' behalf. Even fewer have systematically thought through what measures are needed to ensure that this capital truly constitutes citizens' wealth. This book offered such a blueprint. It argued that for citizens to properly count as owners of sovereign wealth, SWFs must be managed and used in a manner that reflects, promotes and protects the interests and values of their citizen-owners.

There is a way to go before this vision of SWFs as community funds is realized. As a first step, the widespread ambiguity surrounding the ownership status of SWFs in popular and academic discourse and within communities that create such funds demands resolution. Drawing on fiduciary theories of the state, I sought to dispel this confusion by defending a principal–agent conception of the citizen–state relationship. Such a conception implies that governments can only hold sovereign wealth, indeed all public assets, on trust for their principal, the citizenry. Although the citizen–state relationship is not a *legally* recognized fiduciary relationship in any major

jurisdiction at present, the 'deeply fiduciary'[1] character of citizen–state relations is recognized by a growing faction of public law theorists who argue
that the state's legal authority rests on fiduciary foundations and who would
support the creation of a *legal* fiduciary duty between state and citizen.[2] If
this conception of public power is legally entrenched, then fiduciary duty
would require the sole, loyal pursuit of the interests of citizen-principals by
government-managers of SWFs. The state would continue to enjoy legal
and physical possession of sovereign funds, but it would be prohibited from
ultimate ownership of their assets.

Building upon this foundation, the rest of the book sought to identify
the nature and extent of citizen-owner interests in sovereign funds. In
doing so, a core insight of ownership theory was applied: that property
rights consist of both control and benefit privileges. Therefore, citizens
must enjoy control over and benefit from their SWFs. They must do so in
the key areas in which the funds impact upon citizens domestically: in the
management, investment and distribution of sovereign wealth.

Parts II and III explored the potential for popular control and benefit
rights to sovereign wealth respectively. The overall model of citizen
ownership elaborated recommends greater democratic control over the
management and investment of sovereign funds and more direct benefit
for citizen-owners through the distribution of SWF income. In practice,
greater popular control over SWFs implies improved transparency and
citizen awareness of sovereign fund policies and more opportunity to influence their regulation, including the development and enforcement of ethical
guidelines in SWF mandates. Equally, the question of how to distribute
SWF earnings should also be put to the people as it can take a number of
forms, including cash dividends, in-kind payments, budget transfers or
community investment: I argued that there is a reason to prefer dividends
given that, of the four distribution options, they offer the strongest accountability of government-managers to citizen-owners. This mechanism
uniquely endows citizens with both a highly direct form of benefit from
sovereign fund earnings while also encouraging greater interest in and
monitoring of SWF performance by citizens. Compared to growing the
fund perpetually by reinvesting returns into the principal or transferring a
certain percentage back into the general budget, cash dividends more
directly affect citizens, giving them a stronger connection to and, it is hoped,

greater interest in their sovereign fund. In that respect, dividend distribution is more compatible with the measures recommended for improved control over sovereign funds and may even slightly reduce the need for other accountability mechanisms.

Crucially, the principal-agent framework for SWF governance and the enhanced citizen control over and benefit from sovereign wealth it demands does not automatically imply *direct* citizen management of sovereign funds. There may be occasions in more contained communities where direct democratic mechanisms are appropriate and workable. In many cases, though, sovereign funds can be more effective democratic instruments while being professionally managed by expert fund managers and still accommodate substantial citizen input into their overarching policy settings through basic accountability mechanisms. As discussed in Part II, simple measures such as public hearings with a notice and comment period on aspects of SWF regulation and investment are feasible given the established tradition of public parliamentary committee hearings in the democratic tradition on a whole host of policy issues. So, too, are referenda on questions of SWF policy of great importance. Consider that Alaska held a referendum in the 1970s on the basic question of whether to create a sovereign fund to save the state's national resources. Today, some Alaskans argue that, as their Permanent Fund and dividend face a major overhaul that could influence the state finances for many decades to come, questions of how much to save and distribute to citizens should once again be put to the people in a referendum. Such measures can produce equivalent accountability without the costs that sometimes accompany direct citizen involvement, such as common agency costs, the challenge of responding to multiple principals with different views, or insufficient expertise of the principal on more technical matters. Again, basic measures like education campaigns based around sovereign funds can help ensure that citizens are effective principals over their government agents, capable of imposing an informed and engaged general will on the state-manager of sovereign funds.

All of these recommendations were made in full awareness of their demanding and even aspirational nature. For this reason, all suggested reforms were compared to current institutional practice by sovereign funds to test for feasibility and desirability. This revealed a sizeable, although not impossibly large gap between the recommended ideal and reality. Even the best-performing funds in developed democracies – such as Norway, New Zealand and Alaska – fell short of the standard envisaged. But their exemplary performance in many respects offers hope for reform. That reform effort must be incremental and patient. If pursued, sovereign funds could transform into community funds with greatly improved potential for positive impact on the domestic citizen–state relationship.

Reforming the Santiago Principles

Initial steps in a staged reform campaign should target the Santiago Principles. As the standard-bearer for sovereign fund design and management, it is crucial that the principles be updated to reflect the core goal of SWF reform: to ensure sovereign funds are democratically controlled by and provide direct benefit to their citizen-owners within their sponsor communities. To this end, four areas of the Santiago Principles should be targeted:

Definitional reform

First and foremost, the existing definition of an SWF found in the preliminary text to the principles on their objective and purpose must explicitly identify citizen ownership of sovereign funds. The fiduciary nature of government's relationship with its citizens and how this bears on its responsibilities regarding the management of SWFs must also be plainly set out. Accordingly, the current definition of SWFs in the principles should be amended with the following deletions (~~strikethrough~~) and additions (*italicized*):

> [SWFs are] special-purpose investment funds or arrangements that are ~~owned~~ *managed* by the general government *in a fiduciary capacity as agent on behalf of their principal, the citizenry. Citizens own these funds and their underlying assets and their investment returns collectively as a people.* Created by the general government for macroeconomic purposes *that seek to enhance a community's welfare*, SWFs hold, manage, or administer *public* assets to achieve financial objectives, and employ a set of investment strategies that include investing in foreign financial assets.

This amended wording achieves two things. First, it preserves the original definition's emphatic message that SWFs are primarily *financial* entities. The initial definition sought to quell recipient countries' fears that SWFs are purely political instruments created to serve geopolitical purposes through investments. Given that distrust of these entities can produce unnecessary protectionist backlashes in the international investment landscape, the IFSWF's valuable effort to allay those fears by reiterating the funds' commercial objectives must be upheld.

The second goal of this amendment is clarificatory. As conflicts regarding the ownership status of funds persist, the revised wording seeks to dispel any ambiguity that exacerbates these tensions. By replacing the reference to government *ownership* with *management*, as well as incorporating the words 'principal' and 'agent' to describe the citizen–state relationship, the citizen ownership of sovereign wealth becomes emphatic and incontestable.

Enhanced popular control arrangements

Due to the absence of citizen-ownership ideas in the Santiago Principles, they largely omit the concept of democratic control over sovereign funds. Indeed, as noted earlier, there is a general absence of control issues from the principles.

Given my prescriptions for democratizing fund management, requiring popular influence over the setting of an SWF's objectives, shaping of the investment strategy and assessment of management's fealty to those objectives, three amendments are necessary. First, Principle 7 which stipulates that 'the owner should set the objectives of the SWF, appoint the members of its governing body(ies) in accordance with clearly defined procedures, and exercise oversight over the SWF's operations', should be amended. In the explanatory commentary to this principle, the GAPP explains that 'the owner refers to the government as the beneficial and/or the legal owner of the SWF, or assets managed by the SWF, depending on the legal structure of the SWF'.[3] This clarificatory description is now redundant in light of the new proposed definition of SWFs. Accordingly, all references to the 'owner' must distinguish between the government custodian and the citizenry owner. Principle 7 should be reworded as follows:

> The owner, *meaning the citizenry of the SWF-establishing community*, should set the objectives of the SWF, *its overarching investment policy*, appoint the members of its governing body(ies) in accordance with clearly defined procedures, and exercise oversight over the SWF's operations *through participatory democratic mechanisms.*

The explanation and commentary to this principle should be updated to clarify the objectives of this reformed principle. It should underscore that it is up to individual communities as to what participatory mechanisms are used for consulting the people and that such mechanisms may include, but are not limited to, referenda, citizen juries, citizen assemblies, deliberative polling, and direct elections in the case of the board member appointments.

Communities may also vary as to the exact content which they subject to popular determination above a certain minimum threshold. For instance, some communities may wish to precisely stipulate asset class allocation, geographic exposure and risk management strategies, whereas others may prefer to express general parameters on these issues, leaving specification of their detailed content to the SWF board and management. But the overall objective of this amended Principle 7 is that citizens must be consulted on and enjoy a degree of influence over aspects of a sovereign fund's establishment and management.

Second, as for citizens' *ongoing* ability to influence these policy parameters and assess and monitor management's performance in accordance with their popularly determined objectives, the principles that refer to public disclosure obligations must be strengthened. As noted in Chapter 4, seventeen of the twenty-four principles include a requirement for public disclosure, although none of these cover substantive issues such as the fund's investment portfolio (including size, composition, allocation, risk indicators and returns). Those aspects of a fund's behaviour are simply subject to internal accountability mechanisms such as timely, accurate and regular reporting to their government owner. *All seventeen principles* referring to disclosure requirements must be amended to make explicit that any requirements demand full public disclosure *to the citizenry* and not just internal reporting to the *government* custodian. Where there are issues of commercial confidentiality that transparency could negatively affect, these should be clearly set out in the fund's governing documents so the public and government custodian's expectations are clear.

Moreover, as Andrew Rozanov observed, 'the term "transparency" does not appear once in the actual text of the [principles]'.[4] Although the term 'transparent' does appear in the Purpose section of the principles on page 4, and appears frequently in the amplifications, the word should be formally incorporated into the actual principles alongside an explanation of its role in enhancing popular control. An obvious place for this addition is Principle 6, the first principle within the cluster of principles that address issues of 'institutional framework and governance structure':[5]

> The governance framework for the SWF should be sound and establish a clear and effective division of roles and responsibilities in order to facilitate accountability, *transparency* and operational independence in the management of the SWF to pursue its objectives.

Commentary on the principle should elaborate on the primary purpose of transparency in empowering *citizens* to exert control over their sovereign funds, since transparency serves the needs of multiple actors. This point was acknowledged in the precursor document to the Santiago Principles, *Sovereign Wealth Funds – A Work Agenda*: 'Transparency is of interest to very different groups – including the general public, markets, counterparties, recipient countries, and regulators – but their needs differ.'[6] The authors also suggest:

> The case for such a (transparency) focus is two-fold: First, clear govern-ance structures will help foster *accountability and a disciplined and stable investment policy* which reduces fiscal risk and promotes financial stability. Second, transparency contributes to the efficient allocation of resources by ensuring that *markets and the public have information* to identify risks and better assess SWF behavior.[7]

The subsequent absence of the word 'transparency' from the final set of the principles themselves is striking in contrast to this explicit acknowledgement of its importance in the predecessor document. Recent research on the negotiations over the Santiago Principles demonstrates that conflicting cultural ideas over the necessity of transparency undoubtedly contributed to the word's absence. As one Western SWF official reflected on the negotiations:

> I would say most of the concerns were about access of the local public to information. In our context, the people are the fund's owners, as well, so they need to know. In some other places, it is not very clear whether they (the people) have any right to this information . . . to what extent (local) citizens of the country have a need to know; well, there were different opinions on that.[8]

The research goes on to distinguish between the various concerns of the anti-transparency camp, contrasting Middle Eastern funds' worries regarding the local public's need to access information with the Singaporean fund's concern about the business impact of transparency on their fund's operations and returns.[9] While these differing cultural views will continue to challenge democratizing reforms to SWFs and the Santiago Principles, they also underscore how the right of citizens to control their sovereign funds was omitted from the principles, making its rectification all the more vital.

Insertion of an ethical investment obligation

Chapter 6 focused on citizen influence over the investment of sovereign wealth. Having argued against citizens directly investing fund assets, I suggested that a degree of control over investment activities could be achieved through the imposition of democratically determined ethical constraints. This could help ensure citizens' ethical integrity is shielded from undesired complicity in morally objectionable investments given the inherently coercive nature of SWF investment. I argued that governments must impose a statutory obligation on their sovereign funds to invest responsibly as part of their overarching investment mandate.

Such a requirement could be given effect by amending Santiago Principle 19 on the investment policy of sovereign funds:

> The SWF's investment decisions should aim to maximize risk-adjusted financial returns in a manner consistent with its *popularly determined*

investment policy, and based on economic and financial grounds *as well as the ethical obligations of the community.*[10]

Subprinciple 19.1 should also be amended to further explain the operation of the ethical investment obligation. This current version of the subprinciple countenances the possibility of extra-financial considerations in an SWF's investment activity, stating that if 'decisions are subject to *other than* economic and financial considerations, these should be clearly set out in the investment policy and be publicly disclosed'.[11] This subprinciple should be entirely deleted and replaced with a supporting principle that explains the nature of the compulsory ethical investment obligation, including the minimum expectation that the sovereign fund invest sustainably to ensure the protection of future citizens' interests:

> *[Proposed] Subprinciple 19.1: The statutory investment mandate of all funds must include an obligation to invest in a manner consistent with the domestic and international ethical obligations of the owner-state, the content of which should be determined in consultation with the state's citizens and be set out in Responsible Investment Guidelines supporting the mandate. At a minimum, all sovereign funds must incorporate sustainability considerations into their investment decision-making to protect the interests of future generations.*

The supporting commentary on this principle should stipulate that communities should deliberate over the precise content and nature of the ethical constraints to impose upon funds. Clearly, there will be reasonable disagreement on the content of such values within political communities, now and over time, providing even greater justification for regular public consultation on the content of a community's ethical guidelines.

Stipulation of the duty to distribute SWF returns

Part III examined popular benefit rights to sovereign fund income. Chapter 8 set out the case for individualized distribution of this investment income, canvassing the possibility of either direct cash dividends in the vein of the Alaska PFD or indirect cashless payments along the lines of the Mongolian approach.

Again, the Santiago Principles are largely silent on the question of distribution, particularly distribution of SWF investment income. The commentary on Principle 4 on 'Funding and withdrawal rules' simply requires public disclosure on these aspects of a fund's policy. In particular, Subprinciple 4.2 requires public disclosure of '[t]he general approach to withdrawals from the SWF and spending on behalf of the government'.[12] The commentary to Principle 4 observes that '[s]ome SWFs keep their capital and returns while others pay out targeted annual dividends'.[13] This deferential approach to the spending or savings preferences of individual SWFs is in violation of our demand for individualized distribution, whether direct or indirect. The whole section on funding and withdrawal rules is also deficient in terms of properly distinguishing between treatment of investment income and the general principal. As such, a new Subprinciple 4.3 should be inserted to address the treatment of SWF investment income:

> *[Proposed] Subprinciple 4.3: A portion of the income earned on the SWF's investment returns must be distributed to citizen-owners annually, either to individuals through dividends or in-kind benefits, or to the collective through budget transfers or community investment.*

The exact form and amount of the distribution should be determined by the members of respective owning communities, but within the constraint that the distribution will offer the most direct benefit to citizen-owners and the greatest accountability effects if distributed in the form of individualized cash dividends.

These, then, are the main policy implications of my model of citizen ownership and the reforms necessary to transform the Santiago Principles into a framework capable of promoting this popular ownership ideal. But moving from theory to the political practice of citizen ownership of sovereign funds is a complex task. Even if all these reforms to the Santiago Principles are heeded, there is no guarantee that the member sovereign funds which support the principles through their IFSWF membership will amend their own practices and policies in line with the reformed principles. An even trickier task would be getting the majority of sovereign funds that do not enjoy IFSWF membership and which have shown mixed interest in respecting the Santiago Principles as a blueprint for their own design and behaviour to pursue such reforms. But the perfect should not be the enemy of the good. Even partial compliance with some of these reforms will begin to transform SWFs into genuine community funds, democratically controlled by the people, for the people.

The world's sovereign wealth funds (as at April 2016)

Region	Fund name	AUM (US$bn)	Inception	Underlying asset	Regime type[1]
North America and Canada	Alaska Permanent Fund (US)	53.9	1976	Commodity (oil)	Full democracy
	Texas Permanent School Fund (US)	37.7	1854	Commodity (oil & other)	Full democracy
	New Mexico State Investment Council (US)	19.8	1958	Commodity (oil & gas)	Full democracy
	Alberta Heritage Savings Trust Fund (Canada)	17.5	1976	Commodity (oil)	Full democracy
	Permanent University Fund (US – Texas)	17.2	1876	Commodity (oil & gas)	Full democracy
	Permanent Wyoming Mineral Trust Fund (US)	5.6	1974	Commodity (minerals)	Full democracy
	North Dakota Legacy Fund (US)	3.2	2011	Commodity (oil & gas)	Full democracy
	Alabama Trust Fund (US)	2.5	1985	Commodity (oil & gas)	Full democracy
	Louisiana Education Quality Trust Fund (US)	1.3	1986	Commodity (oil & gas)	Full democracy
	West Virginia Future Fund (US – West Virginia)	n/a	2014	Commodity (oil & gas)	Full democracy

	Social and Economic Stabilization Fund (Chile)	15.2	2007	Commodity (copper)	Flawed democracy
	Fiscal Stabilization Fund (Peru)	9.2	1999	Non-commodity	Flawed democracy
	Pension Reserve Fund (Chile)	7.9	2006	Commodity (copper)	Flawed democracy
	Oil Income Stabilization Fund of Mexico[2]	6.0	2000	Commodity (oil)	Flawed democracy
South and Central America	Heritage and Stabilization Fund (Trinidad & Tobago)	5.5	2000	Commodity (oil)	Flawed democracy
	Sovereign Fund of Brazil	5.3	2008	Non-commodity	Flawed democracy
	Fondo de Ahorro de Panamá	1.2	2012	Non-commodity	Flawed democracy
	FINPRO (Bolivia)[3]	1.2	2012	Non-commodity	Hybrid regime
	FEM (Venezuela)[4]	0.8	1998	Commodity (oil)	Hybrid regime
	Fondo Mexicano del Petróleo (Mexico)[5]	n/a	2014	Commodity (oil & gas)	Flawed democracy
	Government Pension Fund Global (Norway)	824.9	1990	Commodity (oil)	Full democracy
	Reserve Fund (Russia)	65.7	2008	Commodity (oil)	Authoritarian regime
	National Welfare Fund (Russia)	73.5	2008	Commodity (oil)	Authoritarian regime
	Samruk-Kazyna JSC (Kazakhstan)	85.1	2008	Non-commodity	Authoritarian regime
	Kazakhstan National Fund	77	2000	Commodity (oil)	Authoritarian regime
	State Oil Fund (Azerbaijan)	37.3	1999	Commodity (oil)	Authoritarian regime
Europe/ Central Asia	Ireland Strategic Investment Fund[6]	23.5	2014	Non-commodity[7]	Full democracy
	Strategic Investment Fund (France)	25.5	2008	Non-commodity	Flawed democracy
	Russian Direct Investment Fund	13	2011	Non-commodity	Authoritarian regime
	Italian Strategic Fund	6.0	2011	Non-commodity	Flawed democracy
	National Investment Corporation (Kazakhstan)	2	2012	Commodity (oil)	Authoritarian regime
	Turkmenistan Stabilization Fund	n/a	2008	Commodity (oil & gas)	Authoritarian regime

	Abu Dhabi Investment Authority (UAE – Abu Dhabi)	773	1976	Commodity (oil)	Authoritarian regime
	Saudi Arabian Monetary Agency (SAMA) Foreign Holdings	632.3	1952	Commodity (oil)[8]	Authoritarian regime
	Kuwait Investment Authority	592	1953	Commodity (oil)	Authoritarian regime
	Qatar Investment Authority	256	2005	Commodity (oil & gas)	Authoritarian regime
	Investment Corporation of Dubai (UAE – Dubai)	183	2006	Non-commodity	Authoritarian regime
	Abu Dhabi Investment Council (UAE – Abu Dhabi)	110	2007	Commodity (oil)	Authoritarian regime
	International Petroleum Investment Company (UAE – Abu Dhabi)	66.3	1984	Commodity (oil)	Authoritarian regime
Middle East	Mubadala Development Company (UAE – Abu Dhabi)	66.3	2002	Commodity (oil)	Authoritarian regime
	National Development Fund of Iran	62	2011	Commodity (oil & gas)	Authoritarian regime
	Development Fund for Iraq	0.9	2003	Commodity (oil)	Hybrid regime
	Emirates Investment Authority (UAE – Federal)	15	2007	Commodity (oil)	Authoritarian regime
	State General Reserve Fund (Oman)	34	1980	Commodity (oil & gas)	Authoritarian regime
	Mumtalakat Holding Company (Bahrain)	11.1	2006	Non-commodity	Authoritarian regime
	Oman Investment Fund	6.0	2006	Commodity (oil)	Authoritarian regime
	Public Investment Fund (Saudi Arabia)	5.3	2008	Commodity (oil)	Authoritarian regime
	RAK Investment Authority (UAE – Ras Al Khaimah)	1.2	2005	Commodity (oil)	Authoritarian regime
	Palestine Investment Fund	0.8	2003	Non-commodity	Hybrid regime

	China Investment Corporation	746.7[9]	2007	Non-commodity	Authoritarian regime
	SAFE Investment Company (China)	541.9	1997	Non-commodity	Authoritarian regime
	Hong Kong Monetary Authority Investment Portfolio (China – Hong Kong)	442.4	1993	Non-commodity	Flawed democracy
	GIC Private Limited (Singapore)	344	1981	Non-commodity	Flawed democracy
	National Social Security Fund (China)	236	2000	Non-commodity	Authoritarian regime
	Temasek Holdings (Singapore)	193.6	1974	Non-commodity	Flawed democracy
	Australian Future Fund	95	2006	Non-commodity	Full democracy
	Korea Investment Corporation (South Korea)	91.8	2005	Non-commodity	Flawed democracy
	Khazanah Nasional Berhad (Malaysia)	41.6	1993	Non-commodity	Flawed democracy
East Asia and Australia	Brunei Investment Agency	40	1983	Commodity (oil)	No ranking
	New Zealand Superannuation Fund	20.2	2003	Non-commodity	Full democracy
	Timor-Leste Petroleum Fund (East Timor)	16.9	2005	Commodity (oil & gas)	Flawed democracy
	China–Africa Development Fund (China)	5.0	2007	Non-commodity	Authoritarian regime
	Revenue Equalization Reserve Fund (Kiribati)	0.6	1956	Commodity (phosphate)	No ranking
	State Capital Investment Corporation (Vietnam)	0.5	2006	Non-commodity	Authoritarian regime
	Government Investment Unit (Indonesia)	0.3[10]	2006	Non-commodity	Flawed democracy
	Western Australian Future Fund	0.3	2012	Commodity (minerals)	Full democracy
	Human Development Fund (Mongolia)[11]	0.3	2009	Commodity (minerals)	Flawed democracy
	Papua New Guinea Sovereign Wealth Fund[12]	n/a	2011	Commodity (gas)	Flawed democracy

	Libyan Investment Authority	66	2006	Commodity (oil)	Authoritarian regime
	Revenue Regulation Fund (Algeria)	50	2000	Commodity (oil & gas)	Authoritarian regime
	Pula Fund (Botswana)	5.7	1994	Commodity (diamonds & minerals)	Flawed democracy
	Fundo Soberano de Angola	5.0	2012	Commodity (oil)	Authoritarian regime
	Nigeria Sovereign Investment Authority	1.4	2012	Commodity (oil)	Hybrid regime
	Senegal FONSIS[14]	1	2012	Non-commodity	Flawed democracy
Africa[13]	Gabon Sovereign Wealth Fund	0.4	1998	Commodity (oil)	Authoritarian regime
	Ghana Petroleum Funds	0.45	2011	Commodity (oil)	Flawed democracy
	National Fund for Hydrocarbon Reserves (Mauritania)	0.3	2006	Commodity (oil & gas)	Authoritarian regime
	Fund for Future Generations (Equatorial Guinea)	0.08	2002	Commodity (oil)	Authoritarian regime
	Agaciro Development Fund (Rwanda)	0.04	2013	Non-commodity (government surplus, citizen contributions)[15]	Authoritarian regime
TOTAL	**79 funds**				

[1] Regime type was classified using the results of the Economist Intelligence Unit Democracy Index 2015. This index uses four categorizations for polities: full democracy, flawed democracy, hybrid regime and authoritarian regime. For state-based sovereign funds, I apply the federal-level regime characterization from the Democracy Index.

[2] Mexico has moved the assets of its Oil Income Stabilization Fund to set up another SWF for the country (Fondo Mexicano del Petróleo). See Preqin (2016), p. 5.

[3] FINPRO: Fondo para la Revolución Industrial Productiva (Fund for Productive Industrial Revolution).

[4] FEM: Fondo para la Estabilización Macroeconómica (Fund for Macroeconomic Stabilization).

[5] See note 2 above.

[6] Formerly National Pensions Reserve Fund, established in 2001.

[7] Funded through annual transfers of 1 per cent of GNP into SWF.

[8] These funds are managed by the Central Bank of Saudi Arabia and on certain definitions would not constitute an SWF. In April 2016, Saudi Arabia announced its intention to establish a dedicated sovereign wealth fund through an IPO of its national oil company Aramco. At the time of writing, the fund had not been legislatively created or seeded.

[9] This number is an informed estimation due to lack of public sources on SAFE's AUM.

[10] Indonesia has all but depleted its fund. See Preqin (2016), p. 5.

[11] The Human Development Fund will be abolished and replaced by the Future Heritage Fund from 2018. See p. 145.

[12] Although the SWF Institute's ranking states that the fund was created in 2011, in its country analysis it found that the SWF was still to be established. According to another report, the Parliament of Papua New Guinea only passed a law sanctioning the creation of an SWF in July 2015. See ABC (2015).

[13] This list excludes recently legislated but not yet operational sovereign funds on the African continent. In 2015, both Zimbabwe and Egypt created government investment funds. In June, Egypt's Cabinet formally approved plans to establish an SWF, and Zimbabwe gazetted its Sovereign Wealth Fund of Zimbabwe Act 2014. Egypt's fund, called Almak, will be state-owned via the National Investment Bank and plans to attract capital from Arabian sovereign funds and the Russian Direct Investment Fund for co-investment in Egypt's communications, logistics and travel sectors. This has stirred debate over whether it is best characterized as an SWF or a state-backed private equity vehicle/regional development bank. Zimbabwe, on the other hand, has created a conventional commodity-based SWF mandated to save and invest 25 per cent of the nation's annual resource royalties. While the fund's board of directors has been appointed, no assets, other than $1 million in working capital, have been entrusted to the fund.

[14] FONSIS: Fonds Souverain d'Investissements Stratégiques (Sovereign Fund for Strategic Investments).

[15] Agaciro is a highly unusual fund in that its funding source is mainly voluntary donations from Rwandan citizens at home and abroad and donations from institutional 'friends of Rwanda'. See http://www.agaciro.org/index.php?id=34. This has caused debate as to its SWF status, with some characterizing Agaciro as a diaspora or solidarity fund. In August 2015, the Rwandan government's announcement that it will contribute a portion of future resource and privatization windfalls to the fund increased its resemblance to a traditional SWF. In March 2016, Agaciro was granted associate membership of the IFSWF. See http://www.ifswf.org/blog/2016-04-04/sovereign-wealth-fund-rwanda-gains-associate-membership-ifswf.

Source: Compiled from SWF Institute (2016), fund rankings (updated April 2016) and Economist Intelligence Unit (2015) Democracy Index. Assets under management (AUM) figures are estimates.

Select sovereign wealth fund definitions

Definition (emphasis added)	SWF owner
There is no single universally accepted definition of an SWF. [In this paper,] the term "SWF" means a *government* investment vehicle which is funded by foreign exchange assets, and which manages those assets separately from the official reserves of the monetary authorities. (US Treasury, June 2007)	government (implicit)
Sovereign wealth funds – or *state* investment funds – are financial vehicles owned by *states* which hold, manage, or administer *public* funds and invest them in a wide range of assets of various kinds. Their funds are mainly derived from excess liquidity in the *public sector* stemming from *government* fiscal surpluses or from official reserves at *central banks*. (Deutsche Bank, September 2007)	state (explicit), public sector (implicit), government (implicit), central bank (implicit)
Sovereign wealth funds are usually funded by the *nation's central bank* reserves and have the objective of maximizing financial returns. (McKinsey Global Institute, October 2007)	nation (implicit), central bank (implicit)
Government-owned investment vehicles funded by foreign exchange assets. (OECD, November 2007)	government (explicit)
Separate pools of international assets owned and managed by *governments* to achieve a variety of economic and financial objectives. (Edwin M. Truman, SWF commentator at Peterson Institute, before the US House Committee on Banking, Housing, and Urban Affairs, November 2007)	government (explicit)

Pools of money derived from a *country's* reserves, which are set aside for investment purposes to benefit the *country's economy and citizens*. The funding for SWFs comes from *central bank* reserves that accumulate as a result of budget and trade surpluses, and even from revenue generated from the exports of natural resources. (Investopedia – influential industry website for Forbes Media, December 2007)	country (implicit), citizens (implicit), central bank (implicit)
An SWF is a government investment vehicle, owned by a *sovereign government*. It is managed separately from funds administrated by the sovereign government's central bank, Ministry of Finance or Treasury (because if it isn't, then other constituencies need not consider it as something different from other agencies of *state*). (Monitor Group, June 2008)[1]	government (explicit)
Sovereign wealth funds are special-purpose investment funds or arrangements that are owned by the general *government* (general government includes both central and subnational government). (International Working Group on SWFs – Santiago Principles, October 2008)	government (explicit)
A Sovereign Wealth Fund is a *state*-owned investment fund composed of financial assets such as stocks, bonds, real estate, or other financial instruments funded by foreign exchange assets. (Sovereign Wealth Fund Institute, 2008)	state (explicit)
SWFs are *government* owned and controlled (directly or indirectly) investment funds that have no outside beneficiaries or liabilities (beyond the government or the *citizenry* in abstract) and that invest their assets ... according to the interests and objectives of the *sovereign* sponsor. (Ashby Monk, Sovereign Wealth Fund commentator, May 2008)[2]	government (explicit), citizenry (implicit)

[1] Miracky et al. (2008), p. 11.
[2] Monk (2008).

Source: Most definitions are from IMF (2008), Annex II, 'Selected Definitions of SWFs', pp. 37–8, unless otherwise indicated in notes.

Truman scoreboard of sovereign wealth funds (2009–12)

TRUMAN ELEMENTS	Average sample score (%)	
	2012	2009
Category 1: Structure		
1. Is the SWF's **objective** clearly stated?	98	95
2. Is there a clear **legal framework** for the SWF?	88	83
3. Is the procedure for **changing the structure** of the SWF clear?	75	73
4. Is the **overall investment strategy** clearly stated?	76	67
5. Is the **source of the SWF's funding** clearly specified?	90	88
6. Is the nature of the subsequent **use of the principal and earnings** of the fund clearly specified?	62	56
7. Are the SWF's operations **appropriately integrated** with fiscal and monetary policies?	56	61
8. Is the SWF **separate** from the country's international reserves?	63	64
SUBTOTAL SCORES	**76**	**73**
Category 2: Governance		
9. Is the **role of the government** in setting the investment strategy of the SWF clearly established?	75	70
10. Is the **role of the governing body** of the SWF clearly established?	81	81

11. Is the **role of the managers** in executing the investment strategy clearly established?	76	74
12. Are **decisions** on **specific investments** made by the managers?	55	45
13. Does the SWF have **internal ethical standards** for its management and staff?	42	24
14. Does the SWF have in place, and make publicly available, **guidelines for corporate responsibility** that it follows?	30	13
15. Does the SWF have **ethical investment guidelines** that it follows?	25	10
SUBTOTAL SCORES	**55**	**45**
Category 3: Transparency and accountability		
Investment Strategy Implementation		
16. Do regular reports on investments by the SWF include information on the **categories** of investment?	73	67
17. Does the strategy use **benchmarks**?	52	44
18. Does the strategy use **credit ratings**?	47	40
19. Are the holders of **investment mandates** identified?	48	45
Investment Activities		
20. Do regular reports on the investments by the SWF include the **size** of the fund?	77	73
21. Do regular reports on the investments by the SWF include information on its **returns**?	59	51
22. Do regular reports on the investments by the SWF include information on the **geographic location** of investments?	47	41
23. Do regular reports on the investments by the SWF include information on **specific investments**?	35	26
24. Do regular reports on the investments by the SWF include information on the **currency composition** of investments?	41	30
Reports		
25. Does the SWF provide at least an annual report on its activities and results?	68	59
26. Does the SWF provide quarterly reports?	40	40
Audits		
27. Is the SWF subject to a regular annual audit?	72	60

28. Does the SWF publish promptly audits of its operations and accounts?	56	40
29. Are the audits independent?	70	56
SUBTOTAL SCORES:	**56**	**47**
Category 4: Behaviour		
30. Does the SWF have an operational risk management policy?	57	30
31. Does the SWF have a policy on the use of leverage?	28	16
32. Does the SWF have a policy on the use of derivatives?	41	38
33. Does the SWF have a guideline on the nature and speed of adjustment in its portfolio?	13	14
SUBTOTAL SCORES:	**35**	**24**
TOTAL SCORE:	**58**	**50**

Note: Each element is formulated as a question with a fund scoring 1 if the answer is 'yes', 0 for 'no', or partial scores of 0.25, 0.5 or 0.75 if they partially satisfy the element. For a discussion of how the Truman scoreboard has evolved since its initial survey in 2007, see Bagnall and Truman (2013), Appendix A.

Source: Bagnall and Truman (2013), Appendix B; Truman (2010), table 5.1.

ENDNOTES

Web addresses in the notes and bibliography were current as of March 2016.

1 Introduction: The Santiago dilemma

1. Moffett (2009). The following few paragraphs draw on this article unless cited otherwise.
2. Chile has two sovereign funds for the management of its copper revenues: the Pension Reserve Fund (PRF), a long-term saving fund, aimed at meeting future pension and social welfare liabilities; and the Economic and Social Stabilization Fund (ESSF), a stabilization fund, aimed at reducing the volatility of the annual fiscal process by helping overcome fiscal deficits when copper revenues decline unexpectedly.
3. Wharton Leadership Centre (2010), p. 16.
4. Moffett (2009).
5. Frankel (2012).
6. IWG (2008).
7. An exception is Fini (2011).
8. See Appendix 1.
9. Truman (2010), p. 2.
10. For an overview of nervous, early policy rhetoric around SWFs in Western economies, see Saxon (2009), pp. 699ff.
11. On SWF investment behaviour and motives, see Kotter and Lel (2011); Barbary et al. (2010); Bortolotti et al. (2009); Avendaño and Santiso (2009); Saxon (2009); Bernstein, Lerner and Schoar (2009); Keller (2009); Miracky et al. (2008); Drezner (2008); Aizenman and Glick (2008).
12. On geopolitical implications of SWFs, see Kimmitt (2008); Truman (2010); Jackson (2008); Aizenman (2007); Beck and Fidora (2008).
13. The two main international policy responses to the rise of SWFs were led by the Organisation for Economic Co-operation and Development (OECD) and the International Monetary Fund (IMF); see OECD (2008a; 2008b; 2008c). In the same year, the IMF agreed to facilitate and coordinate an International Working Group of SWFs (IWG) tasked with identifying best practices for investors and recipients of SWF capital flows. This resulted in the Santiago Principles; see IWG (2008).

14. The most high profile regulatory response occurred in the United States, where the rise of SWFs led to a Congressional hearing; see US House of Representatives Committee on Foreign Relations (2008).
15. Piketty (2014), pp. 44–5.
16. Rozanov first uses the term 'sovereign wealth fund' in a 2005 article in which he refers to these institutional investors as 'sovereign wealth managers'; see Rozanov (2005).
17. The exact number of SWFs in the world is the subject of dispute given the contested definition of 'sovereign wealth fund'. See Chapter 2 of this book and Rozanov (2011) on SWF definitional ambiguity. Appendix 1 provides an author-compiled list of SWFs based on the SWF Institute's 2016 ranking which places the current number at 78; SWF Institute (2016).
18. According to the SWF Institute, 67 per cent of extant funds have been established since the year 2000; SWF Institute (2016). A 2015 study found that '52% of sovereign funds have been in existence for less than a decade'; Preqin (2015).
19. See the SWF Institute's table 'Recent sovereign wealth fund market by size' which shows SWF assets more than doubling in just eight years from $3.5 trillion in 2007 to over $7 trillion at the end of 2015; SWF Institute (2016)
20. Farrell et al. (2007).
21. Corner House (2008), p. 4.
22. For some, the solely domestic focus of the CDC's investments and its obligation to protect struggling French companies from collapse might rule out its characterization as a 'typical' sovereign fund, although it has been described as 'arguably the oldest sovereign wealth fund in the world'; see Hall (2009).
23. As summarized by Miracky et al. (2008), pp. 14–15: 'The oldest (in Kuwait and what is now Kiribati) were set up in the 1950s to manage surplus foreign reserves and offset the eventual decline of natural resource endowments. Another wave in the 1970s and 1980s reflected a spike in energy prices and the rise of the Asian tiger economies. Large funds were established in these decades in Abu Dhabi (the first of several in the United Arab Emirates), Norway (which later converted into a pension fund), and Singapore (Temasek Holdings, 1974, and Government Investment Corporation (GIC), 1981). Another wave in the 1990s brought smaller funds in Asia, Africa, and the Middle East. The major wave, starting in 2000, has led to the formation of nearly twenty funds, most of which are funded by capital inflows based either on high energy prices (especially in the Middle East but also in Russia) or continued large trade surpluses (e.g., in China). Thus the most recent group includes not only funds originating in small, wealthy nations but also in major geopolitical powers.'
24. Holtham (1997).
25. Holtham (1997).
26. Smith (1977), p. 299.
27. Meade (1989).
28. Holtham (1999).
29. Kuttner (1998).
30. Kelly and Lissaeur (2000).
31. White (2003).
32. I believe my MPhil and doctoral theses completed between 2008 and 2013 at the University of Oxford were the first academic works to make the connection.
33. Holtham (2014)
34. Holtham (1999), p. 61.
35. Lansley (2015a; 2016).
36. O'Neill (2016).
37. See Bollier (2003) for a discussion of a variety of collectively owned resources over which there is conflict between citizens, governments and private interests for control.
38. One basis for assessing the increase in and risk of public wealth exposure to financial markets through SWFs is a comparison of sovereign wealth investment with financial

management strategies for other government investment vehicles. Clark and Monk (2012) distinguish SWFs from currency reserve funds and other 'close' cousins within government in light of their 'level of sophistication in [SWF] investment and operations typically not found within government'. That is, SWFs typically outsource to technical experts in the private sector whose greater 'sophistication' in investment style typically means riskier investment strategies.

39. Another policy area where the state has dramatically increased its exposure to financial markets is the pension system. See Blackburn (2006), esp. ch. 5 on the worrying 'financialization' of the public sector, and Blackburn (2002).

40. See Alsweilem et al. (2015), ch. 6.

41. At one extreme of the 'in-house' versus 'outsource' approach to asset management of sovereign funds is the Australian Future Fund, which is legislatively obligated to outsource 100 per cent of its asset investment. At the other extreme is the Canadian Pension Plan Investment Board which at one point managed upwards of 87 per cent of its assets in-house to save on management fees. See Monk (2011b).

42. Bernstein, Lerner and Schoar (2009) looked at the difference between politicians and external managers controlling an SWF in terms of the impact on investment strategy.

43. As Truman (2010) states, because SWFs are 'government institutions' they are 'therefore by construction … political'. This has several consequences, including 'that the boards and managers of SWFs are pressed by the general public and their political authorities to increase their financial returns and to favor certain types of investment, including in the domestic economy' (p. 40).

44. Richardson (2011), p. 2; Bolton, Samama and Stiglitz (2012), esp. chs 4 and 6; Backer (2009); Murray (2011).

45. Backer (2009).

46. The term 'institutional investor' ordinarily refers to organizations whose purpose is to invest significant pools of money on behalf of other actors. Such organizations include pension funds, mutual funds, hedge funds, investment banks, insurance companies, charitable corporations, endowments or investment trusts. They are differentiated from non-institutional investors by their large pooling of assets, longer investment horizons and market sophistication.

47. Murray (2011).

48. Murray (2011), p. 19.

49. Richardson (2011), p. 2.

50. This is today's inflation-adjusted value of the initial seed figure of $734,000. While the APF has historically earned over 10 per cent, these figures imply an annual growth of roughly 34 per cent. The discrepancy is explained if we recall that the APF is augmented each year by at least 25 per cent of Alaska's resource royalties and the unrealized returns on investments (that is, the market value of investments not yet realized). Realized earnings such as stock dividends, bond income, rent, etc., from investments are used to fund the Permanent Fund Dividend. See APFC (2016c). There were also several special appropriations by the legislature including $1.8 billion in surplus oil revenue in 1981, an additional $1.26 billion in 1986, and several hundred million dollars more in the following years; see Olson (2006), p. 165.

51. APFC (2016b).

52. See OMFIF (2016), 'Top 500 Ranking Table'.

53. Norwegian Ministry of Finance (2013), p. 2 (author-calculated currency conversion).

54. SWF Institute (2016).

55. Santiso (2008); Griffith-Jones and Ocampo (2008).

56. World Bank President Robert Zoellick has called for SWFs to direct 1 per cent of assets into investment in African private enterprises through a World Bank-managed equity fund; Zoellick (2010). This vision was partially realized through the April 2010 creation of the Africa, Latin American and Caribbean Fund, a new co-investment vehicle funded mainly from commitments by SWFs and pension funds to help strengthen the

private sector in developing countries through direct investment; Ochoa and Keenan (2011). Former British Prime Minister Gordon Brown also proposed that a mechanism be established to help direct SWF investment to developing country infrastructure; Brown (2009). The most recent advocate of SWF-financed development in poor countries is Microsoft founder Bill Gates, who proposed the creation of an infrastructure fund to be seeded with 1 per cent of SWF assets, creating initial capital of $40 billion; see Lamb (2011).

57. Keenan and Ochoa (2009); Chesterman (2008); Cummine (2014a).
58. Widerquist and Howard (2012a; 2012b); Cummine (2011a).

2 Do sovereign funds make nations richer?

1. Lansley (2015a), p. 566.
2. See HMRC (2016), table 11.11, which covers total UK oil and gas revenues between 1969 and 2014 (excluding funds from a temporary gas levy from 1981 to 1988). Contrast Weyer (2008), who estimates that the UK had received well over £200 billion in North Sea oil and gas revenues by 2008.
3. Calculations and conversions performed with data from Norwegian Ministry of Petroleum and Energy (2016).
4. Atkinson (2015), p. 176. Atkinson's calculations assume that a UK fund was established in 1968 to capture government revenues from the North Sea and only spent its real income after inflation-proofing the fund. Other estimates include that of chief economist at PricewaterhouseCoopers, John Hawksworth, who in 2008 calculated that the UK could have had a fund worth £450 billion if invested in ultra-safe assets, while Sukhdev Johal, professor of accounting at Queen Mary, University of London, thinks the total might well have been £850 billion by 2014; Chakraborrty (2014).
5. Gompertz (2012). See also Chakraborrty (2014).
6. For an account of the UK government's decisions and decision-making process, see Kemp (2008), pp. 584–600.
7. IWG (2008), p. 3, n. 7, emphasis added.
8. *BPM6* (2013), p. 115. See also IMF (2013), p. 5.
9. Note that the term 'sovereign wealth' is not defined as such in any national accounting or SWF documents.
10. We could even add to that list 'government debt', as one of the world's largest SWFs, the China Investment Corporation (CIC), was established through a bond issuance.
11. Das, Mazarei and van der Hoorn (2010), p. xv.
12. Court and McCarthy (2015).
13. Although both Mozambique and Mongolia have experienced substantial domestic delays and recent obstacles in their resource projects.
14. See Alsweilem et al. (2015), ch. 2.
15. Piketty's data for the most recent forty years (1970–2010) is drawn from the United Nations System of National Accounts and supplemented with the author's own sources; Piketty and Zucman (2015), p. 1308.
16. The rest of this section draws on Piketty (2014), pp. 47–9; see p. 48.
17. Piketty (2014), p. 48.
18. It is worth noting that the UN SNA definitions and accounting principles are adopted by the IMF, the European Commission, the OECD and the World Bank. If the UN SNA defines something in a particular way, then that means that all major economic data are defined in that particular way.
19. UN Statistics Division (2003). See also 'Net worth of the total economy', in Eurostat (1996), p. 195 at 8.99, and Bloem, Dippelsman and Maehle (2001), ch. 4.
20. The approaches of the UN and Piketty may produce different readings of national wealth, however. Although the definitions used by Piketty and in international accounting conventions are formally equivalent (because Piketty adopts the SNA

conventions explicitly), there is a difference between how the two measure national wealth: the SNA measures national wealth in terms of book value, whereas Piketty measures it in terms of market value. For a discussion, see Piketty and Zucman (2013), section A.4.2.

21. Piketty (2014), p. 123.
22. Piketty (2014), p. 48.
23. Compare SNA (2008), p. 439.
24. SNA (2008), p. 124.
25. Note also that central bank reserves are a separate type of financial asset of the government to sovereign wealth, even though some SWFs are established with foreign reserves. Reserve assets are shown separately in national accounts from other financial assets because they serve a different function and require a distinct, more conservative type of management that prioritizes safety and liquidity. Official reserves are charged with the special responsibility of meeting balance of payments financing needs and undertaking market intervention to influence the exchange rate. See *BPM6* (2013), p. 111. This is identical to the definition in the UN's SNA (2008), p. 494, and IMF (2013), p. 3.
26. Detter and Fölster (2015), p. 3.
27. Such work is currently being undertaken by the IMF through the Government Finance Statistics Advisory Committee; see IMF (2015a).
28. Such countries deem themselves to have surpassed 'reserve adequacy' and to hold 'excess reserves'. The precise definition and measurement of both concepts are contested, but a basic idea of reserve adequacy requires a central bank to hold sufficient assets to back its domestic currency supply and financial system, cover the cost of imports for a minimum period (typically six months) and pay short-term debt; see Alsweilem et al. (2015). Where reserves exceed these minimum levels, a government may choose to carve out a portion of its 'surplus' foreign reserve holdings and allocate them to an investment vehicle seeking a higher return, like a sovereign fund with a longer term investment horizon and higher risk tolerance. Some countries count such sovereign wealth funds as part of their official reserve assets, but this is discouraged by the Santiago Principles.
29. Such as Norway's fund.
30. Such as Temasek and, in part, Australia's Future Fund.
31. Such as China's CIC.
32. Bremer, Ploeg and Wills (2015).
33. John Hawksworth, 'Dude, Where's My Oil Money?', quoted in Chakraborrty (2014).
34. Wren-Lewis (2013).
35. John Hawksworth, 'Dude, Where's My Oil Money?', quoted in Chakraborrty (2014).
36. Wren-Lewis (2013); see also Carlin and Soskice (2006), pp. 206–9.
37. Chakraborrty (2014).
38. Weyer (2008).
39. Carlin and Soskice (2006), p. 222 and also p. 180.
40. Wren-Lewis (2013).
41. See, for instance, Alsweilem et al. (2015).

3 Whose wealth is it: state's or citizens'?

1. *Greisen v United States*, 831. F. 2d 916, 918 (9th Cir), *cert. denied*, *Beattie v. United States*, 485 U.S. 1006 (1988), para. 11.
2. See http://www.apfc.org/home/Content/dividend/dividendamounts.cfm. This figure only calculates total PFD payments and does not include the one-time special resource rebate of $1,200 per person paid in 2008.
3. Rose and Wohlforth (2008), p. 169.
4. All figures cited in this paragraph are drawn from Knapp (2016). Note that Alaska's fiscal year runs from 1 July 2015 to 30 June 2016.
5. Truman (2010), p. 9.

6. Rozanov (2011), p. 249; Yi-chong (2010), p. 3; Balding (2012), pp. 17–18.
7. Rozanov (2011), p. 251; Balding (2012), p. 15.
8. Murray (2011), p. 2.
9. Keenan (2009), pp. 432–3; Gelpern (2011).
10. Keenan (2009).
11. Gelpern (2011) made a similar observation: definitional disagreements 'reflect the competing interests of the definitions' proponents . . . [E]arly "definers" fell roughly into three groups: market actors whose business was affected by the rise of SWFs; host country governments managing the political fall-out from SWF investments; and academic and civil society observers engaged in policy advocacy. The three groups used the term "sovereign" differently' (pp. 292–3).
12. See Miller (1995), where he argues that despite their superficial conflation, these two terms must be thought of distinctly, with 'nation' referring to a community of people with an aspiration to be politically self-determining, and 'state' meaning a set of political institutions that a people may aspire to possess for themselves (p. 19).
13. Again following Miller's notion of a nation, this clearly can be distinguished from the general understanding of a 'country' as a legally defined territorial entity, yet both are regularly conflated.
14. Steinberger (2004), at pp. 8–13, shows that in both historical and contemporary political discourse, 'state' operates with different meanings, one of which is 'government' as the apparatus of rule. On the ambiguity surrounding the idea of the modern state, see Pierson (2004), esp. ch. 1.
15. See Habermas (1994), who discusses the blurred line between 'the state' and 'the people' on certain conceptions of democracy. See also Pierson (2004), esp. ch. 3 on the distinction between state and society.
16. Balding (2012), p. 19.
17. According to the Economist Intelligence Unit Democracy Index 2015, China and Libya are 'authoritarian regimes', Nigeria is a 'hybrid regime' while Ireland and Australia are both 'full democracies'; see Economist Intelligence Unit (2015), table 2.
18. Irish Times (2015).
19. The Governor's office conducted a three-day workshop on 'Building a Sustainable Future: Conversations with Alaskans' on 5–7 June 2015 during which Alaska's citizens' views were sought on key questions around the reforms, and strategies were developed to take the conversation out to the rest of the state; see http://gov.alaska.gov/Walker_media/documents/20150606_fiscal-stability-conf-design.pdf; and http://gov.alaska.gov/Walker/priorities/new-sustainable-alaska-plan.html.
20. See http://gov.alaska.gov/Walker/priorities/transition-2014/sustainable-future/the-conversation.html#swf.
21. See http://plan4alaska.com.
22. See http://akcommonground.org/programs/video-from-alaskas-fiscal-future-forum/.
23. In the bill, the Preamble refers to the reliance of the 'Nigerian State' on the country's hydrocarbon resources. It is the only time the word 'state' features in the bill, but its presence suggests a conception of at least three different entities with a relationship to the SWF – government, state and people. See NSIF (2010), p. 1.
24. NSIF (2010), para. 3(1)(a).
25. NSIF (2010), para. 29(2).
26. NSIF (2010), para. 29(2).
27. The Fund's tripartite structure also reinforces the Nigerian people's ultimate ownership claim. The Nigeria Infrastructure Fund aims to generate returns on investment in basic infrastructure; the Future Generations Fund involves a rolling five-year investment plan meant to provide future generations with a solid savings base after the exhaustion of the hydrocarbon reserves; and the Stabilisation Fund provides a last-resort source of financing for budget deficits caused by weaker-than-expected commodity prices, affirming current and future Nigerians as the intended beneficiaries.

28. Only four months earlier, the state governors agreed along with all other stakeholders in Nigeria's federal government to allocate a portion of their oil revenues to the new fund. In return, the Governor secured a concession that saw them all become members of the NSIA's Board of Governors; Omachonu (2011).

29. Monk (2011a).

30. Ajayi and Olaleye (2011), emphasis added.

31. The NSIA's predecessor, the Excess Crude Account, was widely recognized as a corrupt, dysfunctional fund, which motivated the need for a proper SWF to manage resource windfalls; Ndanusa (2012).

32. The overall process was very slow due to internal government discord, taking more than fifteen months from when the NSIA Act was signed into law to the unveiling of the board in August 2012.

33. Hutchens (2011a; 2011b); Uren (2011a; 2011b).

34. As Peter Costello, the former federal Treasurer, observed of the Australian SWF debate: 'All of a sudden everyone has a view on whether Australia should establish a sovereign wealth fund ... So it may come as a surprise as you look down the membership of the International Forum [of Sovereign Wealth Funds] to see Australia is listed there. Not only does Australia have a sovereign wealth fund, its fund is so respected that an Australian – the former Commonwealth Bank chief David Murray – was the first chairman of the International Forum'; Costello (2011).

35. Costello (2011), emphasis added.

36. Cummine (2011b).

37. Ironically, '[s]upporters of a sovereign wealth fund say the Future Fund is not a true sovereign wealth fund because it exists solely to fund pension liabilities for public servants'; Colquhoun (2011).

38. See NPRF Commission (2013), p. 6.

39. Investment of the National Pensions Reserve Fund and Miscellaneous Provisions Act 2009 requires the NPRF to invest in certain nominated credit institutions, as directed by the Minister for Finance. The Credit Institutions (Stabilisation) Act 2010 provides for the Minister for Finance to direct the NPRF 'to invest in Irish Government securities' and 'to make payments directly to the Exchequer in the (financial) years 2011, 2012 or 2013 ... in the interests of funding capital expenditure'; NPRF Commission (2013), pp. 6–7.

40. See the Investment of the National Pensions Reserve Fund and Miscellaneous Provisions Act 2009, section 8, at http://www.irishstatutebook.ie/eli/2009/act/7/enacted/en/pdf.

41. Reeves (2010); Slattery (2010).

42. Slattery (2010).

43. See rankings in SWF Institute (2016); ESADEgeo (2015); and the Institutional Investor Sovereign Wealth Center Fund profiles at http://www.sovereignwealthcenter.com/fund-profiles.html.

44. IMF IFS (2015), showing total reserves for 2015, excluding gold (end Dec.).

45. Eaton and Ming (2010).

46. Cummine (forthcoming).

47. Koch-Weser and Haacke (2013), p. 17.

48. Cummine (forthcoming).

49. Liew and He (2010), p. 26.

50. Cummine (forthcoming)

51. Koch-Weser and Haacke (2013), p. 17.

52. Newell (2015).

53. UN Security Council Resolution 1973 (2011), paras 19–21.

54. UN Security Council Resolution 1973, Annex I.

55. UN Security Council Resolution 1973, p. 8.

56. IWG (2008), p. 3.

57. 'The LIA . . . is mandated to manage the financial assets allocated to it by the State.' It aims to provide world class investment management 'for the benefit of the Libyan State' and 'was set up to directly finance domestic infrastructure investments or other public goods or services'; IWG (2008), pp. 39 and 14n respectively.

58. The LIA's mandate is self-described as 'investment management for the benefit of the Libyan state and the long-term future and well-being of its citizens'; IWG (2008), p. 39.

59. Consider this BBC Radio 4 report citing evidence that the LIA was under the direct personal control of Muammar Gaddafi's son, Saif al-Islam: 'The fund is very much the private preserve of the Gaddafi family . . . Saif had no official position, but everybody knew that the LIA is Saif's baby'; Miles (2011a; 2011b). See also Thomas (2011).

60. Behrendt and Sharp (2011), p. 9.

61. Behrendt and Sharp (2011), p. 16. Although some have flagged a more strategic rationale behind asset freezing as a way to draw the Libyan people's attention to the misuse of their assets; Truman (2011).

62. UN Security Council Resolution 1973, p. 5, para. 20.

63. This process commenced with international recognition of a Libya-based National Transitional Council (NTC), a rebel leadership group that fought to oust Gaddafi. World leaders agreed to release $15 billion in frozen assets to those leaders. However, the failure of the NTC to impose order led to a handover of power to the General National Congress in 2012, replaced by a new parliament in 2014 and a preservation of the asset freeze. In March 2016, a new UN-backed 'unity' government was installed in a naval base in Tripoli following a UN-brokered peace deal in October 2015. The new government faces opposition from two rival governments within Libya and their associated investment authorities.

64. For accounts of the competing claims of Breish and Bouhadi to the LIA chairmanship, see Wright (2015a; 2015b).

65. Balzan (2016).

66. There is an analogy here to the public international law doctrine of 'state succession' under which successor governments and their citizens inherit the debts accumulated by predecessor governments: the debts are 'legally glued to the territory, notwithstanding changes of government (constitutional or extraconstitutional), a churning population, or even the disintegration of the state itself'; Buchheit, Mitu Galati and Thompson (2007).

67. BBC (2015a).

68. IWG (2008).

69. According to Yi-chong (2010), '[t]hese definitions suggest that SWFs are a heterogeneous group of funds that share one key feature – government ownership' (p. 4). Rozanov (2011) also supports the development of the IFSWF as driving consensus (p. 256). Evidence of government ownership taking hold in more recent accounts of SWFs can be found in Truman (2010), p. 10; Clark, Dixon and Monk (2013); Bolton, Samama and Stiglitz (2012); Dixon and Monk (2012), p. 105.

70. Reeve (1986), pp. 30–2, 35. Using the label 'public ownership' is not a straightforward move given that some theorists deny this is even a plausible concept. Hannah Arendt (1958) holds that the idea of ownership belongs exclusively to private property since 'the public' cannot exercise ownership rights in any way similar to that of an individual (pp. 256–7).

71. Munzer (1990), p. 25.

72. Reeve (1986), p. 30.

73. Again, see Steinberger (2004), at pp. 8–13, on the historical conflation of 'state' and 'government'.

74. Laslett (1988), p. 367. Although Gough (1973) notes, 'not all commentators on Locke have fully appreciated the implications of his use of [the trust concept], and some have treated it as merely a variety of the theory of contract' (p. 155).

75. For a recent, fully developed fiduciary theory of the state, see Fox-Decent (2011). See also Criddle (2010); Fox-Decent and Criddle (2009); Criddle and Fox-Decent (2009); Criddle (2006); Fox-Decent (2005).
75. The term is Gough's in Gough (1973).
77. Gough (1973); Maitland (1911), p. 403.
78. The dominance of contract as an analytical device in contemporary political philosophy is evident in the theoretical importance of political and moral contractarianism; see Cudd (2008).
79. Both legal and political theorists have observed the historical importance of the trust concept in their respective fields. Purdy and Fielding (2007) note the recent obscurity of private law concepts like trust, agency and wardship in international public law despite their historical centrality in jurisprudential thinking (p. 166). See also Finn (1995). In political thought, John Dunn (1984) argues that 'the attempt to think comprehensively about this conception (of trust in politics) has essentially disappeared from modern political philosophy, both in its Marxist and in its liberal or conservative variants' (p. 279).
80. Birks (2000), p. 8.
81. Fox-Decent (2011), p. 93.
82. Fox-Decent and Criddle (2009), p. 311; see also Fox-Decent (2011), pp. 93–4.
83. Fox-Decent and Criddle (2009), p. 311.
84. Criddle (2010); Fox-Decent and Criddle (2009); Criddle and Fox-Decent (2009); Fox-Decent (2005).
85. The fiduciary concept has been applied to sovereign debt – see Oyola and Sudreau (2013). See also Hebb et al. (2016), ch. 50 on 'fiduciary finance'.
86. In 2012, Rwanda established a sovereign fund, the Agaciro Development Fund (AgDF), as a 'Corporate Trust owned by Rwandan people with governance structure, accountability and transparency mechanisms that adhere to international standards common to all Sovereign Wealth Funds ... The legal personality of the Agaciro Development Fund is that of a Trust with the citizens of Rwanda as its beneficiaries.' See http://www.ifswf.org/members/rwanda. However, AgDF is not a straightforward precedent for my fiduciary ownership framework of sovereign wealth since the bulk of its assets are generated through voluntary donations from Rwandan citizens. See http://www.agaciro.org/index.php?id=39].
87. Slattery (2010).

4 The Tsipras point: control of and benefit from community wealth

1. Mandravelis (2015).
2. Rankin and Smith (2015).
3. In addition to the literature cited in the discussion of the Santiago Principles below, see also Truman (2010), pp. 40–4; Backer (2010); Reed (2009); Feng (2009).
4. Truman (2010), p. 2; Nystuen, Follesdal and Mestad (2011), p. 5.
5. See for instance Bortolotti et al. (2009) and Miracky et al. (2008), both of which assemble longitudinal datasets of SWF investments over the past twenty years to determine whether SWFs take controlling or majority controlling stakes.
6. As Rose (2008) observes: 'Anxious to avoid a political backlash, SWFs have attempted to assure recipient nations that their motives are purely commercial. Thus, the funds intentionally structure their transactions so that they do not acquire a controlling interest in the portfolio firm. Such structures are also designed to avoid adverse regulatory consequences ... [Yet] [w]hile SWFs may not acquire control under the various applicable statutes, they could nonetheless exercise considerable power in the murkier realm of shareholder influence' (pp. 105–6).
7. For attempts to determine SWF investment motives, see Avendaño and Santiso (2009); Blanchard (2011); Raphaeli and Gersten (2008); Reed (2009); Saxon (2009); Gilson and Milhaupt (2008); Kimmitt (2008).
8. See OECD (2009), p. 8; OECD (2010).

9. The Generally Accepted Principles and Practices (GAPP) – the 'Santiago Principles' – in IWG (2008) defines its purpose as increasing the understanding of SWFs in 'home and recipient countries and the international financial markets' (p. 4). This is occasionally linked to the need for greater accountability within a home state, for instance in Subprinciple 1.1 (pp. 11–12).

10. Certain principles refer indirectly to the concept of control. These are Principle 2 and Subprinciple 22.1. Principle 2 requires that the policy purpose of an SWF should be 'clearly defined and publicly disclosed' and explains that excess reserve management is a possible policy purpose. Such assets, it explains, are 'readily available to and controlled by' monetary authorities. Apart from this, the issue of who controls SWF assets is not addressed; IWG (2008), p. 13. Subprinciple 22.1 discusses the need for appropriate control mechanisms as part of risk management. This addresses standard best-practice institutional design, but fails to address who *should* control SWFs; see IWG (2008), p. 15.

11. See Truman (2010), pp. 124–36; Rozanov (2011), p. 261.

12. Rozanov (2011), p. 261.

13. Truman (2010), p. 125.

14. Truman (2010), p. 125.

15. See, for instance, Chesterman (2008) and Velculescu (2008).

16. An exception is Clark and Monk (2010a), who argue that Norway's ethical investment mandate 'transgresses' investment best practice, but still acts as a source of political legitimacy; see also Clark and Monk (2010b). That said, neither article addresses the unique status of *government* investors triggering specific ethical duties.

17. Consider Beck and Fidora (2008) who examined twenty-eight divestments by the Norwegian GPFG in compliance with its ethical investment policy and found no impact on the divested company's stock price (although this is just one outcome sought by ethical investment).

18. IWG (2008), p. 8.

19. IWG (2008), p. 8.

20. 'Some SWFs may exclude certain investments for various reasons, including legally binding international sanctions and social, ethical, or religious reasons (e.g., Kuwait, New Zealand and Norway). More broadly, some SWFs may address social, environmental, or other factors in their investment policy. If so, these reasons and factors should be publicly disclosed'; IWG (2008), p. 22.

21. Murray (2011).

22. Research by Backer (2009) lays a useful foundation by examining how the pursuit of ethical investment by the GPFG challenges the boundaries between public and private responsibility for social and environmental standards, but Backer does not address whether SWFs *should* act in a unique way by virtue of their novel hybrid status in financial markets.

23. Das et al. (2009); Das, Mazarei and van der Hoorn (2010).

24. See, for instance, Dixon and Monk (2011); Gould (2010); Frankel (2010); Davis et al. (2003).

25. Hammer, Kunzel and Petrova (2008).

26. Preqin (2016), p. 5, fig. 1.1.

27. See, for instance, Lansley (2016) and Flomenhoft (2012).

28. Several articles have also pointed to the political (contra policy) purposes SWFs serve in their home states. Hatton and Pistor (2011) have argued that sovereign funds are 'autonomy-maximizing institutions' in which 'ruling elite[s] utilize SWFs to secure their domestic political dominance against both internal and external threats'. Clark, Dixon and Monk (2013) argue that SWFs act 'as a buffer against the risks to autonomy and sovereignty in a global economy' (p. 27).

29. Author interview with SWF officials (2010).

30. IWG (2008), p. 14.

31. IWG (2008), p. 14.

32. IWG (2008), p. 14.
33. See Caney (2006).
34. Pogge (2002) proposes the establishment of a global fund financed by a Global Resources Dividend, a 1 per cent payment on a nation's consumption of resources accumulated in a global fund for the relief of poverty suffered among the world's worst off.
35. Cummine (2014b).
36. Although the valuations of SWF assets of around US$6 trillion are still dwarfed by the holdings of public and private pension funds, even lower SWF estimates still eclipse the US$2.1 trillion in global hedge funds and match those of private equity; Adamson (2012a) and Preqin (2016).

5 No accumulation without representation!

1. BBC (2015b).
2. Fidor, at https://www.fidorbank.uk/about-fidor/about-us#portrait.
3. BBC (2015b)
4. Barber (2015).
5. Property theorists often point to the strict views of legal commentators such as Sir William Blackstone and John Austin as evidence of the 'control' or 'dominium-centred' idea of property. Consider Blackstone's eighteenth-century articulation of property as 'that sole and despotic dominion which one man claims and exercises over the external things of the world, in total exclusion of the right of any other individual in the universe', or John Austin's description of property as 'a right . . . unrestricted in point of disposition – and unlimited in point of duration – over a determinate thing'; see Waldron (2004) and Christman (1994), p. 18.
6. Christman (1991), p. 29.
7. Honore (1961).
8. See, for instance, Barro (1973); Ferejohn (1986); Manin (1997), pp. 170–5; Maskin and Tirole (2004); Fearon (1999); Estlund (2008); Pettit (2012), esp. pp. 153–79.
9. Pettit (2012).
10. Pettit (2012), p. 187.
11. Pettit (2012), p. 241.
12. Pettit (2008), p. 47.
13. Pettit (2012), p. 239.
14. Pettit (2012), p. 243.
15. Pettit (2012), pp. 244–5.
16. Pettit (2012), p. 245.
17. Pettit (2012), p. 249.
18. These provisions could include a requirement that the committee adopt rule-of-law rulings, record its proposals, give members time to object, declare conflicts of interest, submit performance to independent audit and include arrangements for adjudicating and disciplining the committee representatives when there is a breach; see Pettit (2008), pp. 52–3.
19. Papua New Guinea Treasury (2013).
20. Pettit (2008), p. 54.
21. Pettit (2012), p. 259.
22. Backer (2009), p. 182, emphasis added.
23. Not all sovereign funds will precisely emulate this tripartite structure of government-owner/fund board/operational management, but it is recognized as the preferable structure for SWFs, with the Santiago Principles designed on the assumption of this 'arm's-length' distance from government; IWG (2008).
24. Including formulation of the portfolio design, investment strategy, risk framework and performance benchmark; reasons for the selection or termination of investment

managers; the substance of board meetings; the appointment of board members; portfolio exposure (what assets does the fund hold, and where?) and portfolio performance.

25. Skancke (2008), p. 6.
26. Skancke (2008).
27. See Fung (2004; 2006; 2007).
28. Not all sovereign funds follow this approach and some do allow government members on the board or governing body, often the Treasurer or Finance Minister: see Alsweilem (2015), pp. 105–10. These idiosyncrasies aside, the recommended governance approach by the Santiago Principles is for arm's-length management.
29. Board management is to 'implement the SWF[s'] strategies in an independent manner' so as to 'enhance confidence in recipient countries' by ensuring 'that managers' individual investment decisions to implement the SWF's defined strategy [are] *protected* from undue and direct political interference and influence'; IWG (2008), emphasis added.
30. For instance, the board of Papua New Guinea's newly created SWF must consist of non-political appointments, with the seven-member board consisting of a chair (a PNG citizen from the private sector), another five private sector citizens and the Secretary of the Treasury, ex officio; see Papua New Guinea Treasury (2011). The criteria for board appointment is that a potential member be a person of integrity, independence of mind and good reputation, with substantial experience or expertise, professional credibility and significant standing in at least one of the following: investing in financial assets; the management of investments in financial assets; or corporate governance. Board appointments to the Australian Future Fund, South Korea's KIC and the NZSF have similar minimum competency requirements for board members. See Alsweilem (2015), p. 109.
31. Blackburn (1999), p. 63: 'The ideas I have expounded above amount to arguing that workers should, collectively, take over capitalist institutions and run them. I myself believe that such a profound, if also curious, alteration in property relations almost certainly could not be sustained without provoking a fundamental rupture with the capitalist integument.'
32. BBC (2016). In London, the PCC role is taken on by the elected Mayor.
33. Electoral Commission (2016). Other eligibility criteria also include disqualifications, such as bankruptcy and being a police officer.
34. Electoral Commission (2016).
35. BBC (2016).
36. Clark and Monk (2010b), p. 1725.
37. Sunstein (2005); also Sunstein (2002), at pp. 28–52, where he argues that citizens have limited reasoning capabilities due to distorted perceptions of risk, justifying the limitation of the general public's participation in regulation on risk.
38. Research into the performance of citizen trustees on UK pension fund boards in investment decision-making revealed their skills 'were little better than the skills of neophytes'; Clark and Monk (2010b), p. 1725. For an analysis of the original data, see Clark, Caerlewy-Smith and Marshall (2007).
39. Clark and Monk (2010a), p. 15.
40. Clark and Monk (2010b), p. 1726.
41. See Farrell (2012), table 2, where the author identifies six 'people's conventions' of the modern era that took place between 1998 and 2013 on questions of electoral or constitutional reform. Farrell observes that, for the most part, 'the outcome of the deliberations is generally clear' (p. 9).
42. Fung (2012), p. 619.
43. Fung (2012), p. 615.
44. Fishkin (1995), p. 162.
45. Fishkin (1995), pp. 165–8.
46. Similar evidence emerged from the Australian Constitutional Convention in 1998, a forum of 114 citizens and 38 politicians selected to debate different republican models in a week-long convention on the future of constitutional monarchy in Australia. Evidence of the pre- and post-convention attitudes of citizens revealed that when the

convention 'sample became more informed and really discussed the issues, it changed its voting intentions significantly'; Fishkin (2009), p. 8.

47. Harvard Law Review (2011), p. 589.
48. Harvard Law Review (2011), p. 589.
49. Harvard Law Review (2011), p. 594.
50. Truman (2010).

6 Dirty money: generating sovereign wealth ethically

1. Quoted in Thieberger (2015).
2. Di Natale (2012).
3. Bloomberg News (2011). According to Yeates (2012), Greens Senator Richard Di Natale argues that it is 'completely inconsistent for the government to fight big tobacco with "courageous" plain packaging laws, and "then on the other hand to be investing $147 million in large multinationals who make the stuff"'.
4. Yeates (2012).
5. Future Fund (2013).
6. New York Times (2015).
7. Thieberger (2015); Gluyas (2015).
8. The separate but related ethical question of how a community should accumulate the seed capital for an SWF falls outside the scope of this discussion. Here I focus on what can be done to secure citizen control over the investment activities of an already established sovereign fund, irrespective of the origin of the underlying fund assets. I assume for the purposes of the discussion that a community has reflected on its decision to set up an SWF, weighing up the moral trade-offs of generating returns on, for instance, fossil fuels or from privatizing state assets. These are important questions that deserve treatment elsewhere.
9. See Cummine (2014a).
10. Richardson (2011).
11. In February 2012, PNG's parliament unanimously voted to create a sovereign wealth fund to manage its anticipated resource revenues from a new gas project being championed by ExxonMobil. The project seeks to realize the potential of three large gas discoveries in the southern and western highlands of the country. The integrated project includes gas production, processing and liquefaction facilities, as well as offshore and onshore pipelines; see PNG Post-Courier (2012). The SWF's founding law sets out the investment mandate which requires the fund to develop ethical investment guidelines for 'avoiding prejudice to Papua New Guinea's reputation as a responsible member of the world community'. This wording is identical to that of the NZSF's 'responsible investor' clause. See Papua New Guinea Treasury (2011): Organic Law on the Sovereign Wealth Fund, section 7.2(c), p. 4.
12. Rigorous data in this area are difficult to source. This estimate of ad hoc ethical investment obligations is based on the author's reconciliation of two different surveys of responsible investment among SWFs and institutional investors. As these studies cover distinct sample sets and do not fully disclose their methodology for what counts as a sovereign fund *or* ethical obligations, consistency across surveys is problematic. For example, the 2010 Truman Scoreboard finds that of fifty-three government investment funds surveyed, fourteen SWFs had explicit ethical investment guidelines; Truman (2010). In contrast, the 2012 Future Fund Senate submission which reviewed twenty-two 'select' sovereign wealth and pension funds identified the use of exclusions by eleven funds and human rights obligations in operational behaviour within four funds. Personal interview with Future Fund representative (2012). The figure of eighteen funds here comes from reconciling these two surveys and accounting for overlap between funds.
13. The UNPRI is a 2006 initiative by UN Secretary-General Kofi Annan to encourage an international network of investors to put six voluntary and aspirational responsible

investment principles into practice. As of July 2015, there were more than 1,400 signatories from over fifty countries representing US$59 trillion of assets; UNPRI (2015), p. 2.

14. This observation is supported by the 2016 findings of the Asset Owners Disclosure Project, which rates the world's 500 largest asset owners, including sovereign funds, pension funds and insurers, on the extent to which they protect their members from the risks of climate change through their investment activities. SWFs generally perform poorly in the ratings. See Mooney (2016).

15. Backer (2009), pp. 181–2, emphasis added.

16. Kutz (2011), p. 72.

17. On the possibility of assigning responsibility for past injustices to associations rather than the conventional candidates of states, nations or individuals, see Kukathas (2003).

18. Kutz (2011), p. 72.

19. Miller (2007) makes a similar inseparability argument about benefits and burdens in relation to nations inheriting responsibility for past wrongs, observing: 'One cannot legitimately enjoy such benefits [of nationhood] without at the same time acknowledging responsibility for aspects of the national past that have involved the unjust treatment of people inside or outside the national community itself, and liability to provide redress in whatever form the particular circumstances demand' (p. 136, see also pp. 148–51).

20. Kutz (2011), p. 73.

21. New Zealand Superannuation and Retirement Income Act 2001, section 58(2); NZSF (2016a).

22. NZSF (2015a), p. 3.

23. Brundige et al. (2004).

24. The GPFG was instructed by the Council of Ethics to divest its Freeport holdings in 2006 and its Rio Tinto holdings in 2008 on the basis of severe environmental damage caused by the Grasberg mine and the absence of any evidence to suggest that company practices would change; see Norwegian Ministry of Finance (2008a).

25. Abplanalp (2011), p. 41.

26. In October 2011, Indonesian police killed two unarmed striking miners. Strong evidence continued to emerge of corrupt payments to the Indonesian military to facilitate the mining project; Abplanalp (2011).

27. Norwegian Ministry of Finance (2008a).

28. NZSF (2011a).

29. For a discussion on the efficacy of engagement versus exclusion as an RI strategy for SWFs, see Demeyere (2011).

30. Abplanalp (2011), p. 39

31. Quoted in Abplanalp (2011), p. 40.

32. NZSF (2011a), p. 2.

33. NZSF (2012b).

34. Murray (2011), p. 14.

35. Clark and Monk (2010a), at pp. 14–15, have argued that the ethical investment mandate of Norway's GPFG 'actually constrains the fund's functional efficiency' and that 'prioritizing ethics over efficiency may be self-defeating in the long term if it is associated with substandard performance'.

36. Murray (2011), pp. 19–20, emphasis added.

37. Clark and Knight (2011), p. 337. On the unique nature of SWF liabilities, see Rozanov (2011), pp. 253–4. Rozanov expressly distinguishes his typology of SWF liabilities from individual or employer-funded pension fund liabilities (p. 252).

38. The board members of both the Australian and New Zealand sovereign funds are called 'Guardians' as opposed to trustees, the title commonly used for governing members of pension funds. Richardson (2011) notes that in New Zealand, the fund's establishing legislation explicitly declares that the Guardians 'are not a trustee', the purpose of which he suggests 'is to avoid implying any common law fiduciary standards in the manage-

ment of the Fund, and to limit its governance strictly to the terms of the enabling legislation' (p. 17). Clark and Knight (2011) interpret the Australian decision differently, arguing that the 'choice made by the government to label board members "guardians" rather than "trustees"' reflects the government's desire 'to invest the role of its guardians with a higher purpose than that attributed to pension fund trustees' (p. 348).

39. Woods and Urwin (2010), p. 10.
40. Clark and Knight (2011), at p. 345, found evidence of a link between 'the apparent goal of fiscal sustainability ... and the "wellbeing of successive generations"' justifying the establishment of the Australian Future Fund.
41. See, for instance, Grosseries (2001).
42. Brown Weiss (1990), pp. 202–4. For a more general discussion, see Brown Weiss (1989).
43. See Hebb et al. (2016), chs 32 and 46.
44. For some useful attempts to map the diversity of conceptions of sustainability and sustainable development, see Dobson (1999) and Connelly (2007).
45. Woods and Urwin (2010), p. 2.
46. Government Investment Funds Amendment (Ethical Investments) Bill 2011, section 20A.
47. Future Fund (2012), p. 9.
48. Future Fund (2012), p. 13.
49. Hebb et al. (2016), p. 4. Several empirical studies of responsible versus 'conventional' unrestricted investing suggest there are not significant differences in financial performance between the two investment approaches. See, for instance, Goldreyer and Diltz (1999); Statman (2000); Bauer, Derwall and Otten (2007); Galema, Plantinga and Scholtens (2008); Adamo et al. (2010).
50. For arguments against a business grounding of ethical constraints on investment, see Thornton (2008) and Richardson (2009).
51. See, for instance, the 2012 Annual Report for the Norwegian Ministry of Finance where it stated: 'Good long-term financial return is assumed to depend on sustainable development in economic, environmental and social terms, and on well-functioning, efficient and legitimate markets'; Norwegian Ministry of Finance (2013).
52. Richardson (2011), p. 23.
53. For a discussion on the structure of reasonable disagreement, see McMahon (2009), ch. 1.
54. Graver Committee (2003), p. 2.
55. While Amy Gutmann and Dennis Thompson suggest 'economizing on moral disagreement', Henry Richardson suggests 'deep compromise' and Robert Goodin argues for 'democratic deliberation within', all of these approaches involve some form of compromise or mutual accommodation for the purpose of achieving agreement; see McMahon (2009), pp. 22–3.
56. Widerquist (2012), p. 183.
57. Widerquist (2012), p. 184.
58. Casassas and De Wispeleare (2012) p. 183.
59. Widerquist (2012), p. 184.
60. Widerquist (2012), p. 203.
61. For instance, the Universities Superannuation Scheme in the UK.
62. I acknowledge Stuart White for this suggestion.
63. Graver Committee (2003).

7 Role models of community control: Norway and New Zealand

1. Nystuen (2006), pp. 207–8.
2. Reiche (2008), p. 2: Richardson (2011), p. 7.
3. Richardson (2011), p. 8.
4. Author interview with the Council on Ethics (2010). See also Norwegian Ministry of Finance (2008b), p. 29, which summarizes criticisms made by a 2008 review of the

Graver Committee regarding its failure to fully engage the Norwegian public in the formation of the fund's ethical guidelines: 'it is suggested that the process was insular, in the sense that it was not subject to public debate or consultation prior to the adoption of the principles. The report notes that it is recommended, especially when it comes to social and environmental themes, to draw on a broader set of perspectives in order to make the prioritisations viable over time, and in the face of changing political views, changes in the management team of the Fund or a shift in the general public's focus towards new themes.'

5. Norwegian Ministry of Finance (2008b), p. 3.
6. Norwegian Ministry of Finance (2008b), pp. 3–4.
7. See Truman (2010), pp. 94–6, for a critique of alternatives.
8. Bagnall and Truman (2013).
9. Truman (2010), pp. 70–1.
10. The Truman Scoreboard also evaluates a small sample of public pension funds, but the bulk of the analysis focuses on sovereign funds. For ease of comparison, I present Truman's total scores based on the whole sample of public pension funds and SWFs. The inclusion of public pension funds improves the group's average performance as these investors are typically more transparent, accountable and openly governed than SWFs. See Bagnall and Truman (2013), table 5, at pp. 12–13, which separately reports the performance of public pension funds and SWFs on the Scoreboard.
11. According to Rozanov (2011), '[t]he biggest issue that most policymakers and commentators seem to have with many SWFs is their perceived lack of transparency' (p. 258).
12. Bagnall and Truman (2013), p. 1.
13. See Figure 5.1 in Chapter 5 and accompanying discussion.
14. Pettit (2012), p. 239.
15. The New Zealand government is obliged to pay a universal retirement entitlement to all eligible citizens aged sixty-five years and over through a scheme known as New Zealand Superannuation. Following government projections showing that the number and cost of eligible New Zealand retirees between 2005 and 2050 would double, the government set up the fund to help offset its liabilities and smooth the tax burden between generations of New Zealanders. See NZSF (2016a).
16. Richardson (2011), p. 17.
17. New Zealand Superannuation and Retirement Income Act 2001, section 55(1)(a).
18. NZSF (2011b).
19. NZSF (2011b), p. 12.
20. NZSF (2009).
21. The Guardians' original strategy for socially responsible investment focused 'on acting as a responsible shareholder and fostering transparent corporate governance rather than necessarily excluding shares or securities'; see Controller and Auditor-General (2008), para. 3.62.
22. NZSF (2015b), p. 69.
23. NZSF (2015b), p. 70.
24. Richardson (2011), p. 20, quoting the 2010 NZSF Annual Report.
25. NZSF CEO Adrian Orr quoted in Abplanalp (2011), p. 40.
26. NZSF (2012a), p. 40.
27. NZSF (2016b).
28. NZSF (2009), p. 10.
29. Of the 168 excluded companies, 140 are involved in tobacco manufacture; see NZSF (2016b).
30. Controller and Auditor-General (2008), para. 3.74.
31. Controller and Auditor-General (2008), para. 3.768.
32. Mercer (2009), p. 39, para. 3.2.3.
33. Author interview with David Rae, NZSF Head of Investment Analysis (2012).
34. NZSF (2010), p. 2.

35. NZSF (2015b), p. 75.
36. NZSF (2016c).
37. Richardson (2011), p. 19.
38. Act of the Government Petroleum Fund (Lov om Statens petroleumsfond) 1990.
39. Skancke (2003), p. 318.
40. Skancke (2003).
41. See Clark and Monk (2010b), p. 1727; Clark and Monk (2010a), p. 14.
42. Unlike a traditional pension fund, the GPFG does not have a designated beneficiary, its management is not governed by fiduciary duty and it is not acting according to a defined time horizon; Clark and Monk (2010b), p. 1723.
43. Skancke (2003), p. 317.
44. The IMF has argued that the institutional structure of SWFs may take one of three legal forms: a separate legal entity outside of government, a unit within the central bank or a unit within the Ministry of Finance. The first constitutes proper 'arm's-length' governance outside of government, while the latter two structures should still involve independent management but from inside government. Those SWFs sitting within Ministries of Finance are the least independent; Das, Mulder and Sy (2009), p. 13.
45. Clark and Monk (2010b), pp. 1730–1.
46. Clark and Monk (2010b), p. 1729.
47. Clark and Monk (2010b), p. 1724.
48. Skancke (2003), pp. 327–8.
49. Clark and Monk (2010b), p. 1728.
50. Clark and Monk (2010b), p. 327.
51. Skancke (2008), p. 5.
52. Skancke (2003), p. 327.
53. Truman (2010).
54. See all current and historical annual and quarterly reports at NBIM (2016a).
55. See voting records at NBIM (2016b).
56. Clark and Monk (2010b).
57. Skancke (2008), p. 3.
58. Skancke (2008), p. 12.
59. Skancke (2008), p. 6.
60. Personal interview with Martin Skancke (2010).
61. Personal interview with Martin Skancke (2010).
62. Graver Committee (2003), section 2.1.
63. Graver Committee (2003), section 2.1.
64. Graver Committee (2003), section 2.1.
65. For a critique of the GFPG's complicity avoidance approach, see Richardson (2011) and Kutz (2011).
66. Graver Committee (2003), section 3.1.
67. See current guidelines at Council on Ethics (2014).
68. See Norwegian Ministry of Finance (2008), p. 3.
69. Albright Group and Chesterman (2008).
70. See Recommendation 12 in Albright Group and Chesterman (2008), p. 6.
71. The new guidelines allow exclusion 'if there is an unacceptable risk that the company contributes to or is responsible for (a) serious or systematic human rights violations; (b) serious violations of the rights of individuals in situations of war or conflict; (c) severe environmental damage; (d) gross corruption; or (e) other particularly serious violations of fundamental ethical norms'. See Graver Committee (2003), section 6, for original wording.
72. Norwegian Ministry of Finance (2010), p. 24.
73. Richardson (2011), p. 14.
74. Richardson (2011), p. 12.
75. Richardson (2011), p. 16.
76. Council on Ethics (2015), p. 5.

77. Clark and Monk (2010b), p. 1736.
78. Richardson (2011), pp. 6–7.
79. Backer (2009), p. 182.
80. Albright Group and Chesterman (2008), p. 4.
81. Professional stakeholders in participatory democracy 'are frequently paid representatives of organized interests and public officials'; Fung (2012), p. 615.
82. Graver Committee, sections 3.1 and 5.2.3.
83. Norwegian Ministry of Finance (2010), p. 10.
84. Richardson (2011), p. 18.
85. Richardson (2011), pp. 18 and 26.
86. Robert Howell, Head of the Council for Socially Responsible Investment (New Zealand), cited in Richardson (2008), p. 367.
87. Graver Committee (2003), section 3.1.
88. Author interview with Council on Ethics (2010); Graver Committee (2003).

8 Show me the money! Citizen benefit from sovereign wealth

1. Lee Yen Nee (2015).
2. AllAfrica (2015).
3. Honore (1961).
4. Christman's explicit articulation of the control–benefit structure of property rights is one of the most direct formulations of the income-based notion of benefit; Christman (1994). See also Munzer (1990), pp. 97–8; Becker (1977), p. 19; and Meade (1964), who implicitly uses an income-based conception of benefit from property when analysing state versus individual property ownership: 'We are interested . . . in the ultimate destination of income from property and not in the immediate control over property' (p. 68).
5. Christman (1991), p. 30.
6. Honore (1961).
7. Christman (1991), pp. 29–30.
8. Becker (1977), p. 19.
9. Christman (1991), p. 30.
10. Becker (1977), p. 19. While there are pressures for SWFs to move more investment in-house in the wake of the financial crisis due to the high cost of external fund managers, even where that occurs it does not change the control dynamic.
11. Honore (1961).
12. It is of course conceivable that the market does not support a decent level of rent – houses may be so abundant that the market rent is below cost.
13. Martin Skancke, when interviewed in his capacity as Director General of Asset Management at the Norwegian Ministry of Finance responsible for the GPFG, argued that tax cuts and cash handouts both count as citizens enjoying 'direct' access to sovereign fund returns: 'If you have decided that you want to give the population direct access to the cash, then the choice is between tax cuts or cash dividends. I would argue that tax cuts in terms of economic efficiency are better'; author interview with Martin Skancke (2010). The section below challenges the idea that tax cuts constitute direct distribution of SWF returns.
14. See more generally the next chapter. For the significance of calculating the PFD based on *realized* earnings (or losses) as opposed to the entire market value of the Alaska Permanent Fund's income, see Erickson and Groh (2012a), pp. 104–6.
15. Hammond (1984), p. 18, emphasis added.
16. Groh and Erickson (2012), p. 32.
17. Groh and Erickson (2012), p. 32.
18. Groh and Erickson (2012), p. 18; Greely (1977).
19. Groh and Erickson (2012), p. 32.
20. Hammond (1984), p. 18.

21. Groh and Erickson (2012), p. 31.
22. Groh and Erickson (2012), p. 31.
23. APFC (2016c).
24. Erickson and Groh (2012a), p. 42.
25. APFC (2015).
26. Erickson and Groh (2012b), p. 99, emphasis added.
27. Murphy and Nagel (2002), p. 48.
28. Murphy and Nagel (2002), p. 48.
29. In July 2001, substantial deposits of copper and gold were discovered in Mongolia's southern Gobi Desert; see Campi (2012) and Adamson (2012b). Mongolia also has vast coal reserves, and recently re-tendered to maximize production potential; see Isakova, Plekhanov and Zettelmeyer (2012).
30. Tang (2009).
31. Campi (2012); Adamson (2012b).
32. Isakova, Plekhanov and Zettelmeyer (2012), p. 11.
33. Campi (2012).
34. Choi (2009).
35. The government financed the Child Money Programme between 2005 and 2009. At first, payments were targeted, distributed to families with at least three children who lived under the minimum subsistence level. After logistical problems with assessing the eligibility criteria and a further increase in government revenues from climbing commodity prices, the Child Money Programme was made universal in July 2006. The popularity of the universal benefits and Mongolia's continuing growth set the stage for the roll-out of universal payments in the HDF era. See Yeung and Howes (2015a), pp. 9–15.
36. Yeung and Howes (2015a), p. 11.
37. Choi (2009), p. 10.
38. Campi (2012), n. 7.
39. Isakova, Plekhanov and Zettelmeyer (2012), p. 10.
40. Critics point to the inflationary effects of the handouts and increased pork barrelling. As the allocations are not related to the fund's performance and are entirely at the government's discretion, the major political parties have tapped the fund in an undisciplined way to win votes; Adamson (2012b).
41. Yeung and Howes (2015a).
42. Yeung and Howes (2015a), p. 15.
43. Yeung and Howes (2015a), p. 15.
44. Yeung and Howes (2015b).
45. Batkhuyag (2010).
46. Batkhuyag (2010).
47. Campi (2012).
48. Contra Murphy and Nagel, who in their analysis do not consider it relevant from a moral point of view to distinguish between direct and indirect benefit, or individual and collective benefit. Rather, the key question, in their view, concerns the ends of government and whether that should include the general welfare that looks beyond individual benefit or provision of public goods from which everyone benefits; Murphy and Nagel (2002), p. 49.
49. Singapore Ministry of Finance (2016).
50. Singapore Ministry of Finance (2016).
51. Ho Ching (2015).
52. Ho Ching (2015).
53. In national accounting terminology, there is a rough general distinction made between *consumption* spending that benefits individuals, and *investment* spending that tends to promote long-term collective benefit. For a technical discussion of this terminology, see Lequiller and Blades (2006), pp. 249ff. on consumption and p. 232 on investment.
54. Author interview with Martin Skancke (2010), emphasis added.
55. Mubadala (2016a).

56. See, for example, the 2015 consolidated financial statements and full year results of Mubadala; Mubadala (2015).
57. Abu Dhabi Government (2010); Mubadala (2011).
58. Mubadala (2016b); author interview with Mubadala investment manager (2011).
59. Author interview with Mubadala investment manager (2011).
60. Author interview with Mubadala investment manager (2011).
61. For a comprehensive list of potential channels for distributing state wealth to citizens, see El-Katiri, Fattouh and Segal (2011). The authors identify eight main channels of rent distribution for Kuwait's resource wealth (at p. 7). Kuwait possesses an SWF, the Kuwait Investment Authority, which the authors argue forms part of this distributive apparatus, although mainly as a tool for distributing wealth to future generations.
62. Swift and White (2008), p. 55.
63. Swift and White (2008), p. 54. For an explanation of the 'democratic underlabourer' idea, see White (2003), ch. 2.
64. Swift and White (2008), p. 54.
65. Swift and White (2008), p. 54.
66. Erickson and Groh (2012a), pp. 42–3.

9 Owner-state or owner-people: lessons from Alaska

1. Hickel (2002), p. 178, emphasis added.
2. Hammond (1994), p. 319, emphasis added.
3. This summary is mainly taken from Groh and Erickson (2012). For further detail on the creation of the fund, see other chapters in Widerquist and Howard (2012b) and APFC (1997).
4. See Groh and Erickson (2012), p. 24.
5. Groh and Erickson (1997), pp. 29–30.
6. Groh and Erickson (2012), p. 30.
7. Hammond (1984).
8. Groh and Erickson (2012), p. 26, emphasis added.
9. In the conference on the Alaska PFD described below, Fran Ulmer argued that Governor Hammond was strongly opposed to the dividend being viewed as any sort of handout. It was recognition of the fact that 'Alaska's wealth belonged to everyone and each citizen deserved a share of that wealth'; author notes of Fran Ulmer, Exporting the Alaska Model workshop, University of Anchorage, Alaska, 22 April 2011. See also Widerquist (2011), who records Ulmer's views as follows: 'Ulmer and [Rick] Halford argued that few if any legislators at the time intended to create a basic income. Ulmer, who worked in Governor Hammond's administration, argued that he did not and would not have argued for it in those terms. I argued that whatever their intentions, they did create a partial basic income.'
10. Hammond (1984).
11. While the term 'owner-state' was not officially coined until years later, the general notion of the 'state as owner' and, thus, the people as collective custodians and beneficiaries of the state's wealth was core to Hickel's governing philosophy. A detailed notion of the term 'owner-state' and what it entails is set out in Hickel (2002), pp. 5–8.
12. Hickel (2002), p. 91.
13. For a discussion of how Hickel sought to operationalize this, see Hickel (2002), ch. 5.
14. Hickel (2002), p. 7.
15. Hammond (1994), p. 319.
16. Groh and Erickson (2012). For other insider perspectives on the PFD's introduction, see Rose and Wohlforth (2008), esp. chs 11–13.
17. Goldsmith (2012), p. 53.
18. See Alaska Statute §43.23.005.
19. Casassas and De Wispelaere (2012).

20. From 1982 through 2011, the dividend programme paid out almost $19.2 billion to Alaska residents through the annual distribution of dividend checks; see APFC (2011), p. 2. It has trended upward as a share of per capita income at a rate of 1.4 per cent; Goldsmith (2012), p. 50.
21. Vanderborght and Van Parijs (2005), p. 25.
22. Goldsmith (2012), p. 53.
23. Goldsmith (2012), p. 53.
24. Widerquist and Howard (2012a), p. 3.
25. See Widerquist and Howard (2012b); Goldsmith (2012), p. 60.
26. Segal (2012).
27. Zelleke (2012); Carter (2012); Widerquist and Howard (2012a), pp. 5–6.
28. Griffin (2012).
29. Hartzok (2012b), p. 53. See also Howard (2012), who argues for combining basic income goals already achieved through the PFD with a carbon-trading scheme called 'cap-and-dividend'.
30. J. Hickel (2012); Flomenhoft (2012).
31. For instance, Goldsmith (2012) produces evidence of the dividend's equality-promoting impact, while cautioning against its characterization as a basic income or other equality-promoting scheme, since the typical level of the PFD payment falls well below the US poverty line.
32. A day-long conference on the APF and dividend programme in April 2011 brought together academics, former Alaska government officials and policy experts to discuss the origin and operation of the programme. For a summary of proceedings, including perspectives on possible motivations for the dividend, see Widerquist (2011).
33. Goldsmith (2012), p. 49; Goldsmith (2005).
34. Goldsmith (2005), p. 558.
35. Goldsmith (2012), p. 49.
36. Goldsmith (2012), p. 49; also p. 60: 'Because the dividend is viewed as a distribution of wealth rather than a basic income with public policy objectives, and also because it is relatively small both as a share of a basic income and of actual personal income, there have been no analyses of its long-term social effects.'
37. Goldsmith (2012), p. 59.
38. Goldsmith (2012), p. 59.
39. Goldsmith (2005), p. 563.
40. Goldsmith (2005), p. 558.
41. Goldsmith (2005), p. 558.
42. Goldsmith (2005), p. 564.
43. Using a combination of research methods can better reveal differences in attitude within and between demographic groups. See Gamble and Prabhakar (2006), p. 111.
44. Jansen (2010), para. 36.
45. While an atypical setting for qualitative research, the flight offered an ideal environment for this canvassing-style survey seeking to identify the diversity of views among Alaskans. The fact that the carrier was Alaska Airlines meant there was a high probability that Alaska's citizens were on board. The typically diverse composition of passengers on low-cost short-haul flights ensured a random population sample spanning age groups, socioeconomic backgrounds and professions. Perhaps most helpfully, the voluntarily formed nature of the group who were in an enclosed environment of their own volition, and for their own purposes, provided a neat solution to the difficulties of participant recruitment often faced in international research where researchers have no prior knowledge of a community and have limited time and resources for data collation.
46. For discussions on Basic Income versus Basic Capital schemes, see White (2011).
47. Morgan (1988), p. 10.
48. Krueger and Casey (2009), p. 21.

49. Goldsmith (2005; 2012).
50. Goldsmith (2005), p. 558.
51. Goldsmith (2005), p. 558.
52. Knapp (2016).
53. Knapp (2016).
54. Author interview with Cliff Groh (2016).
55. Erickson and Groh (2012a), p. 42.
56. Erickson and Groh (2012a), p. 104.
57. APFC (2012), p. 1.
58. APFC (2012), p. 1.
59. Author interview with Mike Burns, CEO of Alaska Permanent Fund Corporation (2011).
60. APFC (2012), p. 1.
61. Erickson and Groh (2012a) p. 104.
62. Erickson and Groh (2012a) p. 42.
63. Erickson and Groh (2012a), p. 43.
64. Erickson and Groh (2012a), p. 47, n. 7.
65. Author interview with Gregg Erickson, Alaska economist (11 March 2016).

10 Fighting inequality with sovereign wealth

1. Economist (2015).
2. Atkinson (2015).
3. Olin Wright (2006), p. xii.
4. Van Parijs (2006).
5. Newell (2013).
6. Wike (2014).
7. Atkinson, Piketty and Saez (2011); OECD (2014a).
8. See Atkinson (2015), esp. chs 1 and 2. See also Glyn (2006), chs 5 and 8.
9. OECD (2014b), p. 20.
10. Atkinson (2015).
11. Piketty and Zucman (2014); Credit Suisse (2014).
12. Credit Suisse (2014).
13. Davies et al. (2006), p. 2.
14. Piketty and Zucman (2015), p. 1308.
15. Piketty and Zucman (2014).
16. Davies et al. (2010).
17. Credit Suisse (2014). p. 24, fig. 1.
18. Davies et al. (2006), pp. 3–4.
19. Piketty (2014), p. 244.
20. Piketty (2014), p. 2.
21. Lansley (2015a), p. 563.
22. OECD (2015a); UN (2013).
23. See White (2003), p. 4.
24. Smeeding (2004), figs 8 and 9.
25. Mischel, Bernstein and Sheirholz (2008), p. 384.
26. White (2003), p. 5.
27. Glyn (2006), pp. 104–5; for a detailed explanation of the trends influencing the employment prospects of the least qualified, see pp. 105–12.
28. The European Union first set out a Social Inclusion Agenda in 2000. Since 2006, all EU countries, including the UK, have produced a 'National Report on Strategies for Social Protection and Social Inclusion'. The UK now has a dedicated Social Exclusion Task Force, with Australia following suit in 2008, establishing a National Board of Social Inclusion to fight the impact of rising inequality. See Marlier et al. (2007).

29. Lansley (2015a), p. 565.
30. Holtham (2014).
31. Meade (1989)
32. Holtham (2014)
33. Lansley (2015), pp. 568–9.
34. Atkinson (2015), p. 238.
35. Corneo (2015), esp. p. 4.
36. Cummine (2011a).
37. Corneo (2015), p. 5.

11 Past the peak? The future of sovereign wealth accumulation

1. World Bank (2016a).
2. IMF (2015b).
3. Arezki et al. (2015).
4. WTO (2015).
5. OECD (2016).
6. World Bank (2016b).
7. Summers (2014).
8. IMF (2015c).
9. OECD (2016).
10. Elliott and Inman (2015).
11. Davies (2015).
12. OECD (2014b).
13. OECD.Stat (2015).
14. IMF (2015c); World Bank (2015; 2016a).
15. IMF (2015c).
16. Summers (2015).
17. Bouis et al. (2013).
18. Gordon (2015).
19. Davies (2013).
20. OECD (2015b).
21. Krugman (2015).
22. Summers (2014).
23. Hall (2015).
24. Beattie (2015).
25. Summers (2015).
26. Khrais (2016).
27. Rodrik (2015).
28. Corneo (2014).
29. Detter and Fölster (2015).
30. Detter and Fölster (2015), p. 4.
31. Lansley (2015b).
32. Bollier (2003) p. 10.
33. Miceli et al. (2015).
34. Castelli and Tagliapietra (2012); Miceli et al. (2015).
35. Aizenman and Glick (2008).
36. Curto (2010); Triki and Faye (2011).
37. See Appendix 1.
38. Olson (2015).
39. Preqin (2016), p. 5.
40. UNCTAD (2014).
41. Stone (2015).
42. Wriglesworth Consultancy in 2014, cited in Gerrard (2015).

43. Gros and Mayer (2012).
44. Bernanke (2015).
45. Sandbu (2016).
46. See Costello (2016).

12 Transforming sovereign funds into community funds

1. Fox-Decent (2005), p. 259.
2. See Criddle (2010); Fox-Decent and Criddle (2005), pp. 314, 317. Criddle (2010) locates the fiduciary duty with public officials who 'stand in a trust-like relationship toward persons subject to their administrative powers. Just as the common law places trustees and other fiduciaries under legal obligations to honor their beneficiaries' legitimate interests, those who wield powers of public administration likewise bear fiduciary obligations to treat their subjects fairly, reasonably, and non-arbitrarily for public-regarding purposes' (p. 1277).
3. IWG (2008), p. 16, n. 26.
4. Rozanov (2011), p. 261.
5. IWG (2008), p. 15.
6. IMF (2008), p. 26.
7. IMF (2008), p. 24, emphasis added.
8. Mehrpouya (2013), p. 34.
9. Mehrpouya (2013), pp. 34–5.
10. IWG (2008), p. 8.
11. IWG (2008), p. 8.
12. IWG (2008), p. 7.
13. IWG (2008), p. 14.

BIBLIOGRAPHY

References

ABC (2015) 'PNG Passes Sovereign Wealth Fund Bill', *ABC News Online*, 31 July, at http://www.abc.net.au/news/2015–07–30/png-passes-sovereign-wealth-fund-bill/6661162.

Abplanalp, K. (2011) 'Blood Money', *Metro Magazine*, Dec., at www.pmc.aut.ac.nz/sites/default/files/file_bin/201111/Metro_Dec2011_FreeportSuperfund_pp43–49.pdf.

Abu Dhabi Government (2010) *Abu Dhabi Economic Vision 2030*, at https://www.ecouncil.ae/PublicationsEn/economic-vision–2030-full-versionEn.pdf.

Adamo, R., A. Coscarelli, D. Federico and A. Notte (2010) 'The Ethical and Non Ethical Mutual Funds Comparison', *American Journal of Economics and Business Administration*, 2(4): 360–5.

Adamson, L. (2012a) 'Riding a New Wave of Wealth', *Institutional Investor*, 25 Sept., at www.institutionalinvestor.com/Article/3088148/Riding-a-New-Wave-of-Wealth.html.

Adamson, L. (2012b) 'Mongolia Aims to Join the SWF Ranks', *Institutional Investor*, 25 Sept.

Aizenman, J. (2007) *Large Hoarding of International Reserves and the Emerging Global Economic Architecture*, NBER Working Paper 13277 (Cambridge, MA: National Bureau of Economic Research).

Aizenman, J. and R. Glick (2008) *Sovereign Wealth Funds: Stylized Facts about Their Determinants and Governance*, NBER Working Paper 14562 (Cambridge MA: National Bureau of Economic Research).

Ajayi, Y. and O. Olaleye (2011) 'Governors Seek to Stop Sovereign Wealth Fund', *This Day Live*, 21 Aug., at http://logbaby.com/news/governors-seek-to-stop-sovereign-wealth-fund_7965.html#.

Albright Group and S. Chesterman (2008) *Assessment of Implementation of Articles 3 and 4 of the Ethical Guidelines for the Government Pension Fund – Global*, Report submitted to the Norwegian Ministry of Finance, May, at https://www.regjeringen.no/globalassets/upload/FIN/Vedlegg/aff/Albright_Group_Ethical_Guidelines.pdf.

AllAfrica (2011) 'Nigeria: State Governors and Sovereign Wealth Fund', AllAfrica.com, 1 Sept., at www.allafrica.com/stories/201109010821.html.

AllAfrica (2015) 'Namibia: Tucna Calls for Creation of a Sovereign Wealth Fund', AllAfrica.com, 3 Sept., at http://allafrica.com/stories/201509031204.html.

Alsweilem, K., A. Cummine, M. Rietveld and K. Tweedie (2015) *Sovereign Investor Models: Institutions and Policies for Managing Sovereign Wealth*, joint report, Belfer Center for Science and International Affairs and Center for International Development, Harvard Kennedy School, at http://belfercenter.ksg.harvard.edu/files/InvestorModels.pdf.

APFC (1997) *The Early History of the Alaska Permanent Fund: Perspectives on the Origins of Alaska's Oil Savings Account*, Feb. (Juneau, AK: Alaska Permanent Fund Corporation).

APFC (2011) *Annual Report 2011* (Juneau, AK: Alaska Permanent Fund Corporation).

APFC (2012) *Annual Report 2012* (Juneau, AK: Alaska Permanent Fund Corporation).

APFC (2014) 'Permanent Fund Historical Returns FY85–FY13', Alaska Permanent Fund Corporation, at www.apfc.org/_amiReportsArchive/Historical%20returns.pdf.

APFC (2015) 'Annual Dividend Payments', Alaska Permanent Fund Corporation, at www.apfc.org/home/Content/dividend/dividendamounts.cfm.

APFC (2016a) 'Landmarks in Permanent Fund History', Alaska Permanent Fund Corporation, at http://www.apfc.org/home/Content/aboutFund/fundHistory.cfm.

APFC (2016b) 'Fund Market Value', Alaska Permanent Fund Corporation, at www.apfc.org/home/Content/home/index.cfm.

APFC (2016c) 'The Permanent Fund Dividend', Alaska Permanent Fund Corporation, at www.apfc.org/home/Content/dividend/dividend.cfm.

Arendt, H. (1958) *The Human Condition* (Chicago: University of Chicago Press).

Arezki, R., A. Mazarei and A. Prasad (2015) 'Sovereign Wealth Funds in the New Era of Oil', IMF Direct blogpost, 26 Oct., at https://blog-imfdirect.imf.org/2015/10/26/sovereign-wealth-funds-in-the-new-era-of-oil/.

Atkinson, A.T. (2015) *Inequality: What Can Be Done?* (Cambridge, MA: Harvard University Press).

Atkinson, A., T. Piketty and E. Saez (2011) 'Top Incomes in the Long Run of History', *Journal of Economic Literature*, 49(1): 3–71.

Avendaño, R. and J. Santiso (2009) *Are Sovereign Wealth Funds' Investments Politically Biased? Comparison with Mutual Funds*, OECD Development Centre Working Paper 283, Dec. (Paris: OECD).

Backer, L. (2009) 'Sovereign Wealth Funds as Regulatory Chameleons: The Norwegian Sovereign Wealth Funds and Public Global Governance Through Private Global Investment', *Georgetown Journal of International Law*, 41(2): 101–92.

Backer, L. (2010) 'Sovereign Investing in Times of Crisis: Global Regulation of Sovereign Wealth Funds, State-Owned Enterprises and the Chinese Experience', *Transnational Law and Contemporary Problems*, 19(3): 3–144.

Bagnall, A. and E. Truman (2013) *Progress on Sovereign Wealth Fund Transparency and Accountability: An Updated SWF Scoreboard*, Peterson Institute for International Economics (PIIE) Policy Brief 13–19, Aug. (Washington, DC: PIIE), at http://www.iie.com/publications/interstitial.cfm?ResearchID=2454.

Balding, C. (2012) *Sovereign Wealth Funds: The New Intersection of Politics and Money* (New York: Oxford University Press).

Balzan, J. (2016) 'English Court Ruling Confirms Continued Malta Operations of LIA', *MaltaToday*, 18 Mar., at http://www.maltatoday.com.mt/news/world/63275/english_court_ruling_confirms_continued_malta_operations_of_lia#.VxzJaHgrfdk.

Barbary, V., B. Bortolotti, V. Fotak and W. Miracky (2010) *Sovereign Wealth Fund Investment Behaviour: Semi-Annual Report: January–June 2010* (Boston: Monitor Group).

Barber, L. (2015) 'Fidor Launches in the UK as Digital Challenger Bank Expands', *City A.M.*, 18 Sept., at http://www.cityam.com/224597/fidor-launches-uk-digital-challenger-bank-expands.

Barro, R. (1973) 'The Control of Politicians: An Economic Model', *Public Choice*, 14(1): 19–42.

Batkhuyag, B. (2010) 'Human Development Fund Survey Results Revealed', Business-Mongolia.com, 1 July, at www.business-mongolia.com/mongolia/2010/07/01/human-development-fund-survey-results-revealed.

Bauer, R., J. Derwall and R. Otten (2007) 'The Ethical Mutual Fund Performance Debate: New Evidence from Canada', *Journal of Business Ethics*, 70: 111–24.

BBC (2015a) 'Power Struggle over Libya's Sovereign Wealth', *Business Matters*, BBC World Service, 20 Aug., at http://www.bbc.co.uk/programmes/p02yxbs4.

BBC (2015b) 'Interview with Fidor's CEO', BBC 5Live, 21 Sept., at https://www.youtube.com/watch?v=rloto4mksPM.

BBC (2016) 'Q&A: Police and Crime Commissioners', *BBC News*, 21 Apr., at http://www.bbc.com/news/uk-politics–19504639.

Beattie, A. (2015) 'Emerging Markets Will Struggle to Escape Secular Stagnation', *Financial Times*, 22 Apr., at http://www.ft.com/intl/cms/s/0/3900f858-e8ec–11e4–87fe–00144feab7de.html.

Beck, R. and M. Fidora (2008) *The Impact of Sovereign Wealth Funds on Global Financial Markets*, ECB Occasional Paper Series 91, July (Frankfurt: European Central Bank).

Becker, L. (1977) *Property Rights: Philosophic Foundations* (Boston: Routledge & Kegan Paul).

Behrendt, S. and D. Sharp (2011) 'The Libyan Investment Authority: Sanctions and Post-Conflict Resolution', GeoEconomica briefing, Nov.

Bernanke, B. (2015), 'Germany's Trade Surplus is a Problem', Brookings blog, 3 Apr., at http://www.brookings.edu/blogs/ben-bernanke/posts/2015/04/03-germany-trade-surplus-problem.

Bernstein, S., J. Lerner and A. Schoar (2009) *The Investment Strategies of Sovereign Wealth Funds*, NBER Working Paper 14861 (Cambridge, MA: National Bureau of Economic Research).

Birks, P. (2000) 'The Content of the Fiduciary Obligation', *Israel Law Review*, 34(1): 3–20.

Blackburn, R. (1999) 'The New Collectivism: Pension Reform, Grey Capitalism, and Complex Socialism', *New Left Review*, 233 (Jan.–Feb.): 3–65.

Blackburn, R. (2002) *Death or Investing in Life: The History and Future of Pensions* (London: Verso).

Blackburn, R. (2006) *Age Shock: How the System is Failing Us* (London: Verso).

Blanchard, J. (2011) 'China's Grand Strategy and Money Muscle: The Potentialities and Pratfalls of China's Sovereign Wealth Fund and Renminbi Policies', *Chinese Journal of International Politics*, 4(1): 31–53.

Bloem, A., R. Dippelsman and N. Maehle (2001) *Quarterly National Accounts Manual: Concepts, Data Sources, and Compilation*, International Monetary Fund, at http://www.imf.org/external/pubs/ft/qna/2000/textbook/.

Bloomberg News (2011) 'Greens to Push for Future Fund Bar on Tobacco Investment', *Sydney Morning Herald*, 24 Mar., at http://www.smh.com.au/business/greens-to-push-for-future-fund-bar-on-tobacco-investment–20110324–1c7lz.html.

Bollier, D. (2003) *Silent Theft: The Private Plunder of Our Common Wealth* (New York: Routledge).

Bolton, P., F. Samama and J. Stiglitz (eds) (2012) *Sovereign Wealth Funds and Long-Term Investing* (New York: Columbia University Press).

Bortolotti, B., V. Fotak, W. Megginson and W. Miracky (2009) *Sovereign Wealth Fund Investment Patterns and Performance*, Fondazione Eni Enrico Mattei Working Paper 22, at http://www.feem.it/getpage.aspx?id=1880&sez=Publications&padre=73.

Bouis, R., L. Rawdanowicz, J.-P. Renne, S. Watanabe and A.K. Christensen (2013) 'The Effectiveness of Monetary Policy since the Onset of the Financial Crisis', OECD Economics Department Working Paper 1081, at http://www.oecd.org/officialdocuments/publicdisplaydocumentpdf/?cote=ECO/WKP(2013)73&docLanguage=En.

BPM6 (2013) *Balance of Payments and International Investment Position Manual*, 6th edn, International Monetary Fund, at https://www.imf.org/external/pubs/ft/bop/2007/bopman6.htm.

Bremer, T. van den, F. van der Ploeg and S. Wills (2015) 'The Elephant in the Ground: Managing Oil and Sovereign Wealth', OxCarre Research Paper 129, University of

Oxford, June, at https://www.newcastle.edu.au/__data/assets/pdf_file/0019/207145/Sam-Wills-oxcarrerp2013129.pdf.

Brown, G. (2009) *Supporting Global Growth: A Preliminary Report on the Responsiveness and Adaptability of the International Financial Institutions by the Chair of the London Summit* (London: Hayden-McNeil).

Brown Weiss, E. (1989) *In Fairness to Future Generations: International Law, Common Patrimony, and Intergenerational Equity* (Tokyo: United Nations University).

Brown Weiss, E. (1990) 'Our Rights and Obligations to Future Generations for the Environment', *American Journal of International Law*, 84: 198–207.

Brundige, E., W. King, P. Vahali, S. Vladeck and X. Yuan (2004) *Indonesian Human Rights Abuses in West Papua: Application of the Law of Genocide to the History of Indonesian Control*, Apr., at https://www.law.yale.edu/system/files/documents/pdf/Intellectual_Life/West_Papua_final_report.pdf.

Buchheit, L., G. Mitu Galati and R. Thompson (2007) 'The Dilemma of Odious Debt', *Duke Law Journal*, 56(5): 1201–62.

Campi, A. (2012) 'Mongolia's Quest to Balance Human Development in Its Booming Mineral-Based Economy', Brookings East Asia Commentary, Jan., at www.brookings.edu/research/opinions/2012/01/10-mongolia-campi.

Caney, S. (2006) *Justice Beyond Borders: A Global Political Theory* (Oxford: Oxford University Press).

Carlin, W. and D. Soskice (2006) *Macroeconomics: Imperfections, Institutions and Policies* (Oxford: Oxford University Press).

Carter, I. (2012) 'Left-Libertarianism and the Resource Dividend', in K. Widerquist and M.W. Howard (eds), *Alaska's Permanent Fund Dividend: Examining Its Suitability as a Model* (New York: Palgrave Macmillan).

Casassas, D. and J. De Wispelare (2012) 'The Alaska Model: A Republican Perspective', in K. Widerquist and M.W. Howard (eds), *Alaska's Permanent Fund Dividend: Examining Its Suitability as a Model* (New York: Palgrave Macmillan).

Castelli, M. and S. Tagliapietra (2012), 'How Big Could SWFs Be by 2016?', in M. Castelli, M. and F. Scacciavillani, *The New Economics of Sovereign Wealth Funds* (Oxford: Wiley).

Chakraborrty, A. (2014) 'Dude, Where's My North Sea Oil Money?', *Guardian*, 13 Jan., at http://www.theguardian.com/commentisfree/2014/jan/13/north-sea-oil-money-uk-norwegians-fund.

Chesterman, S. (2008) 'The Turn to Ethics: Disinvestment from Multinational Corporations for Human Rights Violations – The Case of Norway's Sovereign Wealth Fund', *American University International Law Review*, 23: 577–615.

Choi, D. (2009) 'Law on Human Development Fund, Mongolia's Sovereign Wealth Fund to Pool in All Revenues from Mineral Resources including OT and TT Has Been Approved', Dale Choi blog, 18 Nov.

Christman, J. (1991) 'Self-Ownership, Equality and the Structure of Property Rights', *Political Theory*, 19(1): 28–46.

Christman, J. (1994) *The Myth of Property: Toward an Egalitarian Theory of Ownership* (Oxford: Oxford University Press).

Clark, G. and E. Knight (2011) 'Temptation and the Virtues of Long-Term Commitment: The Governance of Sovereign Wealth Fund Investment', *Asian Journal of International Law*, 1(1): 321–48.

Clark, G. and A.H.B. Monk (2010a) 'The Norwegian Government Pension Fund: Ethics Over Efficiency', *Rotman International Journal of Pension Management*, 3(1): 14–19.

Clark, G. and A.H.B. Monk (2010b) 'The Legitimacy and Governance of Norway's Sovereign Wealth Fund: The Ethics of Global Investment', *Environment and Planning A*, 42: 1723–38.

Clark, G. and A.H.B. Monk (2012) 'Sovereign Wealth Funds: Form and Function in the 21st Century', in P. Bolton, F. Samama and J. Stiglitz (eds), *Sovereign Wealth Funds and Long-Term Investing* (New York: Columbia University Press).

Clark, G., E. Caerlewy-Smith and J. Marshall (2007) 'The Consistency of UK Pension Fund Trustee Decision Making', *Journal of Pension Economics and Finance*, 6: 67–86.

Clark, G., A. Dixon and A. Monk (2013) *Legitimacy, Governance and Global Power* (Princeton, NJ: Princeton University Press).

Colquhoun, L. (2011) 'Future Fund Asserts Defensive Strategy', *Financial Times*, 25 Sept.

Connelly, S. (2007) 'Mapping Sustainable Development as a Contested Concept', *Local Environment*, 12(3): 259–78.

Controller and Auditor-General (2008) *Guardians of New Zealand Superannuation: Governance and Management of the New Zealand Superannuation Fund*, May (Auckland: New Zealand Government).

Corneo, G. (2014) *Public Capital in the 21st Century*, Social Europe Journal Research Essay 2, Nov., Free University of Berlin, at https://www.socialeurope.eu/wp-content/uploads/2014/11/RE2-Corneo.pdf.

Corneo, G. (2015) *Inequality, Public Wealth, and the Federal Shareholder*, Free University of Berlin, at http://www.wiwiss.fu-berlin.de/fachbereich/vwl/corneo/Forschung/PubCap.pdf.

Corner House (2008) 'Sovereign Wealth Funds: Some Frequently Asked Questions', Corner House Briefing 38, at http://www.thecornerhouse.org.uk/sites/thecornerhouse.org.uk/files/38SWFFAQs.pdf.

Costello, P. (2011) 'Whether Sovereign Wealth or Future, the Fund Needs Funds', *Sydney Morning Herald*, 14 Sept., at http://www.smh.com.au/federal-politics/political-opinion/whether-sovereign-wealth-or-future-the-fund-needs-funds–20110913–1k7l8.html.

Costello, P. (2016) 'Sovereign Wealth Funds: Australia is Not Alaska', *Sydney Morning Herald*, 19 Mar., at http://www.smh.com.au/business/markets/peter-costello-australia-is-not-alaska–20160317-gnlm85.html.

Council on Ethics (2014) 'Guidelines', Council on Ethics for the Norwegian Government Pension Fund Global, 18 Dec., at http://etikkradet.no/en/guidelines/.

Council on Ethics (2015) *Annual Report*, Council on Ethics for the Norwegian Government Pension Fund Global, at http://etikkradet.no/files/2016/03/Etikkraadet_AR_2015_web.pdf.

Court, A. and D. McCarthy (2015) 'Massive Gas Discovery Transforms Mozambique Backwater into Boomtown', CNN, 3 Feb., at http://edition.cnn.com/2015/02/03/africa/pemba-port-mozambique-gas/.

Credit Suisse (2014) *Global Wealth Report 2014*, Research Institute, Oct., at https://publications.credit-suisse.com/tasks/render/file/?fileID=60931FDE-A2D2-F568-B041B58C5EA591A4.

Criddle, E. (2006) 'Fiduciary Foundations of Administrative Law', *UCLA Law Review*, 54: 117–84.

Criddle, E. (2010) 'Mending Holes in the Rule of (Administrative) Law', *Northwestern University Law Review*, 104(3): 1271–80.

Criddle, E. and E. Fox-Decent (2009) 'A Fiduciary Theory of Jus Cogens', *Yale Journal of International Law*, 34: 331–87.

Cudd, A. (2008) 'Contractarianism', in *The Stanford Encyclopedia of Philosophy*, at http://plato.stanford.edu/archives/fall2008/entries/contractarianism/.

Cummine, A. (2011a) 'Overcoming Dividend Skepticism: Why the World's Sovereign Wealth Funds Are Not Paying Basic Income Dividends', *Basic Income Studies*, 6(1): Art. 4.

Cummine, A. (2011b) 'Share the Wealth While It Lasts', *Sydney Morning Herald*, 11 Apr.

Cummine, A. (2014a) 'Ethical Sovereign Investors: Sovereign Wealth Funds and Human Rights', in J. Bohoslavsky and J. Černič (eds), *Making Sovereign Financing and Human Rights Work* (London: Hart).

Cummine, A. (2014b) 'Norway's Sovereign Wealth Fund and Global Justice: A Exchange', *Ethics and International Affairs*, 24 Jan., at http://www.ethicsandinternationalaffairs.org/2014/norways-sovereign-wealth-fund-and-global-justice-an-exchange/.

Cummine, A. (forthcoming) 'A Tale of Two Sovereign Funds: China's Exceptionalism in Sovereign Wealth Management through CIC and SAFE', *International Journal of Public Policy*.

Curto, S. (2010) 'Sovereign Wealth Funds in the Next Decade', in O. Canuto and M. Guigale (eds), *The Day After Tomorrow: A Handbook on the Future of Economic Policy in the Developing World* (Washington, DC: World Bank).

Das, U., Y. Lu, C. Mulder and A. Sy (2009) *Setting Up a Sovereign Wealth Fund: Some Policy and Operational Considerations*, IMF Working Paper 09/179 (Washington, DC: International Monetary Fund), at www.imf.org/external/pubs/ft/wp/2009/wp09179.pdf.

Das, U., A. Mazarei and H. van der Hoorn (eds) (2010) *The Economics of Sovereign Wealth Funds: Issues for Policymakers* (Washington, DC: International Monetary Fund).

Davies, G. (2013) 'The Implications of Secular Stagnation', *Financial Times* blog, 17 Nov., at http://blogs.ft.com/gavyndavies/2013/11/17/the-implications-of-secular-stagnation/.

Davies, G. (2015) 'What the Leaked Fed Forecasts Tell Us', *Financial Times*, 29 July, at http://blogs.ft.com/gavyndavies/2015/07/29/what-the-leaked-fed-forecasts-tell-us/.

Davies, J.B., S. Sandström, A. Shorrocks and E. Wolff (2006) *The World Distribution of Household Wealth*, 5 Dec., at http://www.iariw.org/papers/2006/davies.pdf.

Davies, J., S. Sandstrom, A. Shorrocks and E. Wolff (2010) 'The Level and Distribution of Global Household Wealth', *Economic Journal*, 121(551): 223–54.

Davis, J., R. Ossowski, J. Daniel and S. Barnett (2003) 'Stabilization and Savings Funds for Nonrenewable Resources: Experience and Fiscal Policy Implications', in J. Davis, R. Ossowski and A. Fedelino (eds), *Fiscal Policy Formulation and Implementation in Oil-Producing Countries* (Washington, DC: International Monetary Fund).

Demeyere, B. (2011) 'Sovereign Wealth Funds and (Un)Ethical Investment: Using "Due Diligence" to Avoid Contributing to Human Rights Violations Committed by Companies in the Investment Portfolio', in G. Nystuen, A. Follesdal and O. Mestad (eds), *Human Rights, Corporate Complicity and Disinvestment* (Cambridge: Cambridge University Press).

Detter, D. and S. Fölster (2015) *The Public Wealth of Nations* (London: Palgrave Macmillan)

Di Natale, R. (2012) 'Government Investment Funds Amendment (Ethical Investment) Bill 2011', Second Reading speech, 13 Sept., Commonwealth Senate, Australia.

Dixon, A. and A.H.B. Monk (2011) *The Design and Governance of Sovereign Wealth Funds: Principles and Practices for Resource Revenue Management*, 30 Oct., at www.ssrn.com/abstract=1951573.

Dixon, A. and A.H.B. Monk (2012) 'Rethinking the Sovereign in Sovereign Wealth Funds', *Transactions of the Institute of British Geographers*, 37(1): 104–17.

Dobson, A. (1999) *Fairness and Futurity: Essays on Environmental Sustainability and Social Justice* (Oxford: Oxford University Press).

Drezner, D. (2008) 'Sovereign Wealth Funds and the (In)Security of Global Finance', *Journal of International Affairs*, 62(1): 115–31.

Dunn, J. (1984) 'The Concept of "Trust" in the Politics of John Locke', in R. Rorty (ed.), *Philosophy in History: Essays on the Historiography of Philosophy* (Cambridge: Cambridge University Press).

Eaton, S. and Z. Ming (2010) 'A Principal–Agent Analysis of China's Sovereign Wealth System: Byzantine by Design', *Review of International Political Economy*, 17(3): 481–506.

Economist (2015) 'Mind the Gap', review of Anthony Atkinson, *Inequality: What Can Be Done?*, *The Economist*, 6 June, at http://www.economist.com/news/books-and-arts/21653596-anthony-atkinson-godfather-inequality-research-growing-problem-mind-gap.

Economist Intelligence Unit (2015) 'Democracy Index 2015: Democracy in an Age of Anxiety', at https://www.eiu.com/public/topical_report.aspx?campaignid=Democracy Index2015.

Electoral Commission (2016) *Police and Crime Commissioner Election in England and Wales: Guidance for Candidates and Agents*, at www.electoralcommission.org.uk/__data/assets/pdf_file/0009/148743/PCC-Part–1-Can-you-stand-for-election.pdf.

El-Katiri, L., B. Fattouh and P. Segal (2011) *Anatomy of an Oil-Based Welfare State: Rent Distribution in Kuwait*, LSE Global Governance Research Paper 13, London School of Economics.

Elliott, L. and P. Inman (2015) 'China Syndrome: How the Slowdown Could Spread to the Brics and Beyond', *Guardian*, 22 Aug., at http://www.theguardian.com/business/2015/aug/22/could-china-crisis-spread-to-emerging-markets.

Erickson, G. and C. Groh (2012a) 'Permanent Perhaps: Challenges to the Model in Alaska in Its First 30 Years', in K. Widerquist and M.W. Howard (eds), *Alaska's Permanent Fund Dividend: Examining Its Suitability as a Model* (New York: Palgrave Macmillan).

Erickson, G. and C. Groh (2012b) 'How the APF and the PFD Operate: The Peculiar Mechanics of Alaska's State Finances', in K. Widerquist and M.W. Howard (eds), *Alaska's Permanent Fund Dividend: Examining Its Suitability as a Model* (New York: Palgrave Macmillan).

ESADEgeo (2015) *Sovereign Wealth Funds Ranking 2015*, ESADEgeo-Center for Global Economy and Geopolitics, Madrid, June, at http://esadegeo.maplab.es/ranking.swf.

Estlund, D. (2008) *Democratic Authority* (Princeton, NJ: Princeton University Press).

Eurostat (1996) *European System of Accounts: ESA 1995* (Luxembourg: Office for Official Publications of the European Communities), at http://ec.europa.eu/eurostat/documents/3859598/5826305/CA–15–96–001-EN.pdf/aeec2852-bed2–46d2–9534–5859d3c911d5.

Farrell, D.M. (2012) 'There's More to Democracy Than Polling Day: Citizen Engagement Between Elections', keynote paper at the Australian Electoral Research Forum, 19–20 Nov., Australian Electoral Commission, at www.aec.gov.au/About_AEC/research/caber/keynote.htm.

Farrell, D., S. Lund, E. Gerlemann and P. Seeburger (2007) *The New Power Brokers: How Oil, Asia, Hedge Funds, and Private Equity Are Shaping Global Capital Markets* (San Francisco: McKinsey Global Institute).

Fearon, J. (1999) 'Electoral Accountability and the Control of Politicians: Selecting Good Types versus Sanctioning Poor Performance', in A. Przeworski, B. Manin and S. Stokes (eds), *Democracy, Accountability, and Representation* (Cambridge: Cambridge University Press).

Feng, Z. (2009) 'How Should Sovereign Wealth Funds Be Regulated?', *Brooklyn Journal of Corporate Finance and Commercial Law*, 3(2): 483–511.

Ferejohn, J. (1986) 'Incumbent Performance and Electoral Control', *Public Choice*, 50(1–3): 5–26.

Fini, M. (2011) 'Financial Ideas, Political Constraints: Sovereign Wealth Funds and Domestic Governance', *Competition and Change*, 15(1): 71–93.

Finn, P. (1995) 'The Forgotten "Trust": The People and the State', in M. Cope (ed.), *Equity: Issues and Trends* (Sydney: Federation Press).

Fishkin, J. (1995) *The Voice of the People* (New Haven and London: Yale University Press).

Fishkin, J. (2009) *When the People Speak* (Oxford: Oxford University Press).

Flomenhoft, G. (2012) 'Applying the Alaska Model in a Resource-Poor State: The Example of Vermont', in K. Widerquist and M.W. Howard (eds), *Exporting the Alaska Model: Adapting the Permanent Fund Dividend for Reform Around the World* (New York: Palgrave Macmillan), pp. 85–108.

Fox-Decent, E. (2005) 'The Fiduciary Nature of State Legal Authority', *Queen's Law Journal*, 31: 259–310.

Fox-Decent, E. (2011) *Sovereignty's Promise: The State as Fiduciary* (Oxford: Oxford University Press).

Fox-Decent, E. and E.J. Criddle (2009) 'The Fiduciary Constitution of Human Rights', *Legal Theory*, 15(4): 301–36.

Frankel, J. (2010) *The Natural Resource Curse: A Survey*, Harvard Kennedy School Faculty Research Working Paper Series, RWP10–005J, Feb.

Frankel, J. (2012) 'Chile's Countercyclical Triumph', *Foreign Policy*, 27 June, at http://foreignpolicy.com/2012/06/27/chiles-countercyclical-triumph/.

Fung, A. (2004) *Empowered Participation: Reinventing Urban Democracy* (Princeton, NJ: Princeton University Press).

Fung, A. (2006) 'Varieties of Participation in Complex Governance', *Public Administration Review*, special issue (Dec.): 66–75.

Fung, A. (2007) 'Democratic Theory and Political Science,' *American Political Science Review*, 101: 443–58.

Fung, A. (2012) 'Continuous Institutional Innovation and the Pragmatic Conception of Democracy', *Polity*, 44(4): 609–24.

Future Fund (2012) 'Submission to the Senate Finance and Public Administration Legislation Committee', Inquiry into the Government Investment Funds Amendment (Ethical Investments) Bill 2011, Melbourne.

Future Fund (2013) 'Future Fund Excludes Tobacco Producers', Future Fund media release, 28 Feb.

Galema, R., A. Plantinga and B. Scholtens (2008) 'The Stocks at Stake: Return and Risk in Socially Responsible Investment', *Journal of Banking and Finance*, 32: 2446–54.

Gamble, A. and R. Prabhakar (2006) 'Attitudes of Young People Towards Capital Grants', in W. Paxton and S. White (eds), *The Citizen's Stake: Exploring the Future of Universal Asset Policies* (Bristol: Policy Press).

Gelpern, A. (2011) 'Sovereignty, Accountability and the Wealth Fund Governance Conundrum', *Asian Journal of International Law*, 1(1): 289–320.

Gerrard, B. (2015) 'A New Wave of Support for UK Sovereign Wealth Fund', *Financial Times*, 19 July, at http://www.ft.com/cms/s/0/dcce2e16–2af9–11e5-acfb-cbd2e1c81cca.html#axzz47biz5Eq9.

Gilson, R.J. and C.J. Milhaupt (2008) *Sovereign Wealth Funds and Corporate Governance: A Minimalist Response to the New Mercantilism*, Stanford Law and Economics Olin Working Paper 355, 18 Feb.

Gluyas, R. (2015) 'Future Fund: Peter Costello Pins Hopes on Fossil Fuels', *Australian*, Business Review, 3 Sept.

Glyn, A. (2006) *Capitalism Unleashed: Finance, Globalisation and Welfare* (Oxford: Oxford University Press).

Goldreyer, E.F. and J.D. Diltz (1999) 'The Performance of Socially Responsible Mutual Funds: Incorporating Sociopolitical Information in Portfolio Selection', *Managerial Finance*, 25: 23–36.

Goldsmith, S. (2005) 'The Alaska Permanent Fund Dividend: An Experiment in Wealth Distribution', in G. Standing (ed.), *Promoting Income Security as a Right* (London: Anthem Press).

Goldsmith, S. (2012) 'The Economic and Social Impacts of the Permanent Fund Dividend on Alaska', in K. Widerquist and M.W. Howard (eds), *Alaska's Permanent Fund Dividend: Examining Its Suitability as a Model* (New York: Palgrave Macmillan).

Gompertz, S. (2012) 'Has the UK Squandered its North Sea Riches?', *BBC News*, 8 Oct., at http://www.bbc.com/news/business–19871411.

Gordon, R.J. (2015) 'Secular Stagnation: A Supply-Side View', *American Economic Review*, 105(5): 54–9.

Gough, J. (1973) *John Locke's Political Philosophy*, 2nd edn (Oxford: Clarendon Press).

Gould, M. (2010) 'Managing Manna from Below: Sovereign Wealth Funds and Extractive Industries in the Pacific', *Economic Roundup*, 1: 63–86.

Graver Committee (2003) 'The Report from the Graver Committee', Ministry of Finance, Norway, 7 July, at https://www.regjeringen.no/en/dokumenter/Report-on-ethical-guidelines/id420232/.

Greely, J. (1977) 'The Great Juneau Oil Dollar Giveway', *Alaska Advocate*, 20 Jan.

Griffin, C. (2012) 'Stakeholding through the Permanent Fund Dividend: Fitting Theory to Practice', in K. Widerquist and M.W. Howard (eds), *Alaska's Permanent Fund Dividend: Examining Its Suitability as a Model* (New York: Palgrave Macmillan).

Griffith-Jones, S. and J. Ocampo (2008) *Sovereign Wealth Funds: A Developing Country Perspective*, Columbia University Academic Commons, at http://hdl.handle.net/10022/AC:P:9103.

Groh, C. and G. Erickson (1997) 'The Permanent Fund Dividend Program: Alaska's Noble Experiment', in Alaska Permanent Fund, *The Early History of the Alaska Permanent Fund*, vol. 5 of *The Trustees' Papers* (Juneau, AK: APFC); repr. from *Alaska Journal*, 13(13) (1983).

Groh, C. and G. Erickson (2012) 'The Improbable But True Story of How the Alaska Permanent Fund and the Alaska Permanent Fund Dividend Came to Be', in K. Widerquist and M.W. Howard (eds), *Alaska's Permanent Fund Dividend: Examining Its Suitability as a Model* (New York: Palgrave Macmillan).

Gros, D. and T. Mayer (2012) 'A German Sovereign Wealth Fund to Save the Euro', *Vox*, 28 Aug., at http://www.voxeu.org/article/german-sovereign-wealth-fund-save-euro.

Grosseries, A. (2001) 'What Do We Owe the Next Generations', *Loyola of Los Angeles Law Review*, 35(1): 293–354.

Habermas, J. (1994) 'Three Models of Normative Democracy', *Constellations*, 1(1): 1–10.

Hall, B. (2009) 'French Finance House Reveals First Loss', *Financial Times*, 16 Apr.

Hall, R. (2015) 'Secular Stagnation in the US', *Vox*, 22 Apr., at http://www.voxeu.org/article/secular-stagnation-us.

Hammer, C., P. Kunzel and I. Petrova (2008) *Sovereign Wealth Funds: Current Institutional and Operational Practices* (Washington, DC: International Monetary Fund), at www.imf.org/external/pubs/ft/wp/2008/wp08254.pdf.

Hammond, J. (1984) 'Your Dividend: Here Today, Gone Tomorrow?', *Alaska Public Affairs Journal* (Winter): 18–19.

Hammond, J. (1994) *Tales of Alaska's Bush Rat Governor* (Fairbanks, WA: Epicenter Press).

Hartzok, A. (2012) 'Room for Improvement? Assessing the Strengths and Shortcomings of the Alaska Model in Advance of Export', in K. Widerquist and M.W. Howard (eds), *Exporting the Alaska Model: Adapting the Permanent Fund for Reform around the World* (New York: Palgrave Macmillan).

Harvard Law Review (2011) 'Deweyan Democracy and the Administrative State', *Harvard Law Review*, 125: 580–601.

Hatton, K. and K. Pistor (2011) 'Maximizing Autonomy in the Shadow of Great Powers: The Political Economy of Sovereign Wealth Funds', *Columbia Journal of Transnational Law*, 50(1): 1–81.

Hebb, T., J. Hawley, A. Hoepner, A. Neher and D. Wood (2016) *The Routledge Handbook of Responsible Investment* (Oxford: Routledge).

Hickel, W. (2002) *Crisis in the Commons: The Alaska Solution* (Oakland, CA: ICS Press).

Hickel, J. (2012) 'Constituting the Commons', in K. Widerquist and M. Howard (eds), *Exporting the Alaska Model: Adapting the Permanent Fund for Reform around the World* (New York: Palgrave Macmillan).

HMRC (2016) *Statistics of Government Revenues from UK Oil and Gas Production*, HM Revenue and Customs, London, Jan., at https://www.gov.uk/government/uploads/system/uploads/attachment_data/file/493362/Statistics_of_government_revenues_from_UK_oil_and_gas_production_Jan_2016.pdf.

Ho Ching (2015) 'A Follow-up to My Post on the Singapore Budget', Facebook page of Ho Ching, 8 Sept., at https://www.facebook.com/notes/ho-ching/a-follow-up-to-my-post-on-the-singapore-budget/431796497008190.

Holtham, G. (1997) 'A Community Fund', *Business Strategy Review*, 8(2): 10–13.

Holtham, G. (1999) 'Ownership and Social Democracy', in A. Gamble and T. Wright (eds), *The New Social Democracy* (Oxford: Blackwell).

Holtham, G. (2014) *Payment for Goods: Addressing the Social Democrat's Dilemma*, Institute for Public Policy Research, July.

Honore, A. (1961) 'Ownership', in A. Guest (ed.), *Oxford Essays in Jurisprudence* (Oxford: Clarendon Press).

Howard, M.W. (2012) 'A Cap on Carbon and a Basic Income: A Defensible Combination in the United States', in K. Widerquist and M.W. Howard (eds), *Exporting the Alaska Model: Adapting the Permanent Fund Dividend for Reform Around the World* (New York: Palgrave Macmillan).

Hutchens, G. (2011a) 'Pressure for Sovereign Wealth Fund', *Sydney Morning Herald*, 18 Feb., at http://www.smh.com.au/business/pressure-for-sovereign-wealth-fund–20110217–1ay8m.html.

Hutchens, G. (2011b) 'Heavyweights Call for Sovereign Wealth Fund', *Sydney Morning Herald*, 18 Feb., at http://www.smh.com.au/business/heavyweights-call-for-sovereign-wealth-fund–20110217–1ayb3.html.

IMF (2008) *Sovereign Wealth Funds – A Work Agenda* (Washington, DC: International Monetary Fund), at http://www.imf.org/external/np/pp/eng/2008/022908.pdf.

IMF (2013) *International Reserves and Foreign Currency Liquidity: Guidelines for a Data Template*, International Monetary Fund, at https://www.imf.org/external/np/sta/ir/IRProcessWeb/pdf/guide.pdf.

IMF (2015a) *Report of the IMF Government Finance Statistics Advisory Committee 2015*, International Monetary Fund, 26 Aug., at https://www.imf.org/external/pubs/ft/gfs/gfsac/gfsac15.pdf.

IMF (2015b) *Regional Economic Outlook: Middle East and Central Asia*, International Monetary Fund, Oct., at http://www.imf.org/external/pubs/ft/reo/2015/mcd/eng/pdf/menap1015.pdf.

IMF (2015c) *IMF World Economic Outlook: Uneven Growth: Short- and Long-Term Factors*, Apr., at http://www.imf.org/external/pubs/ft/weo/2015/01/.

IMF IFS (2015) 'Data by Indicator: Reserves (International Liquidity)', *International Financial Statistics*: Data Tables (IFS), at http://data.imf.org/regular.aspx?key=60998126.

Irish Times (2015) 'Why Do We Need the Irish Strategic Investment Fund?', 26 Mar., at http://www.irishtimes.com/business/financial-services/why-do-we-need-the-irish-strategic-investment-fund-1.2153512.

Isakova, A., A. Plekhanov and J. Zettelmeyer (2012) *Managing Mongolia's Resource Boom*, European Bank for Reconstruction and Development Working Paper 138, Jan.

IWG (2008) *Sovereign Wealth Funds: Generally Accepted Principles and Practices: 'Santiago Principles'*, International Working Group of Sovereign Wealth Funds, Oct., at http://www.iwg-swf.org/pubs/eng/santiagoprinciples.pdf.

Jackson, J. (2008) *Foreign Ownership of U.S. Financial Assets: Implications of a Withdrawal*, US Congressional Research Service Rl34319, 14 Jan., at https://www.fas.org/sgp/crs/natsec/RL34319.pdf.

Jansen, H. (2010) 'The Logic of Qualitative Survey Research and Its Position in the Field of Social Research Methods', *Forum Qualitative Sozialforschung / Forum: Qualitative Social Research*, 11(2): Art. 11, at http://nbn-resolving.de/urn:nbn:de:0114-fqs1002110.

Keenan, P. (2009) 'Sovereign Wealth Funds and Social Arrears: Should Debts to Citizens Be Treated Differently than Debts to Other Creditors?', *Virginia Journal of International Law*, 49(2): 431–72.

Keenan, P. and C. Ochoa (2009) 'The Human Rights Potential of Sovereign Wealth Funds', *Georgetown Journal of International Law*, 40(4): 1151–80.

Keller, A. (2009) 'Sovereign Wealth Funds: Trustworthy Investors or Vehicles of Strategic Ambition?', *Georgetown Journal of Law and Public Policy*, 7(1): 333–72.

Kelly, G. and R. Lissauer (2000) *Ownership for All* (London: Institute for Public Policy Research).

Kemp, A. (2008) *The Official History of North Sea Oil and Gas*, vol. I (London: Routledge).

Khrais, R. (2016) 'Saudis Refine Blueprint for Post-Oil Economy', *Al-Monitor*, 26 Apr., at http://www.al-monitor.com/pulse/originals/2016/04/saudi-public-investment-fund-strategy-challenges-income.html.

Kimmitt, R. (2008) 'Public Footprints in Private Markets: Sovereign Wealth Funds and the World Economy', *Foreign Affairs* (Jan.–Feb.).

Knapp, G. (2016) 'Complicated Alaska Budget Crisis Explained in Simple Terms', *Alaska Dispatch News*, 15 Feb., at http://www.adn.com/video/video-complicated-alaska-budget-crisis-explained-simple-terms.

Koch-Weser, I.N. and O.D. Haacke (2013) *China Investment Corporation: Recent Developments in Performance, Strategy, and Governance*, U.S.–China Economic and Security Review Commission staff report, at http://origin.www.uscc.gov/sites/default/files/Research/China%20Investment%20Corporation_Staff%20Report_0.pdf.

Kotter, J. and U. Lel (2011) 'Friends or Foes? Target Selection Decisions of Sovereign Wealth Funds and Their Consequences', *Journal of Financial Economics*, 101(2): 381–411.

Krueger, R.A. and M. Casey (2009) *Focus Groups: A Practical Guide for Applied Research*, 4th edn (Thousand Oaks, CA: Sage).

Krugman, P. (2015) 'Liquidity Traps, Local and Global (Somewhat Wonkish)', *New York Times*, 1 Apr., at http://krugman.blogs.nytimes.com/2015/04/01/liquidity-traps-local-and-global-somewhat-wonkish/?_r=0.

Kukathas, C. (2003) 'Responsibility for Past Injustice: How to Shift the Burden', *Politics, Philosophy and Economics*, 2: 165–90.

Kuttner, R. (1998) 'Rampant Bull', *American Prospect*, 39 (July–Aug.): 30–6.

Kutz, C. (2011) 'Responsibility beyond the Law', in G. Nystuen, A. Follesdal and O. Mestad (eds), *Human Rights, Corporate Complicity and Disinvestment* (Cambridge: Cambridge University Press).

Lamb, G. (2011) 'Technical Note on the Report of Bill Gates to the G20 on Financing for Development', 16 Sept.

Lansley, S. (2015a) 'How Social Wealth Funds Could Help Tackle Inequality', *Political Quarterly*, 86(4): 563–72.

Lansley, S. (2015b) 'If Britain Must Sell off the Family Silver, Let's Put the Proceeds to Good Use at Least', *New Statesman*, 16 June, at http://www.newstatesman.com/politics/2015/06/if-britain-must-sell-family-silver-lets-put-proceeds-good-use-least.

Lansley, S. (2016) *A Sharing Economy: How Social Wealth Funds Can Reduce Inequality and Help Balance the Books* (Bristol: Policy Press).

Laslett, P. (ed.) (1988) *Locke's Two Treatises of Government* (Cambridge: Cambridge University Press).

Lee Yen Nee (2015) 'Reallocation of Government Budget "Can Fund SingFirst Proposals"', *Today* (Singapore), 7 Sept., at http://www.todayonline.com/ge2015/reallocation-govt-budget-can-fund-singfirst-proposals.

Lequiller, F. and D. Blades (2006) *Understanding National Accounts* (Paris: OECD).

Liew, L.H. and L. He (2010) 'Contributing to a Harmonious Society: China's Sovereign Wealth Fund', in X. Yi-chong and G. Bahgat (eds), *The Political Economy of Sovereign Wealth Funds* (New York: Palgrave Macmillan).

Linaburg, C. and A. Maduell (2010) '4Q 2010 Linaburg-Maduell Transparency Index Ratings', Sovereign Wealth Fund Institute, Las Vegas, at http://www.swfinstitute.org/swf-research/4q–2010-linaburg-maduell-transparency-index-ratings-%E2%80%93-public-release/.

Maitland, F. (1911) 'Trust and Corporation', in *The Collected Papers of F.W. Maitland*, vol. 3, ed. H. Fischer (Cambridge: Cambridge University Press).

Mandravelis, V. (2015) 'Tsipras Changes Gov't Tune over Privatization Projects', Ekathimerini.com, 19 Feb., at http://www.ekathimerini.com/167520/article/ekathimerini/business/tsipras-changes-govt-tune-over-privatization-projects.

Manin, B. (1997) *The Principles of Representative Government* (New York: Cambridge University Press).

Marlier, E., T. Atkinson, B. Cantillon and B. Nolan (2007) *The EU and Social Inclusion: Facing the Challenges* (Bristol: Policy Press).

Maskin, E. and J. Tirole (2004) 'The Politician and the Judge: Accountability in Government', *American Economic Review*, 94(4): 1034–54.

McMahon, C. (2009) *Reasonable Disagreement: A Theory of Political Morality* (Cambridge: Cambridge University Press).

Meade, J. (1964) *Efficiency, Equality and Ownership of Property* (London: Allen & Unwin).

Meade, J. (1989) *Agathotopia: The Economics of Partnership* (Aberdeen: Aberdeen University Press).

Mehrpouya, A. (2013) 'Sovereign Wealth Funds, the IMF and Transparency: Are They All Talking about the Same Thing?', Working Paper, Accounting and Management Control Department, HEC Paris, Feb.

Mercer (2009) *Review of the Guardians of New Zealand Superannuation*, report at the request of the New Zealand Treasury, 28 Oct., at http://www.treasury.govt.nz/downloads/pdfs/nzsf-mercer-oct09.pdf.

Miceli, V., A. Wohrmann, M. Wallace and D. Steiner (2015) 'Opportunities or Threats? The Current and Future Role of Sovereign Wealth Funds in Financial Markets', *Deutsche Bank Asset & Wealth Management*, at https://deutscheawm.com/Thought-Leadership/Document-Center/103/Opportunities-or-threats-The-current-and-future-role-of-sovereign-wealth-funds-in-financial-markets.

Miles, H. (2011a) 'Uprisings in Libya', *The Report*, BBC Radio 4, 3 Mar., at http://www.bbc.co.uk/iplayer/episode/b00zf4t1/The_Report_03_03_2011/.

Miles, H. (2011b) 'How Libya's Saif al-Islam Gaddafi Seduced the West', *The Report*, BBC Radio 4, 4 Mar., at http://www.bbc.co.uk/news/world–12626320.

Miller, D. (1995) *On Nationality* (Oxford: Clarendon Press).

Miller, D. (2007) *National Responsibility and Global Justice* (Oxford: Oxford University Press).

Miracky, W. et al. (2008) *Assessing the Risks: The Behaviours of Sovereign Wealth Funds in the Global Economy* (Boston: Monitor Group).

Mischel, L., J. Bernstein and H. Sheirholz (2008) *The State of Working America 2008/2009* (Washington, DC: Economic Policy Institute).

Moffett, M. (2009) 'Prudent Chile Thrives Amid Downturn', *Wall Street Journal*, 27 May, at http://www.wsj.com/articles/SB124337806443856111.

Monk, A. (2008) 'Recasting the Sovereign Wealth Fund Debate: Trust, Legitimacy, and Governance', paper, at http://papers.ssrn.com/sol3/papers.cfm?abstract_id=1134862.

Monk, A. (2011a) 'Did Nigeria's Governors Read the Fine Print?', Oxford SWF Project Blog, 22 Aug., at https://oxfordswf.wordpress.com/2011/08/page/3/.

Monk, A. (2011b) '"Insourcers" Score One against "Outsourcers"', Oxford SWF Project Blog, 28 Mar., at https://oxfordswf.wordpress.com/2011/03/.

Mooney, A. (2016) 'Sovereign Funds Ignore Climate Risk', *Financial Times*, 1 May, at http://www.ft.com/cms/s/0/4881a9fc–0e0d–11e6-b41f–0beb7e589515.html#axzz47hgr35P9.

Morgan, D. (1988) *Focus Groups as Qualitative Research* (London: Sage).

Mubadala (2011) 'Vision, Mission and Values', at http://www.mubadala.com/en/who-we-are/vision-mission-values.

Mubadala (2015) 'Investors', Mubadala 2015 full year results, at http://www.mubadala.com/en/investors.

Mubadala (2016a) 'What We Do', Mubadala, at http://www.mubadala.com/en/what-we-do.

Mubadala (2016b) 'Our Impact', Mubadala, at http://www.mubadala.com/en/our-impact?category=2948.

Munzer, S. (1990) *A Theory of Property* (New York: Cambridge University Press).

Murphy, L. and T. Nagel (2002) *The Myth of Ownership: Taxes and Justice* (Oxford: Oxford University Press).

Murray, D. (2011) 'SWFs: Myths and Realities', keynote address, Global Sovereign Funds Roundtable, London, 5 May, at http://www.ifswf.org/sites/default/files/Publications/london11_0.pdf.

NBIM (2016a) 'Reports', Norges Bank Investment Management, at http://www.nbim.no/en/transparency/reports/.

NBIM (2016b) 'Our Voting Records', Norges Bank Investment Management, at http://www.nbim.no/en/responsibility/our-voting-records/.

Ndanusa, S. (2012) 'The Take-Off of the Nigeria Sovereign Wealth Fund: Things to Watch Out For', 4 Sept., at http://www.articlesbase.com/wealth-building-articles/the-take-off-of-the-nigeria-sovereign-wealth-fund-things-to-watch-out-for-6164732.html.

Newell, J. (2013) 'Obama: Income Inequality Is 'Defining Challenge of Our Time', *Guardian*, 4 Dec., at http://www.theguardian.com/world/2013/dec/04/obama-income-inequality-minimum-wage-live.

Newell, R. (2015) 'Taiwan's SWF Plan Proceeds Despite Opposition', *Asian Investor*, 24 July, at www.asianinvestor.net/News/400116,taiwans-swf-plan-proceeds-despite-opposition.aspx.

New York Times (2015) 'Norway Divests from Coal', editorial, 9 June, at http://www.nytimes.com/2015/06/10/opinion/norway-divests-from-coal.html?_r=0.

Norwegian Ministry of Finance (2008a) 'The Government Pension Fund Divests Its Holdings in Mining Company', Press Release 43/2008, 9 Sept., at www.regjeringen.no/en/dep/fin/press-center/press-releases/2008/the-government-pension-fund-divests-its-.html?id=526030.

Norwegian Ministry of Finance (2008b) 'Consultation Paper – Evaluation of the Ethical Guidelines for the Government Pension Fund – Global', at https://www.regjeringen.no/globalassets/upload/FIN/Vedlegg/aff/evaluation_ethical_Guidelines.pdf.

Norwegian Ministry of Finance (2010) *GPFG Responsible Investment*, Government Pension Fund Global, at https://www.regjeringen.no/upload/FIN/brosjyre/2010/spu/english_2010/SPU_hefte_eng_ebook.pdf.

Norwegian Ministry of Finance (2013) *The Management of the Government Pension Fund in 2012*, Report 27 to the Storting, at https://www.regjeringen.no/en/dokumenter/meld.-st.–27–2012–2013/id721780/?ch=1&q=.

Norwegian Ministry of Petroleum and Energy (2016) 'The Net Government Cash Flow from Petroleum Activities, 1971–2015', updated 16 Mar., at http://www.norskpetroleum.no/en/economy/governments-revenues/.

NPRF Commission (2013) *Annual Report and Financial Statistics*, National Pensions Reserve Fund Commission, 30 June, at http://www.nprf.ie/Publications/2014/AnnualReport2013.pdf.

NSIF (2010) *A Bill for an Act to Establish the Nigerian Sovereign Investment Authority*, Nigerian Sovereign Investment Authority, at http://www.eisourcebook.org/cms/Nigeria%20Sovereign%20Investment%20Authority%20Act.pdf.

Nystuen, G. (2006) 'Investment Policies and Arms Production – Experiences from the Norwegian Pension-Fund Global', in J. Borrie and V. Randin (eds), *Thinking Outside the Box in Multilateral Disarmament and Arms Control Negotiations* (Geneva: United Nations Institute for Disarmament Research).

Nystuen, G., A. Føllesdal and O. Mestad (eds) (2011) *Human Rights, Corporate Complicity and Disinvestment* (Cambridge: Cambridge University Press).

NZSF (2009) *Responsible Investment in Practice Report*, June 2009.

NZSF (2010) *Guardians' Response to Mercer's Independent Review*, updated, New Zealand Superannuation Fund, June, at https://www.nzsuperfund.co.nz/documents/guardians-response-mercers-independent-review.

NZSF (2011a) 'Guardians Respond to Metro Magazine Story, December 2011 Issue', New Zealand Superannuation Fund, 28 Nov., at https://www.nzsuperfund.co.nz/news-media/guardians-respond-metro-magazine-story-december–2011-issue.

NZSF (2011b) *Statement of Investment Policies, Standards and Procedures*, New Zealand Superannuation Fund, 1 July, at http://www.parliament.nz/resource/0000239579.

NZSF (2012a) *Annual Report 2012*, New Zealand Superannuation Fund, at https://www.responsible-investor.com/images/uploads/reports/NZ_Super.pdf.

NZSF (2012b) 'New Zealand Superannuation Fund Excludes Four Companies on Responsible Investment Grounds', New Zealand Superannuation Fund press release,

26 Sept., at https://www.nzsuperfund.co.nz/news-media/new-zealand-superannuation-fund-excludes-four-companies-responsible-investment-grounds.

NZSF (2015a) *Responsible Investment Framework,* New Zealand Superannuation Fund, June, at https://www.nzsuperfund.co.nz/sites/default/files/documents-sys/Responsible%20Investment%20Framework.pdf.

NZSF (2015b) *New Zealand Superannuation Fund Annual Report,* at https://www.nzsuperfund.co.nz/publications/annual-reports.

NZSF (2016a) 'Purpose and Mandate', New Zealand Superannuation Fund, at https://www.nzsuperfund.co.nz/nz-super-fund-explained/purpose-and-mandate.

NZSF (2016b) 'Exclusions', New Zealand Superannuation Fund, at https://www.nzsuperfund.co.nz/how-we-invest-responsible-investment/exclusions.

NZSF (2016c) 'Engagement Reports', BMO annual and quarterly reports, at https://www.nzsuperfund.co.nz/performance-esg-management/engagement-reports.

Ochoa, C. and P. Keenan (2011) 'The IFC's New Africa, Latin America, and Caribbean Fund: Its Worrisome Start, and How to Fix it', Indiana Legal Studies Research Paper 194, 12 May, at ssrn.com/abstract=1839725.

OECD (2008a) *Sovereign Wealth Funds and Recipient Country Policies,* OECD Investment Committee Report, 4 Apr. (Paris: OECD).

OECD (2008b) *OECD Declaration on Sovereign Wealth Funds and Recipient Country Policies,* Ministerial Council Meeting, 4–5 June (Paris: OECD).

OECD (2008c) *OECD Guidelines for Recipient Country Investment Policies Relating to National Security,* OECD Investment Committee Report, 8 Oct. (Paris: OECD).

OECD (2009) *SOEs Operating Abroad* (Paris: OECD).

OECD (2010) *Accountability and Transparency: A Guide for State Ownership* (Paris: OECD).

OECD (2014a) 'Does Income Inequality Hurt Economic Growth?', *Focus on Inequality and Growth,* Dec., at http://www.oecd.org/social/Focus-Inequality-and-Growth-2014.pdf.

OECD (2014b) *Policy Challenges for the Next 50 Years,* OECD Economic Policy Paper 9, July, at http://www.oecd.org/economy/Policy-challenges-for-the-next-fifty-years.pdf.

OECD (2015a) *In It Together: Why Less Inequality Benefits All,* 21 May, at http://www.oecd.org/social/in-it-together-why-less-inequality-benefits-all-9789264235120-en.htm.

OECD (2015b) *Escaping the Stagnation Trap: Policy Options for the Euro Area and Japan,* 15 Jan., at http://www.oecd.org/japan/escaping-the-stagnation-trap-policy-options-for-the-euro-area-and-japan.pdf.

OECD (2016) *OECD Interim Economic Outlook,* 18 Feb., at http://www.oecd.org/economy/economicoutlook.htm.

OECD.Stat (2015) 'Economic Outlook Number 98 – November 2015', at http://stats.oecd.org/Index.aspx?QueryId=51655.

Olin Wright, E. (ed.) (2006) *Redesigning Redistribution: Basic Income and Stakeholder Grants as Cornerstones of a More Egalitarian Capitalism* (New York: Verso).

Olson, D. (2006) 'Fair Exchange: Providing Citizens with Equity Managed by a Community Trust in Return for Government Subsidies or Tax Breaks to Businesses', *Cornell Journal of Law and Public Policy,* 15(2): 102–243.

Olson, R. (2015) 'Sub-Saharan Africa's Sovereign Wealth Funds Struggle in an Era of Low Oil', *Financial Times* blog post, 25 Feb., at http://blogs.ft.com/beyond-brics/2015/02/25/guest-post-sub-saharan-africas-sovereign-wealth-funds-struggle-in-era-of-low-oil.

Omachonu, J. (2011) 'Analysts Condemn Governors Over Sovereign Wealth Fund', *Business Day* (Nigeria), 26 Aug.

OMFIF (2015) *Global Public Investor 2015,* Official Monetary and Financial Institutions Forum, press release, Apr., at http://www.omfif.org/media/1054711/global-public-investor-2015-launch.pdf.

OMFIF (2016) *Global Public Investor 2016: Synopsis,* Official Monetary and Financial Institutions Forum, at http://www.omfif.org/media/1330086/gpi-2016-detailed-synopsis.pdf.

O'Neill, M. (2016) 'The Route to a More Equal Society', York Talks, 10 Feb., at https://www.youtube.com/watch?v=0IuzJU0A6sY.

Oyola, J. and M. Sudreau (2013) 'Fiduciary Relations: Legal Framework and Implications for Responsible Sovereign Debt Management', in C. Esposito, Y. Li and J. Bohoslavsky (eds), *Sovereign Financing and International Law* (Oxford: Oxford University Press).

Papua New Guinea Treasury (2011) 'Organic Law on the Sovereign Wealth Fund', *Papua New Guinea National Gazette* G306, 2 Nov., at http://www.treasury.gov.pg/html/media_releases/files/2011/national.gazette_organic.law.on.swf.pdf.

Papua New Guinea Treasury (2013) *A Sovereign Wealth Fund for All PNG: Information on Sovereign Wealth Fund of Papua New Guinea*, SWF Implementation Secretariat, 20 Feb., at www.treasury.gov.pg/html/public_debt/files/2013/swf/png.swf_public.info_%2022%20Feb%202013.pdf.

Pettit, P. (2008) 'Three Conceptions of Democratic Control', *Constellations*, 15(1): 46–55.

Pettit, P. (2012) *On the People's Terms: A Republican Theory and Model of Democracy* (Cambridge: Cambridge University Press).

Pierson, C. (2004) *The Modern State*, 2nd edn (London: Routledge).

Piketty, T. (2014) *Capital in the Twenty-First Century* (Cambridge, MA: Harvard University Press).

Piketty, T. and G. Zucman (2013) *Capital is Back: Wealth-Income Ratios in Rich Countries, 1700–2010: Data Appendix*, at http://piketty.pse.ens.fr/files/PikettyZucman2013 Appendix.pdf.

Piketty, T. and G. Zucman (2014) 'Capital Is Back: Wealth-Income Ratios in Rich Countries 1700–2010', *Quarterly Journal of Economics*, 129(3): 1255–310.

Piketty, T. and G. Zucman (2015) 'Wealth and Inheritance in the Long Run', in A.B. Atkinson and F. Bourguignon (eds), *Handbook of Income Distribution*, vol. 2B (Amsterdam: Elsevier).

PNG Post-Courier (2012) 'Parlt Passes Sovereign Wealth Fund Bill', *Post-Courier Online* (Papua New Guinea), 23 Feb.

Pogge, T. (2002) *World Poverty and Human Rights* (Cambridge: Polity).

Preqin (2015) *2015 Preqin Sovereign Wealth Fund Review: Exclusive Extract*, June, at https://www.preqin.com/docs/reports/2015-Preqin-Sovereign-Wealth-Fund-Review-Exclusive-Extract-June–2015.pdf.

Preqin (2016) 'Sample Pages', from *The 2016 Preqin Sovereign Wealth Fund Review*, Apr., at https://www.preqin.com/docs/samples/2016-Preqin-Sovereign-Wealth-Fund-Review-Sample-Pages.pdf.

Purdy, J. and K. Fielding (2007) 'Sovereigns, Trustees and Guardians: Private Law Concepts and the Limits of Legitimate State Powers', *Law and Contemporary Problems*, 70(2): 165–201.

Rankin, J. and H. Smith (2015) 'The Great Greece Fire Sale', *Guardian*, 24 July, at http://www.theguardian.com/business/2015/jul/24/greek-debt-crisis-great-greece-fire-sale.

Raphaeli, N. and B. Gersten (2008) 'Sovereign Wealth Funds: Investment Vehicles for the Persian Gulf Countries', *Middle East Quarterly*, 15(2): 45–53.

Reed, B. (2009) 'Sovereign Wealth Funds: The New Barbarians at the Gate? An Analysis of the Legal and Business Implications of Their Ascendancy', *Virginia Law and Business Review*, 4(97): 106–17.

Reeve, A. (1986) *Property* (Atlantic Highlands, NJ: Humanities).

Reeves, P. (2010) 'In Ireland, the Death of the "Celtic Tiger" Leads to Anger, Populist Uproar', National Public Radio, 2 Oct., at www.npr.org/blogs/thetwo-way/2010/10/02/130288328/in-ireland-the-death-of-the-celtic-tiger-leads-to-populist-anger-uproar.

Reiche, D. (2008) 'Sovereign Wealth Funds as a New Instrument of Climate Protection Policy?', Wuppertal Institut 173e, Wuppertal Institute for Climate, Environment and Energy, Dec.

Richardson, B. (2008) *Socially Responsible Investment Law* (Oxford: Oxford University Press).

Richardson, B. (2009) 'Keeping Ethical Investment Ethical: Regulatory Issues for Investing for Sustainability', *Journal of Business Ethics*, 87(4): 555–72.

Richardson, B. (2011) 'Sovereign Wealth Funds and the Quest for Sustainability: Insights from New Zealand and Norway', *Nordic Journal of Commercial Law*, 2: 1–18.

Rodrik, D. (2015) 'From Welfare State to Innovation State', Project Syndicate, 14 Jan., at http://www.project-syndicate.org/commentary/labor-saving-technology-by-dani-rodrik–2015–01#gjGKDTfjYFs4QUEh.99.

Rose, D. and C. Wohlforth (2008) *Saving for the Future: My Life and the Alaska Permanent Fund* (Fairbanks, WA: Epicenter Press).

Rose, P. (2008) 'Sovereign Wealth Funds: Active or Passive Investors?', *Yale Law Journal Pocket Part*, 118: 104–8.

Rozanov, A. (2005) 'Who Holds the Wealth of Nations?', *Central Banking Journal*, 15(4): 52–7.

Rozanov, A. (2011) 'Definitional Challenges of Dealing with Sovereign Wealth Funds', *Asian Journal of International Law*, 1(1): 249–65.

Sandbu, M. (2016) 'How Sovereign Wealth Funds Can Save Capitalism', *Financial Times*, 16 Feb., at http://www.ft.com/cms/s/3/d5cc9ff0-d3c6–11e5–8887–98e7feb46f27.html#axzz47biz5Eq9.

Santiso, J. (2008) 'Sovereign Development Fund: Financial Actors in the Shifting Wealth of Nations', in M. Rietveld (ed.), *New Perspectives on Sovereign Asset Management* (London: Central Banking).

Saxon, M. (2009) 'It's Just Business, Or Is It? How Business and Politics Collide with Sovereign Wealth Funds', *Hastings International and Comparative Law Review*, 32(2): 693–710.

Segal, P. (2012) 'Alaska's Permanent Fund Dividend as a Model for Reducing Global Poverty', in K. Widerquist and M.W. Howard (eds), *Exporting the Alaska Model: Adapting the Permanent Fund Dividend for Reform Around the World* (New York: Palgrave Macmillan).

Singapore Ministry of Finance (2016) 'How Do Singaporeans Benefit from our Reserves?', at http://www.mof.gov.sg/Policies/Our-Nations-Reserves/Section-III-How-do-Singaporeans-benefit-from-our-Reserves.

Skancke, M. (2003) 'Fiscal Policy and Petroleum Fund Management in Norway', in J. Davis (ed.), *Fiscal Policy Formulation and Implementation in Oil-Producing Countries* (Washington, DC: International Monetary Fund).

Skancke, M. (2008) 'Foreign Government Investment in the U.S. Economy and Financial Sector', Submission to the Committee on Financial Services, US House of Representatives, 5 Mar.

Slattery, L. (2010) 'The National Pensions Reserve Fund: An Obituary', *Irish Times*, 30 Nov., at http://www.irishtimes.com/blogs/theindex/2010/11/30/the-national-pensions-reserve-fund-an-obituary/.

Smeeding, T. (2004) *Public Policy and Economic Inequality: The United States in Comparative Perspective*, Luxembourg Income Study Working Paper 367.

Smith, A. (1977) *The Wealth of Nations* (1776) (London: Everyman's Library).

SNA (2008) *System of National Accounts 2008*, United Nations Statistical Commission, at http://unstats.un.org/unsd/nationalaccount/sna2008.asp.

Statman, M. (2000) 'Socially Responsible Mutual Funds', *Financial Analysts Journal*, 56: 30–9.

Steinberger, P. (2004) *The Idea of the State* (Cambridge: Cambridge University Press).

Stone, J. (2015) 'Labour Will Set up a British "Sovereign Wealth Fund" to Make Direct State Investments', *Independent*, 28 Sept., at http://www.independent.co.uk/news/uk/politics/labour-will-set-up-a-british-sovereign-wealth-fund-to-make-direct-state-investments-a6670201.html.

Summers, L.H. (2014) 'Economic Prospects: Secular Stagnation, Hysteresis, and the Zero Lower Bound', *Business Economics*, 49(2): 65–73.

Summers, L.H. (2015) 'Demand Side Secular Stagnation', *American Economic Review*, 105(5): 60–5.

Sunstein, C.R. (2002) *Risk and Reason: Safety, Law and the Environment* (Cambridge: Cambridge University Press).

Sunstein, C.R. (2005) *Laws of Fear: Beyond the Precautionary Principle* (Cambridge: Cambridge University Press).

SWF Institute (2016) 'Fund Rankings', at www.swfinstitute.org/fund-rankings/.

Swift, A. and S. White (2008) 'Political Theory, Social Science and Real Politics', in M. Stears and D. Leopold (eds), *Political Theory: Methods and Approaches* (Oxford: Oxford University Press).

Tang, E. (2009) 'Mongolia Fund to Manage $30 Billion Mining Jackpot', *Bloomberg News*, 11 Sept.

Thieberger, V. (2015) 'Future Fund Brushes off a Divestment Push', *Business Spectator*, 3 Sept.

Thomas, L. (2011) 'Libya's Hidden Wealth May Be Next Battle', *New York Times*, 3 Mar.

Thornton, R. (2008) 'Ethical Investments: A Case of Disjointed Thinking', *Cambridge Law Journal*, 67(2): 396–422.

Triki, T. and I. Faye (2011) *Africa's Quest for Development: Can Sovereign Wealth Funds Help?* Working Paper 142, African Development Bank Group, Dec., at http://www.afdb.org/fileadmin/uploads/afdb/Documents/Publications/WPS%20No%20142%20Africas%20Quest%20for%20Development%20%20Can%20Sovereign%20Wealth%20Funds%20help%20AS.pdf.

Truman, E. (2010) *Sovereign Wealth Funds: Threat or Salvation?* (Washington, DC: Peterson Institute for International Economics).

Truman, E. (2011) *Freezing Libya's Assets: It's Complicated*, Peterson Perspectives, Interviews on Current Topics, 3 Mar., at www.petersoninstitute.org/publications/interviews/pp20110303truman.pdf.

UN (2013) *Inequality Matters: Report on the World Social Situation 2013*, United Nations Department of Social and Economic Affairs (New York: United Nations), at http://www.un.org/esa/socdev/documents/reports/InequalityMatters.pdf.

UNCTAD (2014) *The State of the Commodity Dependence 2014*, United Nations Conference on Trade and Development Report, UNCTAD/SUC/2014/7, at http://unctad.org/en/pages/PublicationWebflyer.aspx?publicationid=1171.

UNPRI (2015) *United Nations Principles for Responsible Investment Annual Report*, July, at https://www.unpri.org/about.

UN Statistics Division (2003) *National Accounts: A Practical Introduction*, at http://unstats.un.org/unsd/publication/SeriesF/seriesF_85.pdf.

Uren, D. (2011a) 'Wealth Fund Will Help the Australian Bond Market', *Australian*, 18 Apr.

Uren, D. (2011b) 'Don't Waste the Mining Boom: IMF', *Australian*, 29 Apr.

US House of Representatives Committee on Foreign Relations (2008) *The Rise of Sovereign Wealth Funds: Impacts on U.S. Foreign Policy and Economic Interests*, 21 May (Washington, DC: US Government Printing Office).

Vanderborght, Y. and P. Van Parijs (2005) *L'Allocation universelle* (Paris: La Decouverte).

Van Parijs, P. (2006) 'Basic Income A Simple and Powerful Idea for the Twenty-First Century', in E. Olin Wright (ed.), *Redesigning Redistribution: Basic Income and Stakeholder Grants as Cornerstones of a More Egalitarian Capitalism* (New York: Verso), pp. 3–27.

Velculescu, D. (2008) 'Norway's Oil Fund Shows the Way for Wealth Funds', *IMF Survey Magazine*, 9 July, at http://www.imf.org/external/pubs/ft/survey/so/2008/POL070908A.htm.

Waldron, J. (2004) 'Property and Ownership', in *The Stanford Encyclopedia of Philosophy*, at http://plato.stanford.edu/archives/spr2012/entries/property.

Weyer, M.V. (2008) 'Why Hasn't Britain Got a Sovereign Wealth Fund?', *Spectator*, 2 Apr., at http://www.spectator.co.uk/features/587341/why-hasnt-britain-got-a-sovereign-wealth-fund/.

Wharton Leadership Center (2010) 'The Brave New World of Sovereign Wealth Funds', University of Pennsylvania, at http://d1c25a6gwz7q5e.cloudfront.net/papers/download/052810_Lauder_Sovereign_Wealth_Fund_report_2010.pdf.

White, S. (2003) *The Civic Minimum: On the Rights and Obligations of Economic Citizenship* (Oxford: Oxford University Press).

White, S. (2011) 'Basic Income Versus Basic Capital: Can We Resolve the Disagreement?', *Policy and Politics*, 39(1): 67–81.

Widerquist, K. (2011) 'A Day-Long Discussion of "the Alaska Model" at the University of Alaska-Anchorage', Alaska Dividend Blog, 10 May, at http://usbig.net/alaskablog/2011/05/a-day-long-discussion-of-"the-alaska-model"-at-the-university-of-alaska-anchorage/.

Widerquist, K. (2012) 'Citizens' Capital Accounts: A Proposal', in K. Widerquist and M.W. Howard (eds), *Exporting the Alaska Model: Adapting the Permanent Fund Dividend for Reform around the World* (New York: Palgrave Macmillan).

Widerquist, K. and M.W. Howard (2012a) 'Introduction: Success in Alaska', in K. Widerquist and M.W. Howard (eds), *Alaska's Permanent Fund Dividend: Examining Its Suitability as a Model* (New York: Palgrave Macmillan).

Widerquist, K. and M.W. Howard (2012b) (eds) *Alaska's Permanent Fund Dividend: Examining Its Suitability as a Model* (New York: Palgrave Macmillan.

Wike, R. (2014) 'With 41% of Global Wealth in the Hands of Less Than 1%, Elites and Citizens Agree Inequality is a Top Priority', Pew Research, 8 Nov., at http://www.pewresearch.org/fact-tank/2014/11/08/with-41-of-global-wealth-in-the-hands-of-less-than-1-elites-and-citizens-agree-inequality-is-a-top-priority/.

Woods, C. and R. Urwin (2010) 'Putting Sustainable Investing into Practice: A Governance Framework for Pension Funds', *Journal of Business Ethics*, 92: 1–19.

World Bank (2015) 'World Bank Commodity Price Forecast', 20 July, at http://www.worldbank.org/content/dam/Worldbank/GEP/GEPcommodities/Price_Forecast_20150722.pdf.

World Bank (2016a) *Commodity Markets Outlook*, Jan., at http://pubdocs.worldbank.org/pubdocs/publicdoc/2016/1/991211453766993714/CMO-Jan–2016-Full-Report.pdf.

World Bank (2016b) *Global Economic Prospects 2016: Spillovers amid Weak Growth*, Jan., at http://www.worldbank.org/en/publication/global-economic-prospects.

Wren-Lewis, S. (2013) 'Safe Assets and Sovereign Wealth Funds: Norway, the UK and Oil', Mainly Macro blog, 1 Feb., at http://mainlymacro.blogspot.co.uk/2013/02/safe-assets-and-sovereign-wealth-funds.html.

Wright, C. (2015a) 'Inside Libya: Interview with LIA Sovereign Wealth Fund Chairman Breish', *Forbes*, 23 Jul., at http://www.forbes.com/sites/chriswright/2015/07/23/inside-libya-interview-with-lia-sovereign-wealth-fund-chairman-breish/#d7050f5554a3.

Wright, C. (2015b) 'Libyan Investment Authority: Bouhadi's View', *Forbes*, 23 Aug., at http://www.forbes.com/sites/chriswright/2015/08/23/libyan-investment-authority-bouhadis-view/#386696ef4f51.

WTO (2015) 'Falling Import Demand, Lower Commodity Prices Push Down Trade Growth Prospects', press release 752, 30 Sept., at https://www.wto.org/english/news_e/pres15_e/pr752_e.htm.

Yeates, C. (2012) 'Heat on Labor over Tobacco Investments', *Sydney Morning Herald*, 9 Jan.

Yeung, Y. and S. Howes (2015a) *Resources-to-Cash: A Cautionary Tale from Mongolia*, Development Policy Centre Discussion Paper 42, 16 Sept., at http://dx.doi.org/10.2139/ssrn.2661202.

Yeung, Y. and S. Howes (2015b) 'Resources-to-Cash: A Cautionary Tale from Mongolia', DevPolicy blog, 22 Oct., at http://devpolicy.org/resources-to-cash-a-cautionary-tale-from-mongolia–20151022/.

Yi-chong, X. (2010) 'The Political Economy of Sovereign Wealth Funds', in X. Yi-chong and G. Bahgat (eds), *The Political Economy of Sovereign Wealth Funds* (New York: Palgrave Macmillan).

Zelleke, A. (2012) 'Basic Income and the Alaska Model: Limits of the Resource Dividend Model for the Implementation of the Unconditional Basic Income', in K. Widerquist and M.W. Howard (eds), *Exporting the Alaska Model: Adapting the Permanent Fund Dividend for Reform around the World* (New York: Palgrave Macmillan).

Zoellick, R. (2010) *The End of the Third World? Modernizing Multilateralism for a Multipolar World* (Washington, DC: World Bank).

Author interviews

Mike Burns, CEO of Alaska Permanent Fund Corporation, APFC offices, Juneau, 28 Apr. 2011.

Council on Ethics, Norway, Oslo, 3 Aug. 2010.

Gregg Erickson, expert Alaska economist (phone interview), 11 Mar. 2016.

Future Fund official (phone interview), 9 Dec. 2012.

Cliff Groh, Permanent Fund dividend expert and Alaska attorney (phone interview), 16 Mar. 2016.

Mubadala investment manager, Abu Dhabi, Oct. 2011.

David Murray, Head of the International Forum of Sovereign Wealth Funds, Sydney, 2 Feb. 2010.

David Rae, Head of Investment Analysis, New Zealand Superannuation Fund (phone interview), Dec. 2012.

Martin Skancke, Director General of Asset Management at the Norwegian Ministry of Finance, Oslo, 3 Aug. 2010.

Sovereign wealth fund officials, International Forum of Sovereign Wealth Funds, Sydney meeting (ten confidential interviews), 9–10 May 2010.

United Arab Emirates sovereign wealth fund officials, Abu Dhabi (seven confidential interviews), Oct.–Nov. 2011.

Legislation, cases and resolutions

Act of the Government Pension Fund (2005), Norway.

Act of the Government Petroleum Fund (1990), Norway.

Constitution of the State of Alaska (1956).

Credit Institutions (Stabilisation) Act 2010, Ireland.

Future Fund Act 2006, Australia.

Government Investment Funds Amendment (Ethical Investments) Bill 2011, Australia.

Greisen v United States, 831. F. 2d 916, 918 (9th Cir), *cert. denied, Beattie v. United States*, 485 U.S. 1006 (1988).

National Pensions Reserve Fund and Miscellaneous Provisions Act 2009, Ireland.

Nation-Building Funds Act 2008, Australia.

New Zealand Superannuation and Retirement Income Act 2001.

Nigeria Sovereign Investment Authority Bill (2010).

Organic Law on the Sovereign Wealth Fund (2011), Papua New Guinea.

United Nations Security Council Resolution 1973 (2011).

INDEX

Abplanalp, Karen 101–3
Abu Dhabi Investment Authority (ADIA) 220
Abu Dhabi Investment Council 220
accountability 2, 11–12, 15, 42, 45, 61, 87, 92, 98, 122, 130, 154, 157, 175, 208–9, 212, 216, 227–8
    and dividends 154, 156, 208–9, 216
    government versus sovereign fund 72, 77–82, 98, 127
    to governments versus citizens 15–16, 61, 79–82, 130, 177, 208, 237
    mechanisms/tools 61, 156, 170, 177, 209, 212, 216
    of SWFs 11–12, 16, 79–82, 98, 109, 115–17, 122–8, 154, 170, 175, 211–13, 227–8
Agaciro Development Fund (Rwanda) 222, 223n14, 237n86
agency
    concept of 237
    costs 209
    ethical *see* ethical agency
    relationship 54, 55
    state 42, 50
agent
    fiduciary *see* fiduciary agent
    government/state as *see* government agent
Alabama Trust Fund (US) 218
Alaska 4, 9, 14, 15, 21–2, 36–8, 41–3, 136, 140–4, 150, 156, 159–83, 190–1, 206, 209–10, 218

and community consultation 42–3, 165–75, 206, 209, 234, 249
conflict over sovereign wealth 4, 9, 36–7, 41, 43, 136, 206
Constitution 37, 163, 178
fiscal crisis 37–8, 42–3, 142, 177–8, 181, 206
natural resources 22, 36–7, 141, 161–4, 169–71, 178, 248
ownership of the sovereign fund 36, 169–71, 248
owner-state versus owner-people *see* owner-state; owner-people
parliament/legislature 37–8, 162
sovereign wealth 21, 248
see also Alaska Permanent Fund
Alaska Permanent Fund 14, 36, 116, 140–2, 161–2, 164–5, 170–4, 176–7, 179–81, 218
    conceptions of 169–72
    court case 36–7, 136
    criticism of 177–81
    dividend 36–7, 42–3, 140–3, 163–73, 175–81, 183, 215, 246, 248
    Earnings Reserve 179
    growth of 14, 231
    history of 161–4, 248, 249
    popular attitudes towards 165–75
    as role model 15, 116, 136, 140–2, 144, 150, 183, 191, 206, 209–10
Alberta Heritage Savings Trust Fund (Canada) 218

Angola 204, 222
see also Fundo Soberano de Angola
Athens 58, 59
Atkinson, Anthony 182, 184, 186, 188, 189
Australia 4, 9, 39, 41, 43, 44, 45, 56–7,
  93–5, 97, 108
  conflict/confusion over sovereign wealth
    4, 9, 39, 41, 43–6, 56–7
  and ethical investment dilemma
    93–7, 108
  see also Australian Future Fund; Western
    Australian Future Fund
Australian Future Fund 28, 93–5, 108,
  206, 221
Azerbaijan 23–4, 219
  see also State Oil Fund (Azerbaijan)

Bachelet, Michelle 1, 2
Backer, Lawrence 98, 127
Bahrain 196, 221
  see also Mumtalakat Holding Company
Balding, Christopher 40
benefit
  concept of 137–8, 246
  distribution 13–15, 30–2, 34, 37, 136,
    140–58, 166
  exclusive right of principal 10, 37–8,
    55–6
  individual versus collective 140–58
  rights in property *see* ownership
  rights to sovereign wealth returns 15,
    111, 136–59
  from sovereign wealth *see* sovereign
    wealth, benefit from
Bernanke, Ben 205
bin Salman, Mohammed 201
Birks, Peter 54
Bollier, David 203, 230
Bouhadi, Hassan 51–2, 236
Breish, AbdulMagid 51, 236
Britain *see* UK
Brown, Gordon 231
Brunei Investment Agency 221

Canada 51, 89, 218
  see also Alberta Heritage Savings Trust
    Fund
Chile 1–4, 9, 28, 42, 45, 116, 219
  see also Social and Economic
    Stabilization Fund; Pension
    Reserve Fund; copper
China 4, 9, 21, 27, 39, 41, 44, 46, 48–50,
  196–7, 200, 202, 204, 221–2

and bureaucratic rivalry 42, 46, 48–50
and conflict over sovereign wealth 4, 9,
  39, 41, 46, 48–50
economic slowdown 4, 196–8, 200,
  202, 204
see also China Investment Corporation;
  SAFE; China–Africa Development
  Fund; Hong Kong; National Social
  Security Fund
China–Africa Development Fund 221
China Investment Corporation 48–50, 56,
  221, 230, 232, 233
Ching, Ho 149
citizen
  competency as SWF voters 85–8
  control *see* control, democratic
  influence *see* community and values,
    influence/input
  owner 11, 15–16, 60, 73–4, 79, 91, 95–6,
    98–9, 103, 139–40, 158–9, 207–8,
    210–11, 216
  principal/trustee 10, 15, 57, 80, 155–6,
    208
  state relationship 3, 4, 10, 14, 34, 41, 50,
    53–7, 60, 74, 81, 207, 210, 211
  wealth *see* citizens' wealth; public wealth
citizens' wealth
  ownership 5, 9, 15, 36, 163–5, 178, 207–11
  and transformation of sovereign wealth
    5, 8–10, 14–15, 60, 188, 197, 207
civil society 128–30, 234
Clark, Gordon 88, 121–2, 127
community and values 95, 99, 100, 105,
  108, 130
  conceptions of 170–1, 175–7
  control 92, 113–15, 116
  global 65–7
  immoral 111–12
  influence/input 66, 72, 84–5, 103, 107,
    116, 124, 126–30, 155–6, 159, 186,
    208, 211–14
  local/domestic 3, 11, 14–16, 59, 82–130
  meaning of 5, 8, 53, 65, 66, 84–5, 210–11
  power over sovereign funds 59–60, 60–7,
    72–3, 81, 106
  property *see* ownership, community/
    collective/common
  as SWF sponsor 3, 4, 5, 8, 9, 11, 13–14,
    23, 40–1, 56, 96, 99, 106
  wealth 59, 106
community fund
  definition of 6–7
  and equality 182–4

funding for 64, 197, 201–5
ideal 66–7, 81, 184, 207–10
and intergenerational equity 65–7
investment 108–12
local benefit from 59, 63–5
local control of 59–63, 72
ownership *see* sovereign wealth fund,
  ownership
potential/development 6–8, 197, 201–3,
  206
and stakeholder trusts *see* Bollier, David
and transformation of SWFs 14–16, 64,
  177, 207–10, 216–17
versus SWF 5–8
control
and benefit rights 137–8, 154, 156–9,
  208, 246; *see also* ownership, and
  benefit rights; ownership, and
  control rights
community *see* control, democratic
concept of 72–4, 137–8
democratic 14–15, 59–60, 65, 72–3,
  74–6, 91–2, 105, 111–12, 114–31,
  154, 208–15, 217
dynamic in sovereign funds 72, 81, 123,
  156, 246
effective/meaningful 95, 102, 114–15
and feasibility of democratic control
  rights 115
by government *see* government, control
and institutional power model
  77–83, 128
objections to democratic control
  83–92
popular *see* control, democratic
by principal 10, 55–7, 157–9
of property 11, 73–6, 208, 239
rights *see* ownership, and control rights
by SWFs 60–1, 237
of SWF income *see* control, and benefit
  rights
of SWF investment 62–3, 92, 95, 102–5,
  110–12, 115, 128–30, 214–15, 241
of SWF management 60–1, 114,
  115–17, 126–8, 209, 211–14
over SWFs 4, 11–12, 14–15, 41, 46,
  47–54, 55–7, 59–61, 65–6, 73–83,
  92, 113–17, 139, 208–15, 225, 231
versus influence 73, 74–7, 78, 84, 156
copper 1, 2, 9, 42
Corbyn, Jeremy 191
Corneo, Giacomo 189–91, 202
Costello, Peter 45, 93
Criddle, Evan 54, 236–7, 251

democracy 2, 44, 64, 74–5, 127, 160,
  218–23
and SWFs *see* control, democratic
democratic
control *see* control, democratic; control,
  and institutional power model
government 5, 41, 72–9, 82–4,
  85–7, 92
processes 92, 96, 110–12, 114–15, 116,
  137, 139, 154, 159, 180, 208,
  209–17
societies 5, 8, 41, 43, 72–9, 103,
  218–25
Detter, Dag 26, 203–4
Development Fund for Iraq 220
Dewey, John 90, 91
Di Natale, Richard 93, 103
dividends
cash 140–3, 144, 153, 154, 156–7, 159,
  161, 162, 166, 167, 176, 183, 189,
  190, 215–16, 246
desirability of 140–3, 158–9
and equality 158–9, 165, 175, 249
individual 137, 140
and ownership rights 140, 163, 166–7,
  175, 178
and recommendations 215–17
social 189
versus collective distribution 150, 153
versus in-kind benefits 143–7
see also Alaska Permanent Fund,
  dividend; Mongolia, and
  distribution of dividends

Egypt 204, 222, 223
Emirates Investment Authority
  (UAE – Federal) 220
endowment 35, 183, 188, 230, 231
equality
intergenerational 35, 57, 112, 113,
  127–8, 157–8, 171, 182
and SWFs 8, 34–5, 64, 136, 145–7, 158,
  162, 165, 175, 182–4, 187–91
see also inequality; dividends, and
  equality; community fund, and
  equality
Erickson, Gregg 142, 163
ethical
agency 104, 128
obligations of government 12, 97, 101,
  104–5, 113, 215
ethical investment
and case for SWFs 97–100
and citizens' ethical integrity 97–100

comparison of Norway and New
  Zealand 117–25, 128–30
and democratic control *see* control,
  democratic
guidelines 101, 104–5, 109–10, 113–14,
  120–1, 124–5, 127–30, 208, 215, 227
lack of by SWFs 96–7
mandate 62–3, 100, 122, 238
of national wealth 97–9
and New Zealand/NZSF 15, 94–7,
  100–4, 108, 114–20, 125–31, 244
and Norway/GPFG *see* Norway
and objections to for SWFs 105–12
obligation 62–3, 94, 214–15
reform 104–6, 108, 214–15
restrictions 94, 97, 103, 109, 214–15, 243
role models 15, 100–5, 113–25, 128–30
by SWFs 12–13, 62–3, 214–15, 241, 277
and UNPRI *see* United Nations
  Principles for Responsible
  Investment

FEM (Venezuela) 219
Fidor 71–2
fiduciary
  agent 10, 43, 53–7, 59, 82, 99–100, 106,
    154–5, 207–9, 210, 236
  beneficiary 43, 53–5
  concept of 53–5, 208, 237
  duty 54–5, 106, 208, 244, 251
  model of SWF ownership 10, 55, 59,
    157, 207–9
  nature of citizen–state relationship 10,
    53–7, 59–60, 207–8, 210, 236
  ownership 43–4, 55, 56–7, 59, 99–100,
    154–5, 157
  principal 10–11, 15, 53–7, 59, 82,
    99–100, 106, 154–5, 157, 207–8,
    210, 251
  relationship/trust 54–5, 100, 106,
    207, 251
FINPRO (Bolivia) 219
Fiscal Stabilization Fund (Peru) 219
Fölster, Stefan 26, 203–4
Fondo de Ahorro de Panama 219
Fondo Mexicano del Petróleo (Mexico)
  219
Fox-Decent, Evan 54
France 184, 219
  see also Strategic Investment Fund
Fund for Future Generations (Equatorial
  Guinea) 222
Fundo Soberano de Angola (Angola) 222
Fung, Archon 84, 89

Gabon Sovereign Wealth Fund 222
Gaddafi, Muammar 50, 51, 235–6
GAPP 3, 6, 20–1, 53, 60–5, 104, 116, 123,
  210–11, 213–14, 216–17, 225
  see also Santiago Principles
Gates, Bill 232
Ghana 204
Ghana Petroleum Funds 222
GIC Private Limited (Singapore) 135,
  148–9, 221
Goldsmith, Scott 164–8, 171–5
governance
  democratic 10; *see also* control,
    democratic
  of SWFs 2, 10, 12, 16, 42, 57, 61, 72,
    77–82, 85, 87, 88, 102, 104, 106,
    114–15, 117, 118–22, 125, 127–30,
    155, 157, 179, 191, 203, 206, 209,
    213, 226, 239, 240, 242, 244
government
  agent 10, 15, 41–3, 53–7, 59, 72, 74, 80,
    82, 99, 100, 154, 209
  concept of 39–40, 53
  control 38, 52, 57, 61, 81
  investment 30–1, 32, 112, 148–9, 152–3,
    154–5, 158, 177, 201–2
  investment vehicle 201–2, 225, 230, 241
  ownership *see* ownership, state/
    government
  versus state 40, 48–50
Government Investment Unit (Indonesia)
  221
Government Pension Fund Global
  (Norway) 14, 33, 96, 98, 101–2,
  104, 116, 120–9, 150, 196–7, 219
  as role model 15–16, 113–1
  see also Norway, Graver Committee
Graver, Hans 113–14
Graver Committee *see* Norway, Graver
  Committee
Groh, Cliff 142, 163

Hammond, Jay 140, 141, 160–4, 170, 176
Hansen, Alvin 199
Harvard Kennedy School 23
Hellenic Republic Asset Development
  Fund 58–9, 60
Heritage and Stabilization Fund (Trinidad
  & Tobago) 219
Hickel, Walter J. 160–1, 163–4, 175, 176
Holtham, Gerald 6–8, 187–8
Hong Kong 49–50, 221
  see also Hong Kong Monetary Authority;
    SAFE

Hong Kong Monetary Authority
(HKMA) 50, 221
   Investment Portfolio 221
Human Development Fund (Mongolia) 221

inequality
   crisis 184–7
   economic 3–4, 8, 35, 64, 145–7,
      184–7, 191
   income 3, 145, 184
   intergenerational 35, 150, 153, 158, 165
   and private ownership 182–3
   of wealth/capital 4, 185–6, 189, 191; see
      also ownership, of wealth/capital
   see also Piketty, Thomas
intergenerational equality see inequality,
      intergenerational; equality,
      intergenerational
International Forum of Sovereign Wealth
   Funds (IFSWF) 6, 51, 63–4, 105,
   116, 211, 216
International Monetary Fund (IMF) 20,
   26, 195, 200
International Petroleum Investment
   Company (UAE) 220
intrastate challenge 4, 46
Investment Corporation of Dubai (UAE)
   220
Ireland 4, 9, 39, 41–2, 46–7, 56, 89, 116,
   199, 219
   conflict over sovereign wealth 4, 9, 39,
      41, 46–7
   economic recovery 42, 47
   sovereign wealth 4, 42, 46–7, 56, 116
   see also Ireland Strategic Investment Fund
Ireland Strategic Investment Fund 47, 219
Israel 205
Israeli Citizen Fund 205
Italian Strategic Fund 219
Italy 51, 199, 220
   see also Italian Strategic Fund

Johnson, Boris 202
justice
   intergenerational 107, 113, 127, 157–8,
      241
   global 65–7, 121
   social 166
   and SWFs 13, 14, 62, 64, 107, 113, 127,
      157–8, 166

Kazakhstan National Fund (Kazakhstan)
   219
Kelly, Gavin 7

Khazanah Nasional Berhad (Malaysia) 221
Korea Investment Corporation (South
   Korea) 50, 221
Kroner, Matthias 71
Kuttner, Robert 7
Kutz, Christopher 99
Kuwait 6, 196, 220
   see also Kuwait Investment Authority
Kuwait Investment Authority 6, 220

Lansley, Stewart 8, 19, 186, 188, 203
Lawson, Nigel 33
Libya 9, 39, 41, 46, 50–2, 56, 222
   asset freeze 50–2
   conflict over sovereign wealth 9, 39, 41,
      46, 50–2
   see also Libyan Investment Authority;
      Gaddafi, Muammar
Libyan Investment Authority 50–2, 222
Lissauer, Rachel 7
Locke, John 10, 53
London 201
Louisiana 21, 218
   see also Louisiana Education Quality
      Trust Fund
Louisiana Education Quality Trust Fund
   (US) 218
Luxembourg 59

Meade, James 6–8, 188
Mexico 2, 21, 219
   see also Oil Revenues Stabilization Fund
      of Mexico; Fondo Mexicano del
      Petróleo
Mongolia 4, 9, 22–3, 144–8, 150, 156,
   215, 222
   benefit from sovereign wealth 144–8
   conflict over sovereign wealth 4, 9
   distribution of dividends 144–8, 150,
      156, 215
   Human Development Fund 144–5,
      147, 156
   misuse of resource revenues 145–6
   see also Fiscal Stability Fund (Mongolia)
Monk, Ashby 88, 121–2, 127, 225
Mubadala Development Company (UAE –
   Abu Dhabi) 220
Mumtalakat Holding Company (Bahrain)
   220
Munzer, Stephen 53
Murray, David 105, 106, 108

Namibia 135–6
National Development Fund of Iran 220

National Fund for Hydrocarbon Reserves (Mauritania) 222
National Investment Corporation (Kazakhstan) 219
national net worth see national wealth
National Social Security Fund (China) 221
national wealth 11, 13, 20–1, 23, 24–5, 35, 72, 94, 105, 110, 114, 135–6, 184, 187–8, 197, 203, 206
  accountability of 11, 45
  definition of 20–4
  distribution of 30–2
  financial and non-financial 24–6
  measurement of 24–5, 232
  ownership of 25–6
  and private versus public 25, 30–4; see also public wealth
  sources of 20–4, 206
  see also Piketty, Thomas
National Welfare Fund (Russia) 219
natural resources
  ownership of 36–7, 66, 135–6, 141, 161, 163–4, 170, 178, 202, 225
  as public wealth 26, 29–30, 64, 202
New Mexico State Investment Council (US) 218
New Zealand 4, 15, 28, 91, 94–7, 100–4, 108, 114–21, 123, 125–31, 210, 222, 238, 242, 244
  see also New Zealand Superannuation Fund
New Zealand Superannuation Fund 28, 91, 94, 100–4, 116, 118–20, 126, 128–30, 221
Nigeria 4, 9, 23–4, 39, 41, 43–4, 56, 204
  see also Nigeria Sovereign Investment Authority
Nigeria Sovereign Investment Authority 43–4, 222
North Dakota 21, 218
  see also North Dakota Legacy Fund
North Dakota Legacy Fund (US) 218
Norway 4, 8, 15, 19–21, 24, 33–5, 62, 83, 91, 94–8, 104, 108–10, 113–17, 219
  compared to New Zealand 97, 108, 113–17, 125–31
  compared to UK 19–20, 21, 24, 33–5
  and conflict over sovereign wealth 4, 109–10, 113
  and ethical investment 62, 97, 108–10, 114, 120–2, 124, 127–9
  Graver Committee 109, 112, 114, 124, 128–30

North Sea oil and gas 19–20, 24, 34–5, 94, 121
  as role model see Government Pension Fund Global, as role model
  and sovereign wealth 8, 20–5, 34, 97–8, 117, 121, 122, 125, 196–7, 206
  and SWFs 8, 19–20, 33–5, 62, 83, 91, 96, 108–9, 113, 116, 121, 125, 190–1, 197
  see also Government Pension Fund Global

Obama, Barack 184
Official Monetary and Financial Institutions Forum (OMFIF) 27
Oil Income Stabilization Fund of Mexico 219
Oman Investment Fund 220
O'Neill, Martin 8
Organisation for Economic Co-operation and Development (OECD) 184, 198–9, 224
Orr, Adrian 102
Osborne, George 202
owner-people 160–1, 164, 176
owner-state 104, 160–1, 163, 164–9, 176, 215, 248
ownership
  and benefit rights 10–11, 15, 111, 136–8, 140, 149, 151, 156–9, 177, 183, 207
  citizen 10, 11, 14, 15–16, 126, 154, 157, 174–5, 177, 207–11
  citizen versus state/government 9–10, 160–9
  collective/community/common 10, 161, 163–5, 166, 167, 170, 176–7, 189
  concept of 39–40, 74
  and control rights 15, 61, 65, 73–4, 78, 79, 81–2, 92, 111, 112, 115, 127, 137–8, 157
  fiduciary see fiduciary, ownership
  popular see ownership, citizen; citizen, owner; citizens' wealth, ownership
  private 183
  public 25, 38–9, 40, 161
  rights 59, 66, 74, 121, 123, 137, 140, 177, 208, 246
  of sovereign wealth see sovereign wealth fund, ownership
  state/government 7, 9, 10–11, 53, 160, 211, 236
  versus property 10, 51–4, 236
  of wealth/capital 4, 182–3, 189, 191

Palestine Investment Fund (Palestine) 221
Papua New Guinea 79, 96, 222
  see also Papua New Guinea Sovereign
    Wealth Fund
Papua New Guinea Sovereign Wealth
  Fund 221
Pension Reserve Fund (Chile) 2, 28, 219
Permanent Fund dividend see Alaska
    Permanent Fund, dividend
Permanent University Fund (Texas) 218
Permanent Wyoming Mineral Trust Fund
  (US) 218
Pettit, Philip 74–5, 77–8, 82, 84
Piketty, Thomas 4, 24–5, 185–6, 188
Police and Crime Commissioners (PCC)
  19, 54, 86
principal
  citizen see citizen, principal/trustee
  control of see control, by principal
  fund/underlying assets of SWF 13, 23,
    63, 110, 149, 152, 157, 159, 162,
    165, 177, 179–81, 196, 216, 226
  in fiduciary relationship see fiduciary,
    principal
principal-agent 10, 15, 55–7, 82, 99–100,
    154, 188, 207, 209
  conception of citizen–state relationship
    207
  control mechanisms 82
  framework for SWFs 10, 55–7
property see ownership
  state 7, 10, 37; see also ownership, state/
    government
Public Investment Fund (Saudi Arabia)
  201, 220
public wealth 4, 6, 7, 11, 14, 24, 24–7
  accountable management of 41, 45, 237
  financial and non-financial 25–6, 29
  future of 200–5
  managers 26, 27
  measurement/definition of 185; see also
    national wealth; Piketty, Thomas
  and relationship to private wealth
    24–5
  size of 27
  sources of 20–1, 26–7
  and sovereign wealth 26, 28–35
  and SWFs 28–33, 66, 91, 138, 147
  see also national wealth
Pula Fund (Botswana) 222

Qatar 196, 220
  see also Qatar Investment Authority
Qatar Investment Authority 220

RAK Investment Authority (UAE – Ras
    Al Khaimah) 220
Reeve, Andrew 53
Reserve Fund (Russia) 195, 219
responsible investment see ethical
    investment
Revenue Equalization Reserve Fund
    (Kiribati) 221
Revenue Regulation Fund (Algeria) 222
Rodrik, Dani 202
Rozanov, Andrew 5, 61, 213
Russia 4, 195, 197, 219–20
  tapping into reserve fund for national
    budget 195–7
  see also Reserve Fund; Russian Direct
    Investment Fund; National Welfare
    Fund
Russian Direct Investment Fund 219
Rwanda 204, 223, 237
  see also Agaciro Development Fund

SAFE (China) 48, 221
Samruk-Kazyna JSC (Kazakhstan) 219
Sanders, Bernie 191
Santiago
  dilemma 3, 16
  Principles 1–3, 6, 9, 16, 20–1, 53, 60–5,
    85, 104, 116, 123, 210–11, 213–14,
    216–17, 225
    and reform 5, 15–16, 96, 104–5, 117,
    209–17
Saudi Arabia 22–3, 195, 201, 220, 221
  and Aramco 201
  Deputy Crown Prince Mohammed bin
    Salman 201
  and sovereign wealth 23, 195, 201
  see also Saudi Arabian Monetary Agency
    Foreign Holdings; Public
    Investment Fund
Saudi Arabian Monetary Agency (SAMA)
    Foreign Holdings 220
Senegal FONSIS 222
Singapore 8, 27, 113, 135–6, 148–9, 157–8,
    204, 214
  see also GIC Private Limited; Temasek
    Holdings
Skancke, Martin 83, 122–3, 150–1
Smith, Adam 1, 6–9, 25, 206–7
Social and Economic Stabilization Fund
    (Chile) 2, 116, 219
South Korea 4, 21, 27, 50, 204
  see also Korea Investment Corporation
    (South Korea)
Sovereign Fund of Brazil 219

sovereign wealth
  benefit from 4, 10, 14–15, 37–8, 44–8,
    51, 54–6, 57, 59–60, 62, 64, 74, 88
  conflict over 9–10, 41–3, 46–52
  confusion over 41–7
  control over 8, 14–15, 73–4, 76, 92, 177
  and deficit reduction 31–2
  definition of 20–1, 25, 39–40
  distribution of 11, 13–14, 15, 136–58,
    208
  ethical investment of *see* ethical
    investment
  global rights to 65–7
  and government consumption 30
  and government investment 30–1
  growth of 14, 200–1
  investment of 62–3, 92, 95, 102–5,
    110–12, 115, 128–30, 214–15, 241
  and national balance sheet 20, 22, 28–30
  ownership *see* sovereign wealth fund,
    ownership; natural resources,
    ownership of
  ownership ambiguity 9, 39, 43–6, 53,
    207, 211
  and public wealth 25–6, 28–30; *see also*
    public wealth
  and secular stagnation 200–1
  sources of 20–3
  and tax cuts 31, 33, 143, 246n13
  versus national wealth 24–5; *see also*
    national wealth
sovereign wealth fund (SWF)
  benefits of 8, 10, 60–5, 98, 100, 104,
    137–8
  control over 4, 73–83, 113–17
  definition of 6, 9, 20, 38–41, 45, 53, 138,
    210–11, 233, 224–5
  democratic control of 72–83, 115–31; *see
    also* control, democratic
  domestic legitimacy of 91–2, 110, 124,
    126, 128, 130, 145, 155, 205–6, 238
  and equality *see* equality, and SWFs
  excess reserves-based 27, 48–50, 66, 149,
    197, 238, 233
  future of 197, 200–5
  government use of 25–6, 28
  growth 5–6, 14, 64, 206, 231n50
  impact on public wealth 28–32, 34–5; *see
    also* public wealth, and SWFs
  influence 13, 61, 119, 237
  investment of returns 152–3, 154
  local impact on citizens 5, 11–14, 29, 32,
    210
  new types of 22, 55, 201–4, 237

number globally 5, 21, 206, 230
  ownership 8, 9–10, 11, 14, 16, 27, 36–40,
    41, 43–4, 46–53, 56–7, 59, 65–6,
    140, 166, 167, 170, 207–11
  resource-based/commodity 63–4,
    204–5
  return distribution 140–58; *see also*
    benefit, distribution
  role model 10, 15–16, 113–15, 116
    117–26, 130–1, 155, 165–6, 178
  role of 4, 8, 11, 12, 14, 25, 28, 34, 178,
    191, 207–8
  and sponsor-community 3, 4, 5, 8, 9, 11,
    13–14, 23, 40, 56, 60, 62, 96, 100,
    117
  trusteeship 105–9, 112
  types of 28, 200–5
  and undue influence over 239
  versus community fund 5–8, 15–16
  versus national wealth fund 203
  versus private funds 12–13
  versus public asset managers 26–7, 28
State Capital Investment Corporation
  (Vietnam) 221
State General Reserve Fund (Oman) 220
State Oil Fund (Azerbaijan) 219
Strategic Investment Fund (France) 219
Summers, Larry 199
SWF *see* sovereign wealth fund

Taiped 58–9
  see also Hellenic Republic Asset
    Development Fund
tax relief 31, 33, 143, 246n13
  see also sovereign wealth, and tax cuts
Temasek Holdings (Singapore) 148, 221
Texas Permanent School Fund (US) 5, 218
Thatcher, Margaret 32–3
TIAA-CREF 98
Timor-Leste Petroleum Fund (East
  Timor) 221
transparency
  limits to SWFs 83–4, 91, 212
  objections to SWFs 83–4
  and Santiago Principles 61, 212–13
  of sovereign funds 11–12, 15, 61, 77, 79,
    82, 83, 91, 114–17, 120, 122, 125–6,
    154–5, 208, 212–13, 227–8, 244
Truman, Ted 61, 115–17, 126, 224, 226
trust
  in citizen–state relationship 41, 207
  legal concept 54, 207, 251
  political metaphor 54, 236–7
  stakeholder 203

trustee
    board 52, 121–2, 242
    citizen 77, 240; *see also* citizen,
        principal
    concept for SWFs 54, 105–7
    definition of 54
Tsipras, Alexis 58–60, 65
Turkmenistan Stabilization Fund 219

UK 19, 51–2, 71–2, 86, 89–90
    compared to Norway 19–20, 21, 24,
        33–5
    economic growth 187, 198
    inequality 19, 33–5, 182, 184, 187,
        189, 191
    North Sea oil and gas 19–20, 24, 29,
        32–5
    public wealth 20, 30–3, 187, 201–3
    SWF 7–8, 19–21, 24, 29–30, 32–5, 182,
        187, 189, 201–2, 205
United Arab Emirates 152, 196
United Nations 20, 25, 50
United Nations Principles for Responsible
    Investment (UNPRI) 97
United Nations System of National
    Accounts 25, 232

USA
    community funds 7, 184
    Court of Appeals 36–7
    economic growth 186, 198, 200
    inequality 165, 184–6
    public assets 21, 36, 203
    sovereign wealth 2, 51, 178, 184, 203
    Supreme Court 36–7
    SWFs 3, 14, 19, 21, 165–6

Velasco, Andrés 1, 2

Walker, Bill 38, 42, 180
West Virginia Future Fund (US – West
    Virginia) 218
Western Australian Future Fund
    (Australia) 221
White, Stuart 7, 154
Widerquist, Karl 110, 248
World Bank 198, 231, 232
Wyoming 21, 218
    see also Permanent Wyoming Mineral
        Trust Fund

Zimbabwe 204, 222–3
Zoellick, Robert 231